PAT BROWN, MBA

Financial Literacy Is Sexy

"Own Your Money, Build Your Confidence, and Redefine What Wealth Looks Like."

ABRAM 47 BROWN

First published by AbramBrown47 2025

First edition

ISBN: 978-1-967737-32-1

This book was professionally typeset on Reedsy.
Find out more at reedsy.com

Contents

Preface

Why We're Having This Conversation Now

Let's be honest.

There's nothing sexy about overdraft fees.

Nothing glamorous about financial anxiety.

Nothing empowering about living paycheck to paycheck when you make good money.

But you know what *is* sexy?

Clarity. Confidence. Control.

Knowing exactly where your money is going.

Watching your investments grow while you sleep.

Being able to say "yes" to what matters and "no" to what doesn't—with zero guilt.

That's why I wrote this book.

Because in a world full of shiny things, loud advice, and endless pressure to "have it all," we're missing something essential: real, honest, approachable financial education that speaks to *you*—the smart, capable person who was somehow left out of every meaningful money conversation.

You didn't miss a memo.

There just wasn't one.

No one taught you how to negotiate your salary, manage debt without drowning, save for a future you actually want, or figure out if your "retirement plan" is more than just vibes.

You were told to work hard, get the degree, show up on time, maybe contribute to a 401(k), and hope for the best.

That's not a plan. That's a wish.

And wishes don't build wealth. Systems do. Strategy does. You do.

What This Book Isn't

This isn't a lecture. This isn't a spreadsheet full of jargon and guilt trips.

This isn't another financial bro yelling at you to cut lattes and live in fear.

Financial Literacy Is Sexy is the opposite.

It's the book I wish existed for every 24-year-old with student loans, every 37-year-old trying to build wealth while juggling life, and every 52-year-old wondering if they'll actually be okay.

It's direct. It's playful. It's honest.

And it's built for real people who want to make real moves—with their money, and their life.

What This Book Is

This is a conversation with someone who's been there.

Someone who knows that budgeting isn't about deprivation—it's about direction.

That investing doesn't require a finance degree—just a decision to start.

That wealth isn't about perfection—it's about patterns, protection, and peace.

This is about understanding your relationship with money—how it was shaped, how it's showing up now, and how to take the wheel and steer it somewhere powerful.

We're going to break things down clearly:

- What debt is actually okay (and what's not)
- How to design a spending plan that reflects your *real* life
- What investing means when you're not a millionaire
- How to avoid money shame and lifestyle traps
- How to protect your income, your future, and your energy
- How to think generationally—even if you're just getting started

This book is about building wealth that feels good.

Not performative. Not pressured. Not punishing.
Just clear. Honest. Intentional.
Sexy.

Why "Sexy"?

Because financial literacy *is* sexy.

It's confidence. It's peace. It's personal power.

It's walking into a room knowing your bills are paid, your savings is growing, and you're not financially handcuffed to any job, partner, or circumstance.

It's the freedom to say "yes" on your terms.

It's the boundaries that protect your energy.

It's the self-respect that says: "I worked for this. I earned this. I'm building this with intention."

That's not just literacy. That's leadership.

And this book will help you build it—one decision, one mindset shift, and one strategy at a time.

Before We Dive In

This book won't fix your finances overnight. That's not the point.

The point is to help you feel *capable. Calm. Clear-headed.*

To put you back in the captain's seat of your financial life.

To help you stop flying blind and start flying bold.

It's okay if you don't know everything.

It's okay if you've made some financial mistakes.

It's okay if you're still figuring it out.

You're not behind. You're just beginning—with better tools, better information, and a whole lot more swagger.

So let's throw out the fear. Let's drop the shame. Let's build something better, brick by brick, budget by budget.

Because when you get your money right?

Everything else gets lighter.

Now let's begin.

— Pat Brown, MBA

Author | Financial Educator

How to Use This Book

This Isn't Just a Book. It's a Mirror, a Map, and a Megaphone.

You didn't pick up *Financial Literacy Is Sexy* by accident.

You picked it up because something in your life—your paycheck, your goals, your stress, your curiosity—said:

> *"I want more clarity. More power. More control over my money—and my life."*

This book was made for that moment.

It's not a textbook. It's not a lecture. It's not about guilt, deprivation, or boring rules.

It's about confidence.

It's about clarity.

It's about building wealth *on your own terms*—with style, swagger, and a strategy.

Here's how to use this book so it actually changes your life—not just your bookshelf.

1. Don't Read It Like a Novel

You can read it cover to cover if you want. But you don't have to.

This book is built in chapters that stand alone and stand strong.

Flip to the chapter that speaks to your current situation:

- Struggling with debt? Start there.
- Ready to invest but feel overwhelmed? Start there.

- Want to protect your income or raise financially literate kids? Start there.

Follow your instincts—not the page numbers.

2. Ask Yourself Bold Questions

Before each chapter, pause and ask:

- What do I wish I understood better about this topic?
- What habits around this area make me proud—or ashamed?
- What would it feel like to be in full control of this?

Write those answers down. Return to them later. That's where your transformation begins.

3. Engage With It—Don't Just Skim It

You are not a passive reader. You are the main character.

Grab a pen. Mark up the margins. Circle things that punch you in the chest.

Write questions you want to ask your partner, your mentor, or your financial advisor.

Dog-ear pages. Reread chapters. Highlight like it's your new gospel.

Because this book? It's about your *real life*. And real life is worth writing all over.

4. Take Action at the End of Each Chapter

Every chapter closes with a clear, unfiltered, unapologetic *call to action*.

Do one thing. Just one. Then do another next week.

Small moves = massive momentum.

Think of it like getting dressed: sexy doesn't happen all at once. It's the slow layering of confidence.

5. Don't Let Perfection Slow You Down

You don't need to master every chapter before moving forward.

You don't need to memorize every acronym or know every detail.

You just need to *move*.

This isn't about being perfect. It's about being intentional.

Perfection is a myth. Progress is magic.

6. Come Back to It When Life Changes

This isn't a "read once and shelve it" kind of book.

Come back when:

- You switch jobs or start a business
- You get married, divorced, or have a baby
- You inherit money or get hit with a financial setback
- You start to wonder if you're on the right path

This book is your financial mirror. Use it to check in. Recalibrate. Keep flying high.

7. Share It Boldly

When something clicks—don't keep it to yourself.

Text a quote to a friend. Buy a copy for your sister. Bring it to your next group chat, brunch, or team meeting.

Financial literacy is sexy. But *shared* financial literacy? That's power multiplied.

Final Note

This book is yours now.

Let it live in your bag. Your nightstand. Your notes app.

Let it start conversations. Let it shift your thinking.

Let it help you build a life that feels *as good as it looks on paper.*

Because being broke isn't sexy.

Being confused isn't sexy.

But confidence? Ownership? Wealth with purpose?

That's as sexy as it gets.

Let's get to it.

— Pat Brown, MBA

info@financialliteracyissexy.com

www.financialliteracyissexy.com

About the Author

Pat Brown, MBA is not your typical financial advisor—and *Financial Literacy Is Sexy* is not your typical finance book.

A former Division I athlete turned wealth manager, Pat has spent over two decades helping professionals, entrepreneurs, and high achievers break free from financial confusion and step into clarity, control, and long-term wealth. He's built a career on translating complex financial topics into real-life strategies that actually make sense—and actually get results.

Pat is the founder of a growing suite of financial literacy platforms, including:

- FinancialLiteracyForPilots.com
- FinancialLiteracyForDoctors.com
- FinancialLiteracyForNIL.com
- FinancialLiteracyForAttorneys.com
- FinancialLiteracyForStudentAthletes.com
- And now, FinancialLiteracyIsSexy.com

But behind every site and every book is one core belief: **financial literacy is not just important—it's empowering. It's freedom. It's legacy.**

Pat has spoken on stages, in locker rooms, in boardrooms, and at hospital conferences. His clients include pilots, physicians, engineers, pro athletes, small business owners, and people who simply want to *finally* stop feeling behind when it comes to money.

He's known for telling the truth with love, explaining money without the jargon, and helping people of all income levels take bold steps toward financial independence.

When he's not writing books or advising clients, Pat is spending time with his wife and daughters, watching a good movie, or shooting hoops in his driveway.

He's walked the walk. Now he's here to help you fly your own financial flight plan—with clarity, swagger, and zero apology.

Let's build wealth that looks good, feels good, and lasts.

— Pat Brown, MBA

info@financialliteracyissexy.com

www.financialliteracyissexy.com

Why I Wrote This Book

I wrote this book because I wanted to make financial literacy **cool**.

I wanted to make it **attractive**.

I wanted to make financial literacy **sexy**.

Yeah—I said it. Sexy.

Not boring. Not stiff. Not "sit through a lecture with your eyes glazed over."

I wanted to spark curiosity. Start conversations.

Make people want to learn about money—not because they're forced to, but because they *want* to.

And I'll be honest...

I also wanted to drop some **cool t-shirts and merch** that say:

"Financial Literacy Is Sexy."

Because it is.

Because understanding your money is hot.

Because confidence at the bank is just as powerful as confidence in the cockpit—or the boardroom—or the bedroom.

So here's the question I've been asking myself:

Can I actually do it?

Can I get people to buy in?

Can I make people want to talk about Roth IRAs the way they talk about new sneakers or new tech or new drops?

Can I make financial literacy sexy?

Am I...

"Bringing Financial Literacy Sexy Back"?

(Let's go.)

This book is me saying: **Hell yes.**

It's packed with tools, tips, stories, checklists, and mindset shifts that make money feel less like a mystery and more like a skill you've already got—you just haven't tapped into it yet.

It's not a textbook.

It's a conversation.

It's a movement.

And it starts with you—flipping this page, wearing that shirt, sending that link to your friend, and saying:

"Yo. This is different. This makes sense. This feels *good.*"

Let's break the stigma.

Let's kill the shame.

Let's make learning about money something you're *excited* to do—not just for your wallet, but for your whole damn life.

Because when you know better, you plan better.

And when you plan better—you build a life that's powerful, confident, generous, and calm.

And *that's* sexy.

Let's build.

Let's flex financial literacy in style.

Let's make it mainstream. Let's make it bold. Let's make it fly.

Let's make Financial Literacy Sexy.

Own Your Money. Design Your Life. Move With Confidence.

This book isn't about skipping lattes or cutting up your credit cards.

It's about **power**.

It's about **confidence**.

It's about **freedom**.

It's about building a financial life that turns heads—not because it's flashy, but because it's **intentional**. Because it feels **good** to be in control.

Financial Literacy Is Sexy was written for anyone who's ever thought:

> *"I make decent money, but I still feel behind."*
>
> *"No one ever taught me how to really manage this."*
>
> *"I just want to feel confident about my future."*

Sound familiar? You're not alone.

You were handed a paycheck—but not a plan.

You were told to "save for retirement"—but no one explained how.

You were handed a 401(k) packet or an insurance brochure and expected to just "figure it out."

This book fills that gap.

Wherever you are—whether you're just getting started, rebuilding, or leveling up—**Financial Literacy Is Sexy** meets you there. With **no shame**, **no fluff**, and **no judgment**.

This is financial literacy without the boredom.

Without the jargon.

Without the lectures.

Just **real talk**. Real strategy. Real empowerment.

You'll learn how to:

- Ditch money shame and build confidence that lasts
- Design a lifestyle that reflects your values—not someone else's expectations
- Invest wisely, even if you're not "into" finance
- Protect your income, assets, and peace of mind
- Actually *understand* insurance, taxes, and retirement accounts
- Say "no" with boundaries and "yes" without guilt
- Build wealth that supports your vision and creates options

This isn't just a book.

It's your financial permission slip.

To plan better. To live freer. To move bolder.

Because **smart is sexy**.

Confidence is sexy.

Clarity is sexy.

And financial literacy?

That's the kind of sexy that never goes out of style.

Let's build. Let's lead. Let's make financial clarity the new flex.

www.FinancialLiteracyIsSexy.com

Questions or speaking inquiries: **info@financialliteracyissexy.com**

Part I: The Mindset — Confidence is Currency

Before we talk budgets, credit, or investing, we start with what really drives financial transformation: your beliefs. This section is all about shifting your internal narrative—from scarcity and shame to abundance and self-worth. You'll learn why financial literacy isn't just about numbers; it's about confidence, control, and breaking generational patterns that no longer serve you.

We'll explore the toxic myths that keep people broke and silent, unpack the emotional baggage we all carry around money, and show how self-awareness becomes your first—and most powerful—financial tool. You'll reframe your mindset around wealth, power, and possibility, and realize that financial confidence isn't arrogant—it's attractive, empowering, and absolutely necessary.

Because before you build wealth, you need to believe you're worthy of it.

Chapter 1: Why Financial Literacy Is the New Sexy

Let's get this straight from the jump: Financial literacy isn't just smart. It isn't just responsible. It isn't just mature.

It's sexy.

Yes, sexy.

There is something magnetic about a person who knows where their money is, where it's going, and why. A person who isn't panicking when rent's due. Who doesn't fumble when the conversation turns to Roth IRAs, credit scores, or insurance deductibles. Who can hold their own whether they're at the dinner table, in the boardroom, or swiping through Zillow.

That kind of confidence? That kind of freedom?

It's not just appealing. It's irresistible.

Let's talk about why.

Reframing Sexy: From Surface to Substance

We live in a culture that constantly sells us a shallow version of sexy: skin-deep beauty, fast cars, flashy clothes, and high-status zip codes. But we're shifting. People are waking up to the fact that sexy isn't about what you wear—it's about how you live. It's about how grounded you are. How steady you are under pressure. How confidently you make decisions.

And nothing reveals those qualities faster than money.

Financial literacy is the modern glow-up.

You know what's sexy?

- Being able to take care of yourself.
- Not flinching when you check your bank balance.
- Being able to say "no" to a toxic job or relationship because your emergency fund has your back.
- Talking about money openly and calmly, not defensively or with shame.
- Being generous on purpose—not out of guilt or social pressure.

Power Is Sexy. And Money Is Power.

Let's drop the fake humility for a minute. You want power. And you deserve it.

Not power over other people. But power over your own damn life.

Financial literacy puts you in the driver's seat. When you understand your money, you stop reacting and start choosing. You're no longer the passenger hoping things work out—you're the one mapping the route.

That power feels good. And when you own it, people feel it.

That's sexy.

Confidence Is the Real Flex

You know what's not sexy? Being scared every time you swipe your debit card. Avoiding your mail because it might have another bill. Ghosting your bank app for three weeks because you know the news isn't good.

Confidence is built one informed decision at a time. Every budget tracked. Every dollar intentionally saved. Every honest money conversation you choose to have.

Financial literacy turns shame into swagger.

And when you're walking around with that quiet confidence? That head-held-high energy?

That's sexy.

Financial Literacy Is About Options. And Options Are Irresistible.

Picture this: You hate your job. Your boss doesn't value you. The culture is toxic.

But you've been saving 20% of your income for years. You have six months of living expenses in cash. Your resume's sharp and your LinkedIn is lit.

So you walk out.

Because you can.

That's what financial literacy buys you: OPTIONS.

When you understand money, you stop asking, "Can I afford it?" and start asking, "Do I even want it?"

Big difference.

Options let you:

- Travel without guilt
- Leave bad relationships
- Support your parents
- Take time off when your mental health needs it
- Start your dream business with real numbers, not vibes

That freedom? It's intoxicating.

Wealth Isn't Just a Number. It's a Vibe.

Let's talk about energy.

There's a kind of glow that comes from people who know their financial life is handled. It's not about being a millionaire. It's about not being at war with your money.

When you're financially literate, you stop dragging financial anxiety around like a ball and chain. You walk lighter. You laugh easier. You move with a sense of calm that makes people wonder what you know that they don't.

Here's the secret: It's spreadsheets. And intentional spending. And a few auto-transfers.

That's the vibe.

The New Sexy Is Sustainable

Let's get real.

Anyone can look rich for a weekend. Designer shoes. Section at the club. First-class ticket once a year.

But can you:

- Sleep peacefully on the first of the month?
- Handle a $2,000 emergency without calling your parents?
- Afford to take time off when life hits hard?
- Invest in your kids' future without sacrificing your own?

Sustainable is the new sexy. It's not a flex if you can't repeat it next month.

Financial literacy builds a life that lasts. And that reliability? That peace of mind?

That's sexy.

Action Steps to Make Your Money Sexy Today

1. Open your bank app. Don't flinch. Know where you stand.
2. Set up automatic transfers to a savings or investment account—even $25 counts.
3. Start a money date with yourself or your partner once a week. Glass of wine, playlist, and a spreadsheet.
4. Track your spending for 30 days. No shame. Just data.
5. Pick one thing to cancel or downgrade that no longer aligns with your goals.
6. Pick one thing to upgrade that supports your future (therapy, gym, a money coach).
7. Learn one new financial term each week. Google it. Understand it. Own it.

Closing Thoughts

You don't have to be perfect with money to be powerful. You don't need a six-figure salary or a finance degree.

You just need to pay attention. To care. To decide that you're worthy of peace, options, and joy.

And if you're reading this?

You're already on the way.

You're not behind. You're just getting started.

Most people don't know this stuff—until they do.

Now you do.
Clarity is confidence. And confidence is sexy.
So tonight, make one money move before you go to bed.
Just one.
And then do another next week.
Because financial literacy isn't just smart.
It's freedom.
It's swagger.
It's self-love.
Financial literacy is the new sexy.
And you wear it well.

Chapter 2: Scarcity Thinking Is Outdated

Stop romanticizing the struggle — abundance is in.

Let's go ahead and say the quiet part out loud: being broke is not a personality trait. Scarcity isn't noble. Financial stress isn't proof of how hard you work or how deeply you love. It's just stress.

And it's time to break up with it.

We've been taught to believe that struggle equals strength. That hustle equals worth. That suffering through your finances somehow makes you more real, more grounded, more "relatable." But that lie has kept too many people small, exhausted, and broke.

Financial literacy changes that. It doesn't just teach you how to budget. It teaches you how to breathe. How to make decisions without fear. How to claim what you actually want—not just what you can scrape together.

Abundance is not a scam. It's a system.

Let's build yours.

Part 1: The Roots of Scarcity Thinking

Most of us didn't learn about money in a classroom. We learned about it at the dinner table. In the silence when the rent was due. In the whispered fights. In the guilt trips. In the generational patterns of fear, shame, or survival.

Scarcity thinking isn't just about not having enough money. It's about believing you'll never have enough. It's the background noise that tells you:

"I better not spend this, even though I need it."

"People like me don't get ahead."

"I don't deserve more."

"If I get money, I'll probably lose it."

Scarcity thinking makes you shrink. It keeps you overworking, under-earning, and self-sabotaging. It makes you say yes when you should say no. It makes you feel like money is the enemy instead of the tool.

But scarcity is a mindset. And mindsets can change.

Part 2: Struggle Is Not the Badge of Honor You Think It Is

We have glamorized the grind. Romanticized the hustle. Turned suffering into virtue. But here's the truth: struggling is not sexy. Not financially. Not emotionally. Not energetically.

You can be driven without being drained. You can work hard without constantly proving that you're worthy. You can want ease and still be ambitious.

Let's stop glorifying the broke college days. The sleeping-on-the-floor startup stories. The sacrifice-your-sanity-for-the-dream culture. We can build wealth with integrity, not martyrdom.

Struggle is not proof of love.

Struggle is not proof of value.

Struggle is not required.

Part 3: Understanding the Shift from Scarcity to Abundance

Scarcity mindset says: There's only one slice of the pie, and if someone else gets a piece, there's less for me.

Abundance mindset says: Let's bake a bigger pie.

The abundance mindset doesn't mean spending recklessly or pretending problems don't exist. It means making decisions from a place of trust and strategy, not fear.

It sounds like:

"I can figure this out."

"There are opportunities out there for me."

"My income can grow."

"I am learning and improving."

Abundance is steady. It's patient. It's quiet confidence in motion.

You build it one choice at a time.

Part 4: Money and Self-Worth

Let's be blunt: Your bank account is not a reflection of your value as a person.

But the way you handle money often reflects what you believe you deserve.

When you chronically undercharge, overspend, give too much, or avoid making financial plans, that's often about worthiness, not math.

You are allowed to want more. Not because you're greedy. Because you're human.

Wanting money doesn't make you shallow.

Building wealth doesn't make you selfish.

Setting boundaries around your time and energy doesn't make you cold.

It makes you clear.

And clear is sexy.

Part 5: Actionable Steps to Shift Into Abundance

Let's get tactical. Here's how you begin moving from scarcity into abundance:

1. Track Your Financial Behavior With Curiosity, Not Criticism
2. Write down everything you spend in a week. Not to punish yourself, but to see clearly. Clarity kills shame.
3. Build Your Emergency Fund
4. Start with $500. Then $1,000. Then aim for 3-6 months of living expenses. You don't need to do it overnight. Just automate a little each month.
5. Name Your Accounts
6. Rename your savings account to "Freedom Fund" or "My Future Home." Make it emotional. Make it motivating.
7. Cancel One Scarcity Habit
8. Maybe it's saying yes to things out of guilt. Maybe it's doom-scrolling Zillow instead of investing in a plan. Cut it out.
9. Create a Monthly "Abundance Audit"

10. Each month, review what you brought in, what you spent, what you saved, and how you felt. Ask: Did I make money decisions that felt powerful?

Part 6: Real-Life Abundance Shifts

Case 1: The Closet Full of Nothing to Wear

Amanda makes $65K and still feels broke. Her credit cards are near maxed. She shops when she's stressed. But none of it brings peace. When she tracks her spending for 60 days, she sees she's spent $900 on clothes—yet feels no closer to confidence. She begins to budget with intention. She starts a capsule wardrobe. She automates $200/month into savings. In 6 months, she pays off one card and starts smiling when she gets dressed.

Case 2: The Six-Figure Struggle

Darius earns $140K but has nothing left at the end of the month. Two car payments, private school tuition, dinners out, subscriptions he doesn't use. He always feels behind. He does an "Abundance Reset" and cuts $1,200 in recurring costs. He downsizes one car. He sets up a Roth IRA. He realizes abundance isn't more spending. It's more breathing room.

Case 3: The Financial Phoenix

Sandra is 61 and divorced after 30 years. She never handled the money. Now she's got a pension, a house, and fear. She takes a free financial literacy course. She hires a fiduciary. She sells her house and moves into something smaller and sunny. She finally opens her own investment account. She says, "I used to be scared of money. Now I'm building something that's mine."

Part 7: Breaking Cultural and Generational Patterns

Some of us inherited more than eye color and cooking skills. We inherited financial trauma. We saw our parents hide bills, avoid the bank, never talk about money unless someone was yelling.

We learned that financial stress is normal.

But it doesn't have to be.

It ends with you.

Break the cycle by:

- Talking about money without shame
- Learning financial vocabulary
- Creating a will or estate plan
- Setting up custodial accounts or college funds
- Teaching your kids to invest, not just save

Changing your family's financial future is the boldest love letter you can write.

Part 8: Building a Personal Abundance Blueprint

You don't need to follow someone else's financial playbook.

You need a system that works for your life, your energy, your goals.

Ask yourself:

- What do I want money to do for me?
- How do I want to feel when I open my bank app?
- What am I tolerating that abundance could eliminate?

Create systems:

- Auto-transfer to savings
- Invest through your employer plan
- Use YNAB, Mint, or a simple Google Sheet
- Check in with your finances weekly

Abundance loves attention.

So pay attention.

Final Words

Scarcity is outdated.

You don't have to earn your worth through exhaustion.

You don't have to prove anything by staying stuck.

Abundance is in.

It's not just a vibe.

It's a decision.

It's a strategy.

It's available.

You're not behind. You're just getting started.

Most people don't know this stuff—until they do.

Now you do.

Clarity is confidence. And confidence is sexy.

Make one move before bed tonight. Cancel something. Automate something. Read something.

Then do another next week.

You're no longer surviving. You're designing.

Scarcity thinking is outdated.

And you?

You're stepping into abundance like it was always yours.

Because it is.

Let's go.

Chapter 3: Money Shame: Break Up with Your Past

Guilt and secrecy keep you broke.

Let's begin with a truth that might sting a little: the money mess you're avoiding isn't the problem. The shame wrapped around it is.

You're not the only one who's made bad money decisions. Not even close. Most of us learned about finances the hard way. Not because we were stupid. But because no one ever taught us differently.

We learned through overdraft fees and debt collections, late-night panic attacks, and saying yes when we should have said no. Through keeping secrets, dodging calls, and pretending everything was fine when it wasn't.

But here's the thing: you can't build wealth on a foundation of shame.

If you're going to step into real financial power—the kind that brings peace, options, and pride—you have to break up with your past.

You can still love the version of you who did their best. But it's time to stop letting that version of you drive the car.

This chapter is about releasing guilt, getting honest, and rewriting the story you've been telling yourself about money.

Because the truth is: shame keeps you small. But ownership sets you free.

Part 1: Shame Is Not a Financial Strategy

Most people aren't broke because they're irresponsible. They're broke because they're carrying financial trauma. Because they've been operating in silence and shame. Because they've been afraid to ask questions.

Shame thrives in secrecy. It keeps you from:

- Opening your bills
- Looking at your bank account
- Asking for help
- Negotiating your salary
- Saying, "I don't know"

It whispers lies like:

"You're bad with money."

"You should be further along by now."

"You messed this up, and now you're stuck."

Shame turns your finances into a haunted house you're scared to walk through.

But what if you turned the lights on?

What if you walked through the fear and found that your past didn't define you—your next move does?

Part 2: The Stories We Inherit

Before you blame yourself for your current situation, take a look at what you were taught.

Were your parents financially secure?

Did anyone talk to you about budgeting, investing, saving, or taxes?

Was money talked about with stress, silence, or fights?

Most of us learned by watching.

We absorbed beliefs like:

"Rich people are greedy."

"Money doesn't grow on trees."

"We can't afford that."

"People like us just get by."

Those messages shape your internal money script. And if you don't challenge them, you start repeating them.

You're not repeating your money mistakes because you're lazy.

You're repeating them because they feel familiar.

But you're allowed to rewrite the story.

Part 3: Guilt Is a Signal, Not a Sentence

Here's what guilt is supposed to do: tell you something didn't align with your values.

That's it.

It's a messenger. Not a judge. Not a prison sentence.

You feel guilty because you spent money when you were sad.

You feel guilty because you let debt pile up.

You feel guilty because you never learned how to budget and now you're 35 and playing catch-up.

Okay. Good information.

Now what?

The question isn't whether you made mistakes.

It's what you do next.

You do not have to drag guilt around like a suitcase. You can unpack it. Learn from it. Leave it behind.

Part 4: Bring It to Light

Secrecy keeps the shame cycle alive.

If you've never told anyone how bad your debt got, or how confused you feel about money, or how embarrassed you are that you still haven't started saving—this is your invitation.

You don't have to tell everyone.

But tell someone.

A therapist.

A friend.

A financial coach.

Your partner.

Say it out loud: "I need help with money."

Because once you say it, you strip shame of its power.

Truth is the beginning of healing.

Part 5: Detach Your Identity from Your History

Repeat after me:

"My past decisions are data. Not destiny."

You are not your student loans.

You are not your credit card balance.

You are not your bounced checks or closed accounts.

You are a whole person who is learning. Growing. Trying.

Just like you wouldn't shame a friend who was learning a new skill, don't shame yourself for not knowing what you were never taught.

You are not bad with money.

You were uninformed. Maybe overwhelmed.

But never beyond repair.

Part 6: Your Money Narrative – And How to Rewrite It

Take out a sheet of paper or open your Notes app.

Answer these:

1. What were you taught about money growing up?
2. What money mistakes have you made that still feel heavy?
3. What do you believe about people who have wealth?
4. What do you believe about yourself and money?
5. What would your financial life look like if you believed you were worthy of abundance?

Then write a new story.

One that starts now.

One that acknowledges the past without letting it run the future.

Example:

Old Story: "I'm terrible with money. I always screw it up."

New Story: "I'm learning new skills every day. My past does not limit my potential."

Part 7: Real-Life Stories of Money Shame and Rebuilding

Jasmin, 27

"I used to lie to my boyfriend about credit card debt. I'd say it was under control, but it wasn't. One day I broke down. He didn't judge me. He helped me make a plan. We paid off $12,000 in 18 months. The shame almost cost me the relationship. Honesty saved it."

Luis, 39

"I felt like a failure because I had to move back home after a layoff. But while I was there, I took free online finance classes, started freelancing, and built a six-month emergency fund. What I thought was a setback was really a setup."

Tanya, 54

"Divorce left me with debt and self-doubt. I thought I was too old to start over. But I got a part-time job, paid off my credit cards, and found a financial advisor who treated me with dignity. Now I own my own place. It's never too late."

Part 8: Action Steps to Break Free from Shame

1. Say it out loud: "I forgive myself for my past financial decisions."
2. Write a letter to your younger self. Thank them for surviving.
3. Make a list of what you've learned from your financial mistakes.
4. Create a financial affirmation. Say it daily. Example: "I am building wealth with clarity and courage."
5. Start a money journal. Track your thoughts and wins, not just numbers.
6. Schedule a 1:1 with a money mentor, advisor, or accountability partner.
7. Take one micro-action: pull your credit report, organize your bills, or read one chapter of a financial book.

Final Words

You can't hate yourself into financial success.

You have to build from love, from grace, from compassion.

You have to talk to yourself the way you would talk to a best friend.

With encouragement.

With honesty.

With hope.

You're not behind. You're just getting started.

Most people don't know this stuff—until they do.
Now you do.
Clarity is confidence.
And confidence is sexy.
Tonight, write down one thing you're ready to release.
Then write one thing you're ready to claim.
Guilt and secrecy will keep you broke.
Truth and action will set you free.
Break up with your past.
You're building something new now.
And it looks damn good on you.
Let's go.

Chapter 4: You Deserve to Be Rich (Yes, You)

Self-worth is the foundation of net worth.

We're going to start this chapter with a sentence that might make you squirm:

You deserve to be rich.

Not because you worked 100 hours last week.

Not because you grew up poor and want to prove a point.

Not because you sacrificed your joy for productivity.

You deserve to be rich because you're human. Because comfort is not a luxury. Because peace of mind is not something you have to earn with pain.

You deserve to be rich because having money is not about greed. It's about freedom, choices, safety, and legacy.

But if hearing that sentence made you uncomfortable, you're not alone.

This chapter is your permission slip to want more—without apology. It's your invitation to stop playing small with your money, your goals, your ambition, and your sense of worth.

Because self-worth isn't just a buzzword. It's the foundation of every money move you make.

Part 1: Reclaiming the Word "Rich"

Let's be real: the word "rich" has baggage. For some, it means excess. Greed. Arrogance. For others, it means security. Freedom. Joy. But if you grew up hearing things like:

"Money changes people."

"They're rich, but they must be doing something shady."

"We don't need all that."

...then somewhere inside you, rich may have started to feel like a dirty word.

So here's a radical reframe: rich isn't about what you have. It's about what you can do.

Can you:

- Take care of your parents?
- Pay for your kids' college without stress?
- Take two weeks off work and not worry about bills?
- Leave a toxic job and breathe for a while?

That's rich.

Let go of the myth that wanting more makes you greedy.

Wanting more makes you human.

Part 2: How Self-Worth Shapes Net Worth

Your net worth is not just a financial metric. It's a mirror of your beliefs, your habits, your boundaries.

If you believe:

"I have to work myself into the ground to deserve money."

"No one will pay me more."

"I'm bad with money."

...then you're going to unconsciously act in ways that reinforce those beliefs.

Self-worth affects:

- How you price your services
- Whether you negotiate your salary
- If you invest, or hoard cash from fear
- Whether you ask for help or suffer in silence
- How you react to windfalls (some people sabotage themselves when

money finally comes)

When you don't feel worthy, you repel wealth.

When you claim your worth, you make space for wealth to stay.

Part 3: The Hustle Lie – You Don't Have to Earn It Through Exhaustion

We've been sold the idea that only the hardest worker wins. That your income must match your output. That sleep is for the weak.

And sure, work ethic matters. But hustle isn't the only ingredient in wealth. In fact, hustling without healing can leave you rich on paper and bankrupt in spirit.

You do not have to:

- Burn out to be worthy of a vacation
- Work two jobs to justify a savings account
- Suffer in silence to prove you're strong

You are allowed to rest.

You are allowed to receive.

You are allowed to build slowly, with intention.

You don't have to prove anything to be rich. You just have to stop apologizing for wanting it.

Part 4: Scarcity Scripts That Keep You Small

Your mindset is the software your financial life runs on. Outdated scripts = system crashes.

Here are some scarcity scripts that quietly sabotage people:

- "I'll never make more than this."
- "If I get money, I'll lose it."
- "People will judge me if I level up."
- "I don't know what I'm doing, so why try?"
- "I should be grateful for what I have and stop wanting more."

Gratitude and ambition can coexist.

Humility and abundance are not enemies.

You don't have to choose between being a good person and a wealthy person.

You can be both.

Part 5: Rich Is Relative. Define It for Yourself.

What does rich mean to you?

Not what your parents said.

Not what your favorite influencer flaunts.

What does it mean to *you*?

Maybe it's:

- A paid-off mortgage
- $10K in the bank
- Traveling twice a year
- Not panicking when your kid needs braces
- Retiring your mom

Personal finance is personal.

Define rich in a way that feels aligned—not performative.

Because if you're chasing someone else's version of success, you'll never feel full.

Part 6: How to Start Believing You Deserve Wealth

This is where mindset becomes muscle.

1. **Audit Your Money Beliefs**
2. Write down every sentence that comes to mind when you hear: "You deserve to be rich." Notice the resistance.
3. **Name Your Fear**
4. Are you afraid you'll be judged? Lose friends? Become someone you don't like? Bring it to the surface.
5. **Flip the Script**
6. Old: "People like me don't get rich."

7. New: "People like me change everything."
8. **Practice Worthy Habits**

- Negotiate your pay
- Invest even if it's just $50/month
- Set money boundaries
- Create a financial vision board
- Learn one new financial skill a month

1. **Speak Wealth Into Your Life**
2. Repeat affirmations like:

- "I am worthy of financial abundance."
- "I attract opportunities that build my legacy."
- "I can hold wealth without fear."

Part 7: Real-Life Stories of Worthiness-Driven Wealth

Leah, 32

"I grew up thinking rich people were jerks. So I always undercharged. One day, I realized I was exhausted and broke. I doubled my prices, lost a few clients, gained better ones. I stopped chasing validation and started chasing value."

Devin, 41

"I stayed in a job for ten years that drained me. I didn't think I deserved more. Finally, I applied for a role that paid $40K more. I got it. I cried on my first paycheck. I'd been the only thing in my way."

Jamila, 59

"After divorce, I thought my money life was over. But I hired a coach, learned to invest, and in five years built a $300K portfolio. It wasn't luck. It was permission."

Part 8: Action Steps to Claim What You Deserve

1. Write your personal definition of rich

2. List 3 things you've done that show resilience and growth
3. Automate savings/investing even if it's $25/month
4. Practice one worthiness affirmation daily
5. Set a bold income goal and reverse engineer it
6. Watch your language. Stop saying:

- "I'm so broke."
- "I could never afford that."
- "I'm not good with money."
- Replace with:
- "I'm learning to manage money with power."
- "I'm building new habits."
- "I make aligned financial decisions."

Final Words

You don't have to earn the right to financial peace through suffering.
You already have the right.
You're not behind. You're just getting started.
Most people don't know this stuff—until they do.
Now you do.
Clarity is confidence.
And confidence is sexy.
Tonight, look in the mirror and say: "I deserve to be rich."
Say it again tomorrow. And the next day. Until you stop flinching.
Then act like it's true.
Because it is.
Let's go.

Chapter 5: Financial Foreplay: Talking Money in Relationships

Conversations that build trust, not tension

Let's get real: talking about money with your partner can feel more intimate than sex and more terrifying than a tax audit.

And yet, if you're going to build a future with someone—a real one, not just a fantasy—you have to talk about money. Not once. Not when it's already a problem. But regularly, openly, with compassion and clarity.

This chapter is about making money talk sexy. Not stressful. It's about learning to connect over goals instead of disconnecting over guilt. It's about setting the mood with transparency. And most of all, it's about recognizing that financial intimacy is emotional intimacy.

Money touches everything in a relationship:

- Where you live
- How you vacation
- What kind of lifestyle you can sustain
- How safe you feel
- What dreams you pursue together

Avoiding money talk doesn't keep the peace. It delays the pain.

But the couples who thrive? They don't just budget together. They dream together. They plan together. They face hard truths together. And then they win—together.

This chapter is your step-by-step guide to making money conversations feel less like interrogations and more like invitations.

To trust. To clarity. To partnership.

Because the couples who talk money often? They have more of it. And more peace while they build it.

Part 1: Why Talking About Money Feels So Vulnerable

Money isn't just math. It's emotion. It's history. It's power.

That's why conversations about money can make your palms sweat.

When you talk about money with your partner, you're talking about:

- Your past
- Your fears
- Your dreams
- Your insecurities

And if your financial past is filled with shame, mistakes, or scarcity, opening up can feel like undressing your soul.

But let's be clear: you can't build emotional intimacy while keeping financial secrets.

It doesn't matter how compatible you are in bed, on vacation, or in public. If you can't trust each other with dollars, you're building on shaky ground.

Part 2: How to Start the Conversation (Without Making It Weird)

You don't have to open the conversation with a spreadsheet. Start with a story.

Try something like:

"I realized no one ever taught me how to talk about money, and I want to get better at it. Want to help me practice?"

or

"I want us to feel like a team when it comes to money. Can we make space to talk about what we both want financially?"

Make it collaborative, not confrontational. You're not trying to interrogate them. You're inviting them into a shared vision.

Timing matters too. Don't launch into a deep financial discussion during a fight or in the middle of brunch with their parents. Choose a calm moment. Pour a drink. Light a candle. Make it a vibe.

Financial foreplay starts with emotional safety.

Part 3: Money Types and How They Clash (and Complement)

There are spenders and savers. Hustlers and security-seekers. Givers and accumulators.

Knowing your money personality—and your partner's—is like knowing your love language.

Here are some common archetypes:

1. **The Saver** – Loves security. Hates risk. Finds joy in coupon codes and paid-off credit cards.
2. **The Spender** – Finds joy in experiences and things. Believes money is meant to be enjoyed.
3. **The Avoider** – Doesn't look at statements. Feels overwhelmed. Hopes problems will fix themselves.
4. **The Controller** – Wants full oversight. Tracks every penny. Gets anxious if things feel messy.

Every type has strengths. Every type has blind spots.

Talking about your money type creates awareness, not blame.

Try saying:

"I think I lean toward being an Avoider. It helps me to talk about money in small doses. How about you?"

Understanding how your partner *feels* about money is more powerful than knowing their FICO score.

Part 4: Financial Red Flags and Green Lights in Relationships

Before you merge lives (or bank accounts), know what to look for.

Red Flags:

- Hiding purchases or accounts
- Refusing to talk about debt
- Gaslighting you about your financial questions

- Shaming you for your income or financial goals
- Using money to control or manipulate

Green Lights:

- Willingness to talk, even if it's uncomfortable
- Shared vision for the future
- Openness about debt, credit, and goals
- Mutual respect for boundaries and autonomy
- Desire to grow financially together

Healthy financial conversations are less about agreement and more about honesty and alignment.

Part 5: Scripts for Tricky Conversations

1. Talking About Debt:

"There's some debt I want to be upfront about because I see us building something real. I don't need you to fix it—just want to share it with transparency."

2. Talking About Income Differences:

"We make different amounts, but I don't want that to create weirdness. Let's figure out a way to split things that feels fair to both of us."

3. Talking About Budgeting:

"Can we try setting a weekly spending check-in? I don't want to micromanage—I just want to make sure we're staying on the same page."

4. Talking About Future Goals:

"Where do you see us in 5 years financially? I want to start aligning what we do today with where we want to go."

These conversations don't have to be perfect. They just have to be real.

Part 6: Building Shared Goals Without Losing Yourself

You can be a couple and still have your own financial identity.

In fact, it's essential.

Here are a few ways to structure money as a couple:

1. **All In** – Fully joint accounts and shared everything
2. **Yours, Mine, Ours** – Separate accounts + one joint account for shared bills
3. **Fully Separate** – Each person handles their own finances and agrees on a split

None of these is right or wrong. The key is agreement and transparency.

If one person resents the structure, it's not working.

Define goals together like:

- Travel budget
- Down payment fund
- Kids' education
- Retirement targets

Create a vision board. Make it fun. Talk numbers, but dream big.

Money planning can feel like planning a life—because it is.

Part 7: Money Dates – Turning Talk Into Intimacy

Make it a ritual.

Set a weekly or monthly money date.

Do it over wine or mocktails. Light a candle. Play music. Make it feel safe and warm.

Agenda for a money date:

1. Review spending
2. Celebrate a win (big or small)
3. Discuss a short-term and long-term goal
4. Identify one thing to improve
5. Set next action steps

This isn't just about numbers. It's about connection.

Money dates build consistency. Trust. Shared language.

And they make it way less likely you'll end up surprised or blindsided later.

Part 8: Forgiving Financial Mistakes in Relationships

Maybe your partner made a money mistake.

Maybe you did.

Forgiveness doesn't mean forgetting. It means moving forward with boundaries and clarity.

If there's been secrecy, debt accumulation, or irresponsible choices:

1. Have an honest conversation
2. Ask for full transparency
3. Set up a plan together
4. Decide how trust will be rebuilt

Shaming your partner won't fix the problem.

But enabling it won't either.

Forgiveness is a team rebuild.

Part 9: Long-Term Planning Together

As your relationship grows, so will your financial responsibilities.

Topics to discuss:

- Estate planning
- Insurance
- Beneficiaries
- Children's education
- Financial care for aging parents
- Retirement age and vision

These conversations might not feel sexy, but the peace of mind they bring is incredibly attractive.

Start small.

Build consistently.

And remember: love is not just feelings. It's planning for each other's futures.

Final Words

Money is not the enemy.

Silence is.

Talk often. Talk gently. Talk truthfully.

You're not behind. You're just getting started.

Most people don't know this stuff—until they do.

Now you do.

Clarity is confidence.

And confidence is sexy.

Tonight, make a money date.

Ask your partner a financial question you've been avoiding.

And just listen.

You deserve a relationship where money is a bridge, not a battlefield.

Let's build that.

Part II: Your Money, Your Rules

This section is your unapologetic permission slip to take full ownership of your financial life—on your terms, not anyone else's. Whether you grew up counting pennies or blowing paychecks, this part of the book invites you to reprogram the rules you've inherited, absorbed, or accepted about money. It doesn't just teach you how to save, invest, and spend wisely—it helps you rewrite the emotional code that drives every financial decision you make.

From breaking up with money shame and scarcity thinking, to building a bold belief in your worthiness to be wealthy, Part II turns personal finance into a power move. You'll learn how to create systems that feel sexy and sustainable. You'll redefine rich for yourself. And you'll stop asking for permission to build the life you want.

Because the truth is: when you stop outsourcing your financial decisions to fear, culture, or someone else's opinion, you don't just get better with money—you get freer, fiercer, and fully in control.

Ready to be the CEO of your life?

Let's go.

Chapter 6: Budgeting Without Feeling Broke

Sexy Doesn't Mean Restrictive

Let's start by destroying the myth: Budgeting is not about cutting joy out of your life. It's about assigning purpose to your money. And purpose? Purpose is sexy.

When you hear the word "budget," you might imagine spreadsheets, scarcity, or saying no to everything fun. But budgeting done right? It's not punishment. It's power. It's not about restriction. It's about intention. It's not about saying no to everything. It's about knowing when, why, and how to say yes—without guilt.

This chapter is your roadmap to a budget that doesn't feel like a diet. It feels like a strategy. Like a plan that lets you fund your dreams, protect your peace, and still enjoy life.

Because financial freedom doesn't mean depriving yourself forever. It means giving yourself the structure to thrive—now and later.

We're going to walk through:

- The mindset shift that turns budgeting into empowerment
- Why most people fail at budgeting (and how to fix it)
- Different budgeting styles, and how to choose the one that fits you
- Real-world examples of sexy, flexible budgets
- Actionable steps to start (or restart) your budget today
- Scripts and tips to make budgeting work with your partner

- How to make your budget sustainable, not suffocating

Budgeting isn't about limitation. It's about liberation.

Let's make it feel that way.

The Mindset Shift: From Scarcity to Strategy

You know what's not sexy? Living paycheck to paycheck while pretending you're not stressed. Or spending blindly and then feeling guilty about it in silence. Or telling yourself that budgeting is for broke people.

You know what is sexy? Clarity. Confidence. Options. A plan.

Budgeting is not about giving up everything you love. It's about being honest about what you actually want—and creating a structure to afford it. That's the power shift.

When you stop seeing budgeting as a punishment and start seeing it as your game plan for freedom, everything changes.

Think of your budget like GPS. It's not telling you where you can't go. It's just helping you avoid traffic, tolls, and wasted time so you can get to your destination faster.

You are still the driver. The budget is just your map.

Why Most Budgets Fail (And How to Fix It)

Here's what trips most people up:

1. **They treat budgeting like a crash diet.**
2. Cutting out everything cold turkey, trying to go from chaos to monk-level discipline in a week. Unsustainable.
3. **They don't track the truth.**
4. Budgeting only works if you know your real numbers. Not your Instagram-worthy ones.
5. **They confuse frugality with success.**
6. Being cheap is not the same as being strategic. You can't shrink your way to wealth.
7. **They use someone else's formula.**
8. A budget is not one-size-fits-all. It should match your values, lifestyle, and goals.

9. **They forget to include joy.**
10. If your budget has no room for the things you love, you'll sabotage it within a month.

Fixing your budget starts with being honest about how you live, what matters to you, and what you want to change—without shame.

Popular Budgeting Styles (And How to Pick Yours)

Let's walk through a few approaches. Each one has its pros, cons, and best use case.

1. The 50/30/20 Rule

- 50% Needs
- 30% Wants
- 20% Savings/Debt

Great for: Simplicity lovers who want balance without over-tracking.

2. Zero-Based Budgeting

- Every dollar has a job.
- Income minus expenses equals zero.

Great for: Control freaks, detail lovers, and anyone cleaning up past financial messes.

3. Percentage-Based Buckets

- Customize your own ratios: 70/10/10/10 or 60/20/10/10

Great for: Entrepreneurs or folks with variable income who want to automate systems.

4. Envelope or Digital Envelope Method

- Allocate money into specific categories and stop spending when the envelope is empty.

Great for: Visual learners, overspenders, or anyone needing structure.

Your budget should match your personality. Don't force a system that feels like a prison. Find one that supports your flow.

How to Start (or Restart) Your Budget Today

1. **Know Your Net**
2. Start with what's actually hitting your account after taxes and deductions.
3. **Track Honestly for 30 Days**
4. No judgment. Just observe. Where is your money actually going?
5. **Categorize Your Life**
6. Instead of just bills, food, and savings, try categories like:

- Joy
- Security
- Essentials
- Growth
- Flex

1. **Set Intentional Percentages**
2. Don't just react. Decide: How much do you *want* to put toward each category?
3. **Automate Wherever You Can**
4. Treat your savings like a bill. Automate your transfers before you ever see the money.
5. **Adjust Monthly**
6. Budgets are not static. They flex with your life. Review and adapt.
7. **Name Your Money Goals**
8. Give your budget a purpose:

- Vacation in 6 months
- Pay off a credit card
- Save $5K emergency fund

- Invest $300/month

A goal without a plan is a wish.

A goal with a budget? That's a strategy.

Making Budgeting Feel Empowering (Not Embarrassing)

Budgeting isn't something you hide. It's something you lead with.

Instead of saying, "I can't afford that," try:

- "That's not in my current strategy."
- "I'm prioritizing something else right now."
- "I'm building something bigger."

You're not broke. You're focused.

Own your plan. Protect your peace.

Budgeting with a Partner: Love + Logic

Money is one of the biggest sources of tension in relationships. But it doesn't have to be.

If you're budgeting together:

- Pick a time where you both feel calm
- Avoid blame or past-focused language
- Focus on shared goals
- Create a joint money date ritual
- Have autonomy AND transparency

Try:

"Let's figure out a budget that honors both of our priorities."

Shared budgets are less about math and more about values.

When Life Throws Curveballs (Budgeting Through Chaos)

Got laid off? Big medical bill? A surprise expense?

Here's how to shift fast:

1. Cut back to your essentials category

2. Pause wants, but keep one joy line if possible
3. Communicate early if bills need to be deferred
4. Prioritize emergency savings and income rebuilding

The most powerful budgets are flexible.

Budgeting When You Have Inconsistent Income

Freelancers, entrepreneurs, gig workers—this is for you.

Your budget must be based on your *lowest* predictable income month.

Then:

- Save more during high months
- Automate transfers to savings and taxes
- Build a 3-6 month business buffer fund
- Live on last month's income (if possible)

Inconsistent income just means you need more planning, not more panic.

Creative Budgeting Categories That Make It Fun

- "Badass Business Fund"
- "Weekend Joy Money"
- "Glow Up Budget"
- "Family First"
- "Self-Care Savings"
- "Hot Girl Summer Stash"
- "Emergency Exit Fund"

This is your life. Label your money in ways that excite you.

Final Encouragement

You're not behind. You're just getting started.

Most people don't know how to budget in a way that feels good.

Now you do.

Budgeting isn't about saying no forever.

It's about knowing what you're saying yes to.

And yes—you deserve a life that feels abundant, intentional, and free.
Clarity is confidence.
And confidence is sexy.
Make one money move before you go to bed tonight.
Just one.
And then do another next week.
Your bank account will thank you.
Your future self will thank you.
And the version of you that doesn't feel broke anymore?
They'll be living proof that budgeting is beautiful.
Because financial literacy is sexy.
And so are you.

Chapter 7: The 50/30/20 Rule Remix

Customize Spending in a Way That Feels Good and Works

Let's get one thing straight: Personal finance is personal.

Yes, there are timeless money principles. Yes, there are systems that work. But the moment a budget feels like it belongs to someone else—a Pinterest mom, a finance bro, or your accountant uncle who hasn't smiled since 2007—you're not going to stick with it.

So let's remix something classic. The 50/30/20 Rule. You've probably heard of it. It's a popular budgeting framework:

- 50% of your income goes to needs
- 30% to wants
- 20% to savings and debt

Simple. Elegant. But maybe... too generic?

Because what counts as a "need" when your mental health depends on yoga class?

What's a "want" when it helps you network, build your brand, or show up with confidence?

What if your life doesn't break down into these neat little boxes?

This chapter is here to help you remix the 50/30/20 Rule into something that doesn't just look good on paper—but feels good in your real life.

The History and Logic Behind the Rule

The 50/30/20 Rule was popularized by U.S. Senator Elizabeth Warren in her book *All Your Worth: The Ultimate Lifetime Money Plan.* It was designed to be a simple structure for people to manage their income without feeling overwhelmed.

- 50% Needs: rent, groceries, utilities, insurance
- 30% Wants: dining out, streaming subscriptions, travel
- 20% Savings/Debt: emergency funds, retirement, paying down debt

The appeal? It's simple. Straightforward. It doesn't require complex spreadsheets or tracking every dollar.

But here's the catch: life is rarely this clean.

We live in a world of blended expenses. Uber rides that double as business transportation. Dinner dates that double as networking. Self-care rituals that double as mental health necessities.

So while the 50/30/20 framework is a great starting point, it might need a remix to reflect your real values, habits, and goals.

Why It Works for Some (And Not Others)

For people with stable income and average living costs, the original rule can be empowering. It provides:

- Clarity
- Balance
- Simplicity

But what if you live in a high-cost city? What if you're caring for aging parents? What if you're juggling gig work and your income changes monthly?

That 50% "needs" number? It might be 65% of your budget. And that's not a failure—it's reality.

This is where the remix comes in.

Redefining Needs, Wants, and Savings

Let's talk about how you define these categories for *you.*

Needs: Anything that keeps you safe, healthy, or employed. That could include:

- Rent or mortgage
- Groceries
- Internet (yes, it's essential now)
- Therapy
- Childcare
- Gas or transit

Wants: Things that add pleasure, convenience, or enrichment:

- Dining out
- Travel
- Designer clothes
- Subscriptions
- Upgraded phone

Savings/Debt: Anything that increases your net worth or reduces financial pressure:

- 401(k) contributions
- Roth IRA
- Emergency fund
- Credit card debt
- Student loan payments

Here's where it gets sexy: you can move these boundaries. Your version of a "want" might be someone else's "need." That's the point. Make it yours.

Customizing Your Own Ratio

Here are a few popular remixes of the 50/30/20 Rule:

60/20/20

- For people with high fixed costs (e.g. living in New York, supporting family)

40/30/20/10

- Needs: 40%
- Wants: 30%
- Savings: 20%
- Giving/Fun/Other: 10%

30/30/30/10

- A "rule of thirds" with 10% buffer for flexibility

70/10/10/10

- Works well for entrepreneurs or inconsistent income folks

You don't need to be rigid. The goal is to create a ratio that lets you:

- Meet your responsibilities
- Enjoy your life
- Build for the future
- Sleep at night

Real-Life Scenarios

Scenario 1: The Single Millennial with Side Hustles

- Monthly Net: $4,000
- Remix: 45% Needs ($1,800), 25% Wants ($1,000), 20% Savings ($800), 10% Business Investment ($400)

Scenario 2: Married Parents with Two Kids

- Monthly Net: $6,500
- Remix: 60% Needs ($3,900), 20% Wants ($1,300), 15% Savings ($975),

5% Giving ($325)

Scenario 3: 55-Year-Old Divorced Woman Rebuilding

- Monthly Net: $3,200
- Remix: 50% Needs ($1,600), 20% Wants ($640), 25% Savings ($800), 5% Emergency Buffer ($160)

See? Same rule. Different life. Different remix.

How to Use the Rule With Variable Income

When your income changes month-to-month, budgeting can feel impossible.

Here's the trick: budget off your *lowest consistent income month.*

If your income ranges from $3,000 to $6,000, plan your core budget around $3,000. Use the extra as follows:

- First: Build an emergency fund
- Next: Pay extra toward debt
- Then: Save or invest the rest

Consider:

- Creating a "hill and valley" account to smooth income
- Separating your business and personal finances
- Using percentages instead of fixed dollar amounts

Building Your Remix From Scratch

1. Track 3 months of real spending
2. Categorize by need, want, save
3. Calculate your real percentages
4. Adjust by 5% at a time
5. Test your remix for 90 days

Give yourself grace. You're not trying to impress a spreadsheet. You're building something that reflects your life.

Quick Tips for Making It Stick

- Automate your savings FIRST
- Use two checking accounts: one for bills, one for fun
- Label your savings accounts by goal
- Review and adjust monthly
- Celebrate small wins

And yes—budgeting can be sexy. Because what's sexier than control, clarity, and being able to say:

"I'm good. I got it covered."

Final Encouragement

You're not behind. You're just getting started.

The 50/30/20 Rule is a template. A guideline. A blueprint.

But the house you build? That's yours.

Make it beautiful. Make it bold. Make it yours.

Clarity is confidence. And confidence is sexy.

Make one money move before you go to bed tonight.

Just one.

And next week? Remix it again.

Because your money, your rhythm, your rules.

And the beat sounds a lot like freedom.

Financial literacy is sexy.

And so are you.

Chapter 8: Impulse Control Is Hot

Why Delayed Gratification Builds Real Power

Let's be honest: that swipe, that click, that buzz of a delivery notification feels good. Real good.

It's dopamine. It's convenience. It's the feeling that you're in control, treating yourself, making moves. But let me tell you something revolutionary:

Real control isn't about saying "yes" all the time. It's about knowing when to say "not yet."

Impulse control is the grown-up version of sexy. It's quiet confidence. It's power. It's walking into a room knowing your bills are paid, your investments are growing, and your peace is intact.

This chapter is about that power.

We're going to explore:

- Why impulse spending is so tempting (and so normal)
- How marketing is designed to make you feel behind if you don't spend
- The science of delayed gratification and wealth-building
- How to spot your financial triggers
- How to build real muscle around "not now"
- What impulse control actually looks like in real life
- How to flex this power without living like a monk

Because sexy isn't about never having what you want. It's about having *options.*

It's about designing a life that turns you on—not one that turns your credit card into a cry for help.

Impulse Spending Isn't a Character Flaw — It's a Design Feature

We live in a world engineered for consumption. Every app, every commercial, every popup ad is whispering the same message: "You need this now."

Social media makes it worse. The influencer you follow just posted a luxury skincare haul. Your college roommate is on their third vacation of the year. That girl from high school is driving a Tesla.

So you think, "Why not me? Why not now?"

Impulse spending isn't just emotional; it's biochemical. Every time you click "Add to Cart," your brain releases a hit of dopamine. It's the same feel-good chemical that lights up when you fall in love or eat chocolate.

In the short term, spending feels like winning.

In the long term, it can quietly strip away your power.

The Lies That Keep You Clicking

Here are some lies our culture feeds us:

- "You deserve this."
- "You can always make more money."
- "It's only $20."
- "Buy now, worry later."
- "This sale won't last."
- "Everyone else is doing it."

Those messages are designed to bypass your logic and go straight for your lizard brain. The part that fears missing out, the part that wants pleasure *now,* the part that doesn't like waiting.

But here's the truth:

You deserve peace.

You deserve freedom.

You deserve to build a life that gets richer, not more chaotic.

The Power of Delayed Gratification

There's a reason all the OGs in finance talk about compound interest. It's not just about money. It's about *momentum.*

Delayed gratification means saying:

"I could have that now... but I choose to wait because something better is coming."

That's not boring. That's powerful.

It means you're playing the long game.

It means you're in charge.

It means you're choosing legacy over likes.

How to Know Your Triggers

Let's do some self-awareness work.

When do you spend impulsively?

- Late at night scrolling?
- After a stressful workday?
- When you're bored, lonely, or anxious?
- After an argument?
- Right after payday?

Track it. Pattern it. Understand it.

Impulse spending isn't random. It's a coping mechanism.

Once you know your triggers, you can interrupt the pattern.

Build the Muscle of "Not Yet"

Impulse control isn't about never spending. It's about building a pause.

Try this:

1. **The 24-Hour Rule**

- Wait 24 hours before buying anything over $50 (or $20, or whatever your threshold is).
- Nine times out of ten, the urge fades.

1. **Make a "Lust List"**

- Create a note in your phone titled: "Stuff I Might Want to Buy."
- Put everything there. Revisit it monthly.

1. **Use a Wishlist Extension**

- Sites like Pinterest or browser plug-ins let you "save" items without buying.
- Just seeing the list scratches the same mental itch—without draining your account.

1. **Celebrate the Flex**

- When you skip a purchase, mark it down.
- Use a tracker, journal, or app.
- Treat impulse control like a win—because it is.

What It Looks Like in Real Life

Let's break this down with a few real scenarios:

Scenario 1: The Daily Coffee Fix

- Old You: $6 latte five days a week
- New You: $6 latte twice a week, and a bomb homemade coffee setup the rest
- Money saved over a year: ~$750

Scenario 2: The Online Shopping Spiral

- Old You: Scroll, click, regret
- New You: Wishlist it, check back in a week, buy only if it still feels like a yes
- Peace of mind: Priceless

Scenario 3: The Payday Splurge

- Old You: Bought clothes to feel rewarded
- New You: Transfers $100 to Roth IRA before shopping
- You still get the thrill, but now you're building wealth with it

Delayed Gratification = Real Wealth

When you delay gratification, three things happen:

1. You stay liquid.
2. You stay calm.
3. You stay ready.

You're not maxed out. You're not reactive. You're positioned to *pounce* on a good opportunity—a new investment, a dream trip, a surprise emergency—without panic.

That's power. That's real freedom.

Flexing Without Deprivation

Let's be real: You don't need to live like a hermit to build wealth.

Impulse control isn't about punishment. It's about *intention.*

Spend on what lights you up. Just *own it.*

Build a budget that includes joy.

Make room for the dinner dates, the massages, the fly shoes.

But make sure they're a choice, not a default.

Hot tip: Build a "Play Money" fund.

- Load a debit card every month with your fun money.
- When it's gone, it's gone.
- No guilt. No overdraft. Full control.

Final Thoughts: Control Is the New Cool

Impulse control isn't about being boring.

It's about being unstoppable.

It's about knowing you can buy something—but choosing to wait because you've got bigger plans.

That's hot.

That's grown.

That's sexy as hell.

Before You Go

You're not behind.

You're just getting started.

Most people don't know this stuff—until they do.

Now you do.

Clarity is confidence. And confidence is sexy.

Make one money move before you go to bed tonight.

Just one.

Pause before buying. Open a new savings account. Write down a goal.

Then do another next week.

Because impulse control isn't a killjoy.

It's a superpower.

And the richest people in the room?

They're not impulsive.

They're intentional.

And so are you.

Chapter 9: Financial Boundaries Are Attractive

Saying "No" Is a Flex

Let's start with a truth bomb: boundaries are sexy.

Not just in your romantic life, not just in friendships, not just in your career. Boundaries with your money are the ultimate form of self-respect. And respect is hot.

Saying "no" to financial obligations that don't serve you isn't rude. It's responsible.

Turning down a dinner invite you can't afford? That's strength.

Refusing to co-sign your cousin's sketchy car loan? That's wisdom.

Not joining every group trip, birthday dinner, destination wedding, and shopping spree? That's discipline. That's clarity. That's power.

And power, my friend, is magnetic.

Why Boundaries Matter

Most of us are taught to avoid conflict. To people-please. To not rock the boat. Especially when it comes to money.

We're told: If you have it, share it. Don't be selfish. Don't be greedy. Don't make people uncomfortable.

But let's flip that script.

Financial boundaries aren't about hoarding money. They're about protecting your peace.

They're about making sure your future self doesn't hate your present-day people-pleasing self.

They're about ensuring that generosity comes from overflow, not obligation.

They're about building a financial life that reflects your values, not your guilt.

And most importantly, they're about living authentically—without financial anxiety simmering under every smile.

What Financial Boundaries Actually Look Like

You don't need to announce your budget on a billboard. But you do need to get honest about what you can and can't afford—and what you want to spend your money on.

Financial boundaries can look like:

- Having a set monthly budget for giving—and sticking to it.
- Saying "I'm not in a place to contribute right now" when friends ask you to chip in for something.
- Choosing not to lend money to people who haven't paid you back in the past.
- Opting for dinner at home instead of a $200 night out.
- Declining to cover someone else's expenses "just this once" if it stretches you thin.

You are not a bad person for saying no.

You are a person who values their stability.

The Pressure to Say "Yes"

Let's be real: saying "yes" often feels easier. It keeps things smooth. It avoids awkwardness.

But ease in the moment can lead to resentment later.

You shouldn't be financially punishing yourself to keep up appearances, maintain friendships, or avoid a hard conversation.

This isn't about becoming stingy. This is about becoming aligned.

Aligned with your goals. With your peace. With your power.

The Real Cost of People-Pleasing

Let's do the math.

Say you spend $300 a month on stuff you don't actually want to do, but feel obligated to:

- Dinner invites
- Wedding gifts
- GoFundMes
- Brunches
- Group trips
- Baby showers

That's $3,600 a year.

Over a decade? $36,000.

That's a down payment on a home. That's a fully funded emergency fund. That's a Roth IRA that could grow into six figures by retirement.

That's the cost of never learning how to say "no."

Scripts That Make Saying "No" Easier

You don't need to write a novel. You just need a line or two that's clear, kind, and final.

Try these:

- "That sounds fun, but it's not in my budget right now."
- "I'm focusing on some financial goals this year, so I'm going to pass."
- "I wish I could, but I'm not in a position to contribute."

- "That's not something I can do at the moment."
- "Let's do something more low-key next time."

You don't owe anyone an explanation. But if you want to give one, do it on your terms—with boundaries intact.

When It's Family Asking

This one's the hardest. We're conditioned to think blood means unlimited access.

But setting boundaries with family isn't betrayal.

It's maturity.

It's breaking the cycle where one person succeeds and then becomes the family ATM.

You can love your family and say no to being financially drained by them.

Try this:

- "I'm working on building stability for my own household. I can't help right now."
- "I've set a budget for family gifts and support. I'm at my limit this month."

It's okay to pause before agreeing. It's okay to say no without guilt.

Boundaries in Romantic Relationships

This is where boundaries and vulnerability really collide.

Money is a form of intimacy. If you're constantly spending to impress, accommodate, or smooth things over—you're not in a partnership. You're in a performance.

True connection means honesty.

Set expectations early:

- "Let's talk about what our date nights will look like budget-wise."
- "Can we split this trip in a way that feels fair to both of us?"
- "Here's what I'm comfortable spending right now."

Financial boundaries don't kill the romance. They protect it.

They build trust. They keep resentment out of your bedroom.

What to Do With Pushback

Yes, some people won't like your boundaries. Especially if they benefited from you not having any.

That's not your problem to fix.

It's your pattern to break.

Stand firm.

Hold your line.

You don't have to be cruel. But you do have to be clear.

And anyone who respects you will respect your boundary.

The Long-Term Benefits of Financial Boundaries

Let's zoom out.

Here's what strong boundaries give you over time:

- **Peace:** No more lying awake worried about how to pay for someone else's choices.
- **Clarity:** You start spending based on your goals, not guilt.
- **Consistency:** Your financial habits become predictable and powerful.
- **Confidence:** You become the kind of person who respects their money—and demands others do, too.

Action Steps

- Write down your top 3 financial priorities right now. Use them to guide your "yes" and "no."
- Create a giving budget. Decide in advance how much you'll contribute monthly or annually.
- Practice one boundary-setting script this week in a real-life situation.
- Make a list of people, events, or habits that consistently cost you more than they're worth.
- Visualize your future self thanking you for the "no's" you said today.

You're Not Behind. You're Just Getting Started.

There's no shame in having lacked boundaries before. Most of us weren't taught how to set them.

But now you know better. And that means you can do better.

Every "no" today is a "yes" to your future.

Every clear line you draw is a step toward peace.

Every time you choose you—you build wealth that isn't just financial, but emotional.

Clarity Is Confidence. And Confidence Is Sexy.

The hottest version of you?

The one who's not afraid to disappoint others in order to honor themselves.

The one who can go to bed with a balanced budget, a calm mind, and zero regret.

The one who knows that boundaries aren't walls—they're doors to the life you actually want.

So flex your "no."

Not out of anger.

Not out of fear.

Out of love.

Out of purpose.

Out of power.

And then watch what happens when your money, your mind, and your relationships all align with your boundaries.

That's real wealth.

That's real sexy.

That's real freedom.

You're not behind.

You're just getting started.

Now go make one bold money move before bed tonight.

Just one.

Then do another next week.

Your mirror will thank you.

Your bank account will thank you.

And your future self?

They'll be in awe.

Chapter 10: Leveling Up = Leaving the Financial Friend Zone

Growth Means Letting Go of Stagnant People and Habits

Let's get real: nothing holds your money back like the people and patterns you refuse to outgrow.

That might sting a little. But it's the truth.

And truth is sexy.

You're not just here to budget your lattes or open a savings account. You're here to level up—to stop playing small with your money, your mindset, and your environment. To stop apologizing for wanting more, doing better, and expecting financial respect from the people around you.

Let's talk about what it really takes to rise. Not just in dollars, but in how you carry yourself. In what you tolerate. In how you protect your energy, your assets, and your future.

Because leveling up financially means leaving behind more than just bad spending habits. It means leaving the financial friend zone—that blurry space where people smile at your ambition but never support your growth. Where people praise your hustle but secretly hope you never pass them.

This chapter is about making peace with your evolution.

Even if it makes others uncomfortable.

Even if it means outgrowing people you love.

Even if it means admitting that your old habits—the ones that felt cozy, familiar, and safe—are part of what kept you stuck.

Let's go there. Let's talk about how to grow without guilt.

And how to love yourself enough to leave the financial friend zone behind.

When Familiar Becomes a Financial Trap

You know what's harder than budgeting? Letting go of comfort. Letting go of the friends who don't want to talk about investing because it "feels too bougie." The cousin who calls you "rich" because you said no to brunch this weekend. The job that keeps paying you less than you're worth—but feels stable. The lifestyle you curated because it made you fit in, not because it actually fed your soul.

The financial friend zone is a comfort trap. You're in the circle. You're accepted. You don't rock the boat. But your wallet is tight. Your goals are blurry. Your confidence is quiet. And somewhere deep down, you know you're meant for more.

Growth demands discomfort. It demands change. And change is often lonely at first.

But loneliness is not a life sentence.

It's a short-term fee you pay to break free.

Why People Fear Your Financial Growth

Let's unpack why your glow-up feels threatening to some folks.

It's not just about the money.

It's about what your growth reflects back at them.

When you level up, you disrupt the narrative. You become a mirror. Your ambition challenges their excuses. Your discipline confronts their denial. Your progress reminds them of their procrastination.

And not everyone is ready for that.

But that doesn't mean you should shrink.

That means you hold your posture, keep walking, and let their discomfort be their own to manage.

From People Pleasing to Progress Making

Saying yes to every invite, loan request, or "let's split this" dinner can quietly kill your financial future. There's a cost to constant accommodation. There's a cost to always being the one who gives, explains, adjusts, and picks up the slack.

Financially leveling up means learning the power of no:

No, I can't loan you money right now.

No, I'm not going out to eat three times this week.

No, I'm not co-signing that lease.

No, I'm not booking that vacation until my emergency fund is solid.

You don't need to be rude. You just need to be clear.

Your money boundaries are not mean.

They are mature.

Let's Talk About Lifestyle Creep

You're making more money, but where is it going?

That's lifestyle creep.

It's when you get a raise and suddenly your clothes, car, home, and habits all level up—but your savings stays flat.

You're not building wealth. You're just looking wealthier. That's a trap.

Here's the remix: Let your income go up. Let your habits stay grounded. Budget like you're rich in wisdom, not just in dollars.

Every new level of income is a new chance to:

- Build a gap between what you earn and what you spend
- Increase your investments
- Max out that Roth IRA
- Knock down debt
- Secure your freedom, not just flex your style

Redefining Your Circle

Not everyone is meant to go with you.

That doesn't mean you don't love them.

It just means you love your future more.

When you start having money goals, some friendships shift. Some grow with you. Others fade quietly. You may find yourself craving new conversations. You might start feeling restless around small talk, drained by complaining, turned off by recklessness.

You're not being bougie.

You're evolving.

Start creating space for people who:

- Celebrate your wins without making it weird
- Talk about budgeting and investing like it's normal
- Respect your boundaries
- Push you to think bigger

That's your new tribe. And they're out there.

You just have to leave the old room to find the new one.

How to Have Hard Money Conversations

It starts with honesty.

Here's how to say it:

"Hey, I'm working on some financial goals right now. That means I'm being more intentional with my money."

That's it.

You don't owe anyone a spreadsheet. You don't need to apologize. You don't need to make excuses.

You're allowed to choose your priorities.

And anyone who makes you feel guilty for that might not be rooting for you the way you thought they were.

The Sexy Side of Saying No

Saying no isn't just responsible. It's magnetic.

Clarity is sexy. Boundaries are hot.

When you honor your money, you show the world you honor yourself.

You attract people who respect that.

You attract opportunities that align with that.

You build a life that supports that.

Your yes becomes more powerful because it means something.

Growth Means Grieving Too

Here's the part nobody tells you:

Leveling up is emotional.

You might grieve:

- The friends who stop calling
- The version of you that used to feel carefree
- The parties you don't attend
- The identity you built around "just getting by"

Let yourself feel it.

But don't stay there.

Because on the other side of that grief is glory.

Build. Bloom. Become.

You are not behind. You are just getting started.

Most people don't know this stuff until they do.

Now you do.

Clarity is confidence. And confidence is sexy.

Make one money move before you go to bed tonight.

Just one.

And then do another next week.

Leave the friend zone.

Step into your power.

Your glow-up is not just financial. It's spiritual. It's emotional. It's relational.

Own it.

The future you deserves nothing less.

Part III: Credit Is Your Financial Glow-Up

Welcome to the part of the book where your money reputation gets a makeover. Credit isn't just a three-digit number—it's a reflection of how confidently you handle financial responsibility, and it can either open doors or quietly shut them. In Part III, we're not just talking about credit scores. We're digging into the mindset, the mechanics, and the money moves that turn credit into your personal power tool.

We'll explore how to build credit from scratch, repair it after mistakes, and use it to your advantage instead of feeling like it's a judgment hanging over your head. We'll debunk myths, break down terms like APR and utilization rate in plain language, and show you how to flirt with credit responsibly—no shame, no fear.

This isn't about being perfect. It's about being prepared. Whether you're trying to qualify for your first mortgage, get better insurance rates, or stop co-signing for folks who don't pay you back, this section will give you the knowledge and swagger to walk into any room—and any loan application—like a boss.

Because in a world where credit matters, clarity is power. And power? Is always sexy.

Chapter 11: Credit Scores Are Like Dating Profiles

Let's be real. If your money had a Tinder bio, your credit score would be the first impression. It's not your whole story, but it tells the algorithm a lot. Just like a dating profile, your credit score is a snapshot that helps others decide whether to swipe right on your financial life. Banks, landlords, car dealerships, and sometimes even employers are looking at that number to determine if you're responsible, stable, and trustworthy.

But here's the sexy truth: You get to shape the narrative. Your credit score is not a verdict. It's a reflection of your past behavior, and it can be rewritten with intention, strategy, and time. This chapter is about breaking down how credit actually works, how to fix it if it's a mess, and how to use it to your advantage without selling your soul to debt.

Why Credit Scores Are a Big Deal (But Not a Dealbreaker)

Let's start with the basics. Your credit score is a three-digit number that lenders use to assess how likely you are to repay borrowed money. It usually ranges from 300 to 850. A higher score means you're considered less risky.

Here's the breakdown of what your credit score affects:

- Your interest rates on loans and credit cards
- Whether you get approved for an apartment

- Your car insurance premiums
- Whether you qualify for certain jobs (yes, seriously)
- Your ability to get a mortgage and how much you pay for it over time

So yeah, it matters. But it's not permanent. And it sure as hell doesn't define your worth.

The Anatomy of a Credit Score (Plain Language Version)

Ever been confused about why your score went down when you paid off a card? Or why closing that store card from 2007 made things worse? Here's a simple breakdown of what makes up your score:

1. Payment History (35%)

This is your "I show up on time" section. Late payments? That's like ghosting your date. Not a good look.

2. Credit Utilization (30%)

This is the balance you carry versus your total limit. Ideally, you want to keep your usage under 30% of your available credit. Under 10% is even better. Maxing out your cards is the financial equivalent of showing up to a date bragging about your ex.

3. Length of Credit History (15%)

The longer your accounts have been open, the more it helps your score. It shows consistency and reliability.

4. Credit Mix (10%)

This is about diversity. Credit cards, car loans, mortgages, student loans—having a mix shows you can handle different types of relationships (with debt).

5. New Credit (10%)

Opening a lot of accounts in a short period? That's like speed dating—a red flag.

What Your Score Actually Says About You

- **Under 580**: You've made some questionable choices. Maybe you ghosted a lender. But that doesn't mean you're not relationship material. It just means you've got work to do.
- **580–670**: You're dating again, but people still check your Instagram history. Not terrible, but not earning trust yet.
- **670–739**: This is a solid place to be. You're financially dateable. People are ready to make long-term plans.
- **740+**: You're a catch. You show up, follow through, and you've probably got great credit boundaries.

Sexy Credit Habits to Build

- **Pay your bills on time** like your future depends on it—because it does.
- **Use autopay** for at least the minimum payment to avoid slip-ups.
- **Keep old accounts open**, even if you don't use them.
- **Ask for credit limit increases**, especially if your income has gone up. (Just don't increase your spending too.)
- **Check your credit reports** at least once a year. (You can get them free at AnnualCreditReport.com.)

Real-Life Scenario: Fixing a Fumbled Score

Let's say you were young, broke, and forgot to pay that $200 credit card bill. Now it's in collections, your score is in the low 600s, and you're trying to adult.

What do you do?

- Call the creditor and ask for a "pay for delete" agreement.
- Pay off any collections or late accounts in full.
- Get a secured credit card and use it responsibly.

- Set up payment reminders or use apps like Mint or Credit Karma.
- Be patient. Credit repair is like healing a broken heart—it takes time and consistency.

Credit and Commitment: What to Know in a Relationship

Before you share finances, share credit reports. Seriously.

Have a "money date" where you both:

- Pull your credit reports and scores
- Discuss debts, savings, and goals
- Set boundaries on co-signing and joint accounts

Love is great. So is honesty. Combine the two.

Let's Talk About Credit Shame

You are not your credit score.

Read that again.

Maybe your parents never taught you this stuff. Maybe life hit you hard. Maybe you used credit to survive. Shame doesn't build wealth—strategy does. Give yourself the grace to learn, grow, and build.

Final Word

Your credit score is a tool. It can be sharpened. It can be improved. It can be used to build the life you want. It doesn't mean you're behind, and it doesn't mean you're not worthy.

You are.

So go pull that credit report. Review it like your next date is asking for the truth. Build it like you're preparing for the love story of a lifetime—with yourself and your money.

And remember:

Clarity is confidence. And confidence is sexy.

Now make one money move before bed tonight. Just one. Check your score, pay a bill, or set up autopay. Then next week? Do it again.

You're leveling up. Keep going.

Chapter 12: How to Fix Bad Credit Like a Boss

Opening Hook

You are not your credit score. Read that again. Let it sink in. Your credit score isn't your IQ. It's not your value. It's not your future. It's a snapshot of your past decisions and, in many cases, your survival strategies. But here's the sexy truth: you can change it. And you don't need a miracle. You just need information, intention, and action.

Let's be clear from the jump—there is zero shame here. If you're in a season of repair, you're not behind. You're taking your power back. That's boss energy.

Why This Chapter Matters

Credit impacts everything: your ability to rent a home, get a car, lock in low insurance rates, even land a job in some industries. It's not just about borrowing. It's about credibility.

Bad credit can feel like walking around with a scarlet letter stamped to your chest. But the truth is, millions of people have dealt with this. Life happens—medical bills, layoffs, financial trauma, or just not knowing what you didn't know. Now you do.

So now we fix it. Together.

This chapter walks you through the steps to repair your credit like the boss you are—without judgment, jargon, or BS. We're not going to make you feel bad. We're going to make you feel empowered.

Step 1: Face It Like a Grown-Up

Before you can fix anything, you need to know what you're working with. That means checking your credit reports from all three bureaus—Equifax, TransUnion, and Experian.

Go to AnnualCreditReport.com and request your free reports. You can do this once a year from each bureau. During the pandemic, you could check weekly. As of now, it's still more than once annually for most folks—use it.

What to Look For:

- Missed payments
- Collections
- Charged-off accounts
- Accounts that aren't yours
- Inaccurate information (wrong addresses, duplicate accounts, etc.)

This step can be triggering. If you feel overwhelmed, take breaks. But don't avoid it. This is the part where you reclaim the narrative.

Step 2: Dispute What's Not Yours

Mistakes happen all the time. If there are errors on your report, you have the legal right to dispute them.

You can do this online or by mail. Keep it simple:

- Identify the mistake
- Attach any supporting documents (optional but helpful)
- Send the dispute to the bureau that reported it

Once submitted, they have 30 days to respond. If they don't, or if they rule in your favor, the item must be removed.

That's right—you've got rights.

Step 3: Pay Off Collections Strategically

Collections accounts are one of the biggest credit killers. But not all are created equal.

Some tips:

- Don't rush to pay until you know the impact.
- If an account is more than seven years old, it may fall off soon. Don't awaken sleeping giants.
- Negotiate a "pay for delete" agreement—this means they remove the item after you pay.
- Get everything in writing before sending money.

Paying collections can boost your score *if* done strategically. Random payments without a game plan? Not sexy.

Step 4: Bring Past-Due Accounts Current

Late payments hurt. But recent late payments hurt more than older ones. If you're behind:

- Call the creditor. Ask for hardship options.
- Set up a payment plan to bring accounts current.
- Request they stop reporting you late if you've brought things back into good standing.

Sometimes, just calling and asking for help can make a bigger impact than you'd expect.

Step 5: Use the Credit-Building Trifecta

Rebuilding your credit means showing lenders you've changed your habits. Here's your toolkit:

1. **Secured Credit Card** – You put down a deposit, then use the card like a normal one. After a few months, it reports positively.
2. **Credit-Builder Loan** – You "borrow" a small amount (usually $300–$1000), but the bank holds the money in a savings account. You make payments over time, then get the money back.
3. **Authorized User Status** – Someone with good credit adds you to their card (no spending needed), and you benefit from their history.

Start with one or two. Use them responsibly. Watch your score grow.

Step 6: Automate Everything

Life is busy. Forgetting a payment shouldn't tank your score.

Set all your bills to auto-pay—at least the minimums. Use reminders, budgeting apps, or a simple calendar alert.

Lenders don't care why you missed a payment. They just see the result. Automate and protect your score like it's sacred. Because it is.

Step 7: Keep Your Utilization Low

Credit utilization = how much of your available credit you're using.

Rule of thumb: keep it under 30% per card. Want to be extra sexy? Aim for under 10%.

Example: If your credit limit is $1000, never let your balance hit more than $300.

This one factor accounts for about 30% of your credit score. It's big. Keep it tight.

Step 8: Build New Habits, Not Just New Credit

This isn't just about fixing the number. It's about becoming the version of you who respects money, who honors your future self, who doesn't confuse generosity with self-neglect.

Financial glow-ups come from identity shifts. Not just debt payoffs.

Real Talk: What to Avoid

- Don't close old accounts unless they charge fees. Older credit = better score.
- Don't open too many new accounts at once. Each hard inquiry dings you.
- Don't pay for shady "credit repair" services promising overnight miracles.
- Don't let shame stop you from asking for help.

Boss Moves to Make This Week

- Pull your credit reports
- Dispute one error

- Open a secured credit card
- Set up one auto-pay
- Pay off a small balance
- Create a "credit wins" journal to track your progress

Small steps. Big impact.

Final Thoughts

You don't need a perfect score to have a powerful life. You need progress, momentum, and knowledge.

Every on-time payment is a flex. Every low balance is a love letter to your future. Every new limit, every paid collection, every strategic move—it's you rewriting your story.

And the new story? It's not just richer. It's smarter. It's bolder. It's sexy.

End This Chapter With:

You're not behind. You're just getting started.

Most people don't know this stuff—until they do. Now you do.

Clarity is confidence. And confidence is sexy.

Make one money move before you go to bed tonight. Just one. And then do another next week.

Your future self? They're cheering already.

Let's go, boss.

Chapter 13: The Art of the Credit Card

Credit cards: seductive, powerful, and—if used correctly—downright rewarding. But let's be clear from the jump: this isn't about glorifying debt. This is about understanding how to use credit cards like a boss, not a victim.

Because when done right, credit cards aren't a trap. They're a tool. A flex. A jet stream of financial leverage that can level up your life, help build your credit, fund your vacations, protect your purchases, and, yes, even earn you money. But when done wrong? They're shackles.

So let's talk about how to master the art. Not just survive it.

Why This Chapter Matters

If you were never taught how credit cards work, welcome to the club. Most people only learn after making a mistake. Missed payments. Maxed-out limits. Collections. Credit score nosedives. That's how the majority of folks get initiated.

We're doing it differently.

This chapter exists to help you skip the shame spiral and go straight into the strategy. To make your credit cards work for you. To decode what you were never taught, demystify the rewards systems, and highlight the sexy discipline of intentional swiping.

Because here's the truth: The problem isn't the plastic. It's the lack of a plan.

You're about to get one.

The Real Power of Plastic

Let's start by busting the myth: Credit cards are not inherently evil.

They are:

- A fast way to build credit when used right
- A safety net in emergencies
- A method for tracking expenses
- A portal to points, cashback, travel perks, and buyer protections

But they are also:

- A high-interest trap if you carry a balance
- A confidence killer when used emotionally
- A debt spiral waiting to happen if not used intentionally

Let's be clear: the card isn't the problem. It's the behavior. So let's learn the behavior that makes the card work for you, not against you.

How Credit Cards Work (Plain and Simple)

Every credit card has the same core anatomy:

- **Credit Limit**: The maximum amount you're allowed to borrow
- **Available Credit**: What you haven't spent yet
- **Statement Balance**: What you owe for the month
- **Minimum Payment**: The smallest amount you must pay to avoid late fees
- **Due Date**: The day your payment is due
- **APR (Annual Percentage Rate)**: The interest charged if you don't pay in full

The golden rule? Pay your balance in full and on time. Every. Single. Month.

If you can't do that, pause. Don't swipe. You're spending future you's peace of mind.

Rewards Without Regret: Understanding the Perks

Here's where things get fun.

Credit card rewards can be:

- **Cashback**: 1% to 5% back on your spending
- **Points**: Redeemable for travel, gift cards, or statement credits
- **Miles**: Airline points that can cut flight costs drastically
- **Sign-Up Bonuses**: Often $100–$1000+ after meeting a spend threshold
- **Perks**: Lounge access, concierge service, travel insurance, extended warranties

Used smartly, these rewards can make credit cards a net gain, not just a convenience.

Hacks for Maximizing Credit Card Benefits

1. **Use the Right Card for the Right Purchase**

- Grocery card for groceries.
- Travel card for flights.
- Cashback card for everyday expenses.

1. **Automate Your Payments**

- Set up auto-pay for full balances. No interest. No missed payments. No stress.

1. **Track Rewards and Redemption Dates**

- Points can expire. Know your expiration dates. Use apps like AwardWallet or Mint.

1. **Stack Rewards with Cashback Portals**

- Use Rakuten, Honey, or credit card shopping portals to double-dip on rewards.

1. **Monitor for Annual Fees**

- Not all fees are bad. Just make sure the value you get exceeds the cost.

The Red Flags You Should Never Ignore

- **Only making minimum payments**: You're renting your past purchases.
- **Using cards to cover basic living expenses**: This is a budget red flag, not a card perk.
- **Opening too many cards at once**: Your score can dip, and it signals risk to lenders.
- **Not knowing your APR**: It's usually 15% to 29%+. That's loan shark territory.
- **Being seduced by rewards and ignoring your cash flow**: Don't spend $1000 to earn $50 if you didn't need to spend the $1000.

Real-Life Scenarios

Scenario 1: The Vacay Trick

You have a trip coming up. You open a travel card with a $600 sign-up bonus after spending $4,000 in 3 months. You book flights, hotels, and food on it—things you'd already planned to spend on. Pay it off in full. Boom: free flight next time.

Scenario 2: The Credit Newbie

You're 22, just got your first job. You open a no-annual-fee cashback card. You automate Netflix, gas, and groceries on the card, then automate the full payment from your checking account. After 12 months, your credit score jumps 100+ points.

Scenario 3: The Emergency Lifeline

You lose your job. You have $0 savings. A credit card helps you cover essentials until unemployment hits. Not ideal, but lifesaving. You pay it down over 6 months, now with a repayment plan in place. A lesson, not a failure.

Action Steps (Do These Today)

1. **Check Your Credit Score and Credit Card APRs**
2. **List All Your Cards and Their Rewards Structures**
3. **Pick One Card to Maximize This Month**
4. **Automate the Payment in Full**
5. **Set a Monthly Reminder to Review Spending & Rewards**
6. **If You're Carrying Debt: Stop Swiping. Start Snowballing.**

Pros and Cons of Credit Card Use

Pros:

- Builds credit when used right
- Offers rewards, points, and perks
- Protects purchases and extends warranties
- Useful in emergencies
- Safer than debit for fraud protection

Cons:

- High-interest rates if unpaid
- Easy to overspend emotionally
- Potential to wreck credit if mismanaged
- Annual fees if not offset
- Late fees, over-limit fees, foreign transaction fees

Let's Be Real: Emotional Triggers Around Credit Cards

A lot of credit card use isn't financial. It's emotional.

You're not buying things. You're buying:

- Comfort after a long week

- Status in front of your friends
- Security you didn't grow up with
- A dopamine hit to feel less numb

When you learn to pause and ask, "What am I *really* buying?", you slow down the swipe. That's when power begins.

Closing the Confidence Gap

You don't have to be rich to use credit cards well.

You just need:

- Awareness
- Intentionality
- A system
- A plan

And you're building all of that right now.

Final Thoughts

Credit cards are neither heroes nor villains. They're mirrors. They reflect how you think, feel, and act around money.

But now you see the playbook.

Now you've got a grip on the game.

Now it's not scary anymore.

You can own the art of the credit card.

Swipe smart. Earn big. Build sexy credit.

You're not behind. You're just getting started.

Most people don't know this stuff—until they do. Now you do.

Clarity is confidence. And confidence is sexy.

Make one money move before you go to bed tonight. Just one. And then do another next week.

Chapter 14: Debt: The Unsexy Kind

Debt. Let's be honest—it's not the sexiest word in the financial dictionary. It's not glamorous. It doesn't make you feel powerful. And most of the time, it comes with stress, shame, and silence. But here's the truth: getting out of debt? That's sexy as hell. Taking control of your financial story, rewriting the ending, and saying, "I'm not going to be owned by my past choices or current bills anymore"? That's empowerment in its rawest form.

So let's talk about debt. The unsexy kind. The kind that creeps up on you in your twenties, keeps you up at night in your thirties, and can quietly drain your dreams in your forties and fifties if you let it. But we're not going to let it. Not anymore. This chapter isn't about making you feel bad for your credit card balance or student loans. This is about giving you the tools, mindset, and method to fix it—and fix it like a boss.

The Real Talk: Types of Debt

Not all debt is created equal. Some debt can actually work in your favor. Other debt? It needs to go.

1. High-Interest Debt (Credit Cards, Payday Loans)

This is the emergency room of debt. It's bleeding money fast, and you need to triage it.

2. Medium-Interest Debt (Auto Loans, Personal Loans)

Not catastrophic, but still not ideal. If it's above 5-7% interest, it's costing you.

3. Low-Interest Debt (Mortgages, Student Loans)

This is more of a long-game debt. Manageable, especially if you're building assets or investing in your future.

4. Toxic Debt (Title Loans, Rent-to-Own, Buy Now Pay Later Traps)

Predatory and designed to trap you. These aren't just financial potholes—they're sinkholes.

The Debt Mindset Detox

Before we even touch a spreadsheet or calculate an APR, let's address the internal stuff. Because debt isn't just numbers. It's emotional.

Guilt, embarrassment, fear—those emotions love to hide behind minimum payments. They whisper lies like "you'll never be free" or "everyone else has it together but you." Lies.

Let's rewrite that narrative:

- You are not your debt.
- You're not behind.
- You're about to do something most people avoid their whole lives: face it head-on.

Step 1: Know What You Owe (Even If It Hurts)

Pull every balance. Credit cards, car loans, student loans, the furniture you financed 3 years ago. Write it down. Create your full picture. Then add:

- Balance
- Interest Rate
- Minimum Payment
- Due Date

Seeing it all in one place? That's power.

Step 2: Choose Your Paydown Strategy (Snowball vs. Avalanche)

The Snowball Method:

Pay off the smallest debt first for a quick win, then roll that payment into the next.

- Great for motivation.
- Feels rewarding fast.

The Avalanche Method:

Pay off the highest interest rate first.

- Mathematically saves you the most.
- Takes more discipline.

Choose what works for *you*. What keeps you moving? What makes you feel in control?

Step 3: Find Your Financial Fire

Every extra dollar counts. Can you:

- Cancel a subscription?
- Cook more at home?
- Sell something you don't use?
- Pick up a freelance gig?
- Redirect your tax refund?

You don't have to go extreme. But redirecting even $100/month makes a difference over time.

Step 4: Negotiate Like a Boss

Call your creditors. Yes, seriously. You can:

- Request lower interest rates
- Settle for a lump sum (if you have the cash)
- Set up a hardship plan

Your voice is powerful. Use it.

Step 5: Automate and Celebrate

Set up automatic payments. No more missed due dates. No more late fees. Then, celebrate small wins:

- First card paid off? Wine night.
- Cut a loan in half? Spa day.

This journey deserves joy.

Sexy Scenario: The Couple Who Tackled $52K in Debt Together

Jasmine and Malcolm had six credit cards between them and $18K in student loans. They were making decent money but constantly arguing about spending. They decided to treat debt payoff like a team sport. Every Friday was a "money date" with snacks, Spotify, and real talk. Two years later, they were debt-free. And their relationship? Stronger than ever.

Red Flags to Watch For

- **Consolidation scams**
- **Debt settlement companies promising miracles**
- **Borrowing from retirement accounts to pay credit cards**

- **Using new credit to pay old credit**

If it sounds too easy, it's not the solution.

When to Consider Professional Help

If you feel stuck, overwhelmed, or in crisis, get support. Options:

- Credit counseling agencies (non-profit)
- Financial planners
- Bankruptcy attorneys (last resort, but sometimes a valid one)

There is no shame in asking for help.

Let's Talk About Student Loans

Student loans can feel endless. But here's how to break them down:

- **Know your servicer.** (Log in and get clear.)
- **Explore forgiveness programs** if you qualify.
- **Consider income-driven repayment** plans.
- **Make peace with the timeline.** Sometimes slow and steady wins.

Final Word: Debt Isn't Your Identity

Paying off debt is not about punishment. It's about possibility.

- You are not less worthy because you owe money.
- You are not a failure because you financed a mistake.
- You are powerful enough to change your story.

Every payment is progress. Every dollar sent to a balance is a brick in your foundation. Every "no" to an impulse purchase is a "yes" to your future.

Your glow-up starts here. Not with a six-figure savings account. Not with an inheritance. But with this moment. This decision. This chapter.

You got this.

End With:

- You're not behind. You're just getting started.
- Most people don't know this stuff—until they do. Now you do.
- Clarity is confidence. And confidence is sexy.
- Make one money move before you go to bed tonight. Just one. And then do another next week.

Your debt isn't sexy.

But your financial power?

Now *that*'s hot.

Chapter 15: Student Loans Don't Have to Be a Life Sentence

Let's get one thing out of the way: you are not your student debt. That balance you see on your loan statement doesn't reflect your worth, your intelligence, or your potential. It's just a number—and numbers can change.

But if that number has ever made your chest tighten, your stomach drop, or your future feel a little out of reach, you're not alone. In this chapter, we're going to talk about student loans with honesty, clarity, and zero shame. Whether you owe $10,000 or six figures, whether you've defaulted or just started paying, there's a way forward. And we're going to walk it, step by step, together.

This is not about drowning in debt for the next 30 years. This is about liberation. This is about power. And yes—this is about strategy.

Why This Chapter Matters

Student loans are one of the most common financial burdens in modern life. They can quietly shape our job decisions, delay our milestones, and cloud our sense of freedom. But here's the truth: you can outsmart your student loans. You can pay them off without pausing your life, and you can build wealth while doing it. The key? A plan that feels possible, not punishing.

Step 1: Get Honest with the Numbers

Let's rip the Band-Aid off. Log in to your loan servicer's site. Make a spreadsheet or grab a notebook. List out:

- Total loan balance(s)
- Interest rates
- Loan types (federal or private)
- Monthly minimum payments
- Current repayment plan
- Servicer contact info

Knowledge is power. And power is sexy.

Step 2: Understand Your Options

Federal Loans

If you have federal student loans, you've got options—many of which don't get discussed in the fine print.

Income-Driven Repayment Plans (IDR)

These plans base your monthly payment on your income and family size. Some popular IDR plans:

- PAYE (Pay As You Earn)
- REPAYE (Revised Pay As You Earn)
- IBR (Income-Based Repayment)
- ICR (Income-Contingent Repayment)

Payments can be as low as $0/month, and after 20–25 years, the balance may be forgiven.

Public Service Loan Forgiveness (PSLF)

Work in public service? Nonprofit? Government? After 10 years of qualifying payments under an IDR plan, your remaining balance can be forgiven—tax-free.

Pro tip: Submit your Employment Certification Form yearly.

Temporary Programs (Limited PSLF Waiver, SAVE plan, Fresh Start)

Sometimes, the government rolls out temporary programs that offer relief or fresh chances. Check StudentAid.gov regularly for updates.

Private Loans

You've got fewer forgiveness options here—but that doesn't mean you're stuck. What you need is:

- A clear repayment plan
- Possibly refinancing (but only with the right terms)

Step 3: Prioritize Payments Strategically

Debt Avalanche

Focus on the loan with the highest interest rate. Once that's paid off, move to the next highest. This saves the most money in the long run.

Debt Snowball

Focus on the smallest loan first. Pay it off fast, then use that momentum for the next one. This builds motivation.

Either strategy is better than no strategy.

Step 4: Consider Refinancing

Refinancing can lower your interest rate and save you thousands—but only do it if:

- You have good credit (or a co-signer who does)
- You have a stable job
- You don't need federal protections like IDR or PSLF

Once you refinance, federal loans become private—and those government perks vanish. Don't give them up lightly.

Step 5: Know the Traps

- Deferment and forbearance are temporary tools—not long-term solutions
- Default wrecks your credit and increases your balance
- Watch out for predatory refinancing offers
- Avoid paying fees for things you can do yourself (like loan consolidation)

Step 6: Balance Payoff with Building Wealth

You don't have to pick between paying off debt or investing. You can do both. Here's how:

- Pay the minimum on low-interest federal loans
- Put extra toward high-interest debt
- Still invest in your 401(k)—especially if there's a match
- Start small. $50/month in an index fund is still building wealth.

Step 7: Make It Automatic (and Emotional)

- Automate your payments—on-time is everything
- Name your debt-free account something juicy: "Freedom Fund" or "Quit My Job Plan"
- Celebrate your progress. Every $500 down deserves a high-five

Real-Life Scenarios

Scenario 1: The Early Grad

You owe $25,000, make $40K/year, and want to start investing. Consider PAYE, make extra payments when you can, and contribute 5% to a Roth IRA.

Scenario 2: The PSLF Path

You're a social worker with $85K in loans. Enroll in REPAYE, file your PSLF forms, and relax—your forgiveness is coming.

Scenario 3: The Six-Figure Warrior

You've got $150K in private loans. You've built credit and got a job. Refinance to 4.5%, pay extra each month, and negotiate like a boss.

Bonus: How to Talk to a Loan Servicer Without Losing It

- Be calm. Be clear. Take notes.
- Ask for written confirmation.
- Keep records of every call.
- If you get a bad rep? Hang up. Call again.

Action Steps Before You Sleep Tonight

1. Pull your full loan list from studentaid.gov
2. Calculate your total loan balance
3. Write down your current monthly payment
4. Pick either the snowball or avalanche strategy
5. Set a reminder to review this in one week

You Got This

Student loans can feel heavy. But they're not your forever story. You're not stuck. You're not behind. You're just getting started.

And the way you show up for your money now? That's power. That's sexy. That's growth.

Final Words

You don't have to hustle in silence or suffer in shame. You deserve peace. You deserve freedom. And yes—you deserve financial literacy that makes you feel unstoppable.

Make one money move before bed tonight. Just one. And then do another next week.

Your mirror will thank you.

Your bank account will thank you.

And your future self?

They'll be blown away.

Part IV: Saving That Stuns – Where Strategy Meets Security

Welcome to the part of your financial glow-up that turns calm into confidence. Part IV is all about saving—but not in the boring, eat-ramen-and-hoard-every-penny kind of way. This is saving that feels luxurious. Purposeful. Sexy. Whether you're stacking your first $1,000 or setting aside six figures, this section helps you ditch guilt and build wealth on your terms.

We'll break down how to build an emergency fund that actually fits your lifestyle (not someone else's), how to save for short-term fun and long-term freedom, and how to automate your money moves like a boss. You'll learn the power of naming your savings accounts, designing your own "peace of mind" fund, and saving without feeling deprived.

This isn't about restriction—it's about expansion. It's about options. And it's about making sure that when life throws you something wild, you don't crumble—you flex.

Let's make saving feel strong, empowered, and aligned with the life you're building.

Chapter 16: Emergency Funds = Peace of Mind

Let's start with this: Security is sexy. Feeling safe is underrated. Knowing that you can breathe—really breathe—if life throws you a curveball? That's not just powerful. That's peace of mind. And that peace of mind starts with something that isn't flashy, doesn't go viral, and won't get you likes on Instagram: an emergency fund.

I know, I know. "Emergency fund" sounds about as exciting as socks on Christmas. But hear me out. The emergency fund is your backstage pass to financial confidence. It's what lets you walk into work knowing you can leave if the vibe gets toxic. It's what lets you sleep when your car makes a weird noise. It's the quiet flex you keep in your bank account, whispering: "I got me."

Why Emergency Funds Matter

An emergency fund isn't just about money. It's about freedom. It's about dignity. It's about having the power to make decisions based on values, not panic. Without it, you're one layoff, one vet bill, or one dental surprise away from a full-blown crisis. With it, you're calm, collected, and in control.

The goal here isn't to create fear. It's to create resilience. Life is unpredictable. But your response doesn't have to be.

How Much Should You Save?

The classic answer: 3 to 6 months of expenses.

But here's the remix: start where you are.

If saving $10,000 feels impossible, start with $100. Then get to $500. Then $1,000. Then keep going. Every dollar is a deposit into your peace-of-mind account. And that account is the foundation for all your next money moves.

Customize your number. A single person in a low-cost city might only need $4,000. A family of four in a high-cost area? More like $20,000+. The point is: don't chase someone else's number. Build your own.

Where to Keep Your Emergency Fund

This is not money you invest.

This is not money you risk.

This is money that sits. Safely. Quietly. And waits to be useful.

Use a high-yield savings account. One with no fees, FDIC insurance, and easy online access. Label it something that feels good: "Peace of Mind," "Safety Net," "F*ck You Fund," or "Grown-Up Cushion."

And keep it separate from your checking account. Out of sight = out of temptation.

What Counts as an Emergency?

Real emergencies:

- Job loss
- Medical bills
- Car repairs
- Emergency pet surgery
- Unexpected travel (like a funeral)

Not emergencies:

- Last-minute concert tickets
- Black Friday deals
- A random "treat yourself" urge
- Vacations you didn't plan for

Remember: this isn't a slush fund. It's a safety net. Protect it like your future depends on it—because sometimes, it really does.

How to Build It (Without Feeling Broke)

1. **Automate It**

- Set up an automatic transfer from your checking to savings every payday.
- Even $25 a week builds over time.

1. **Name It**

- Literally. Give it a nickname in your banking app that makes you smile.

1. **Round Up**

- Use apps that round up your purchases and stash the change.

1. **Redirect Windfalls**

- Got a bonus? Tax refund? Side hustle money? Throw a chunk into your emergency fund.

1. **Cut One Thing**

- Just one recurring expense (subscription, delivery, etc.) and redirect that money.

Real-Life Story: Maya's Safety Net

Maya, 32, was laid off during a company reorg. But she had $8,000 in an emergency fund. Instead of spiraling, she paused. Took a few weeks to rest. Then negotiated her next role with confidence.

"That fund wasn't just money. It was my permission to breathe."

That's the vibe we're going for.

Common Emergency Fund Questions

Q: Should I pay off debt before saving an emergency fund?

A: Start with $500-$1,000 while paying down debt. Then build it up once high-interest debt is under control.

Q: Can I use a credit card instead?

A: You *can*. But that creates more debt. Cash > Credit.

Q: What if I keep pulling from it for non-emergencies?

A: Put it in a separate bank. Make access just a little inconvenient. Future you will thank you.

Sexy Takeaways

- Security is a vibe. Safety is a flex.
- An emergency fund turns chaos into inconvenience.
- It's not the amount. It's the habit.
- Every dollar saved is a vote for your future self.
- Don't just think about saving. Set it on autopilot.

Action Steps

1. **Open a separate high-yield savings account.**
2. **Set up automatic transfers.**
3. **Name your account something powerful.**
4. **Make a list of your monthly expenses to calculate your target fund.**
5. **Celebrate every milestone—even $100.**

Final Words

You're not behind. You're just getting started.

Most people don't have an emergency fund. Not because they're lazy. Because no one ever told them why it matters or how to make it doable.

Now you know. Now you're empowered.

Clarity is confidence. And confidence is sexy.

Make one money move before bed tonight. Just one. Then another next week.

Start your peace-of-mind fund now.

Because financial freedom isn't a finish line. It's a feeling. And that feeling starts with a single deposit into your security.

Let's build it.

Let's protect it.

Let's own it.

Your future self will be so damn proud.

Chapter 17: Automating Your Savings: Set It and Flex

Let's start with a truth that feels radical in a world full of hustle and grind: Wealth is built not by working harder every day, but by making your money work while you're not even paying attention. That's the magic of automation.

Not just for your calendar reminders or smart home routines—we're talking about your money. Your savings. Your investments. Your future. Set it. Flex it. Let it run.

Because here's the truth: Most people don't struggle with money because they're lazy. They struggle because they're overwhelmed. Life gets busy. Emergencies happen. Discipline wears thin. But automation? That's discipline that doesn't depend on willpower. It's strategy in autopilot. And it is *sexy*.

Why Automate?

Because when money moves itself, your goals get real. You stop relying on good intentions. You start relying on systems. You stop saying, "I'll save what's left over." You start saying, "I pay myself first."

Automation isn't about restriction. It's about rhythm. It's about flow. It's the financial version of muscle memory. You build it once. You flex it forever.

Start With the Essentials

1. **Emergency Fund First**
2. Automate a fixed amount every paycheck into a high-yield savings account. Name it something fierce: "Peace of Mind," "Freedom Fund," or "No Drama Savings."
3. **Retirement Contributions**
4. If your job offers a 401(k) or 403(b), you want that money coming out before you even see your paycheck. Match? Yes, always. Max it if you can.
5. **Roth IRA or Traditional IRA**
6. You can set up a recurring transfer to fund your Roth IRA monthly, quarterly, whatever works. Don't leave this to end-of-year stress. Break it down. Make it digestible.
7. **Short-Term Goals**
8. Vacation? Down payment? New car? Automate savings into sub-accounts. It adds up without effort.

Real-Life Story: Dani's Glow-Up

Dani was 28, a freelance graphic designer with inconsistent income. She never saved because she "never knew what she'd make." Once she automated a flat $50 into a savings account the same day each month, something clicked. She adjusted her lifestyle to what was left. Within a year, she had $1,200 saved. That $50 didn't feel like much at first. Now it feels like momentum.

The Tech That Makes It Effortless

- **Direct Deposit Splits**: Some employers let you split your paycheck into multiple accounts. Use that.
- **Bank Auto-Transfers**: Set up rules to move money weekly or monthly.
- **Apps Like Qapital, Chime, or Ally**: Round-ups, goals, savings

buckets.

- **Payroll Deductions**: HR can help route your money smartly.

The Emotional Win: Less Guilt, More Control

When you automate, there's no "oops, I forgot to transfer it this month." You don't have to choose between guilt and gratification. You've already made the right move—consistently, quietly, and powerfully.

What to Watch Out For

- **Overdrafts**: Always schedule transfers the day after payday.
- **Too Many Transfers**: Don't overcomplicate. Start small.
- **Forgetting to Adjust**: Raise your transfers as your income grows.

Action Steps to Set It and Flex

1. Pick one goal.
2. Choose the amount.
3. Set the automation.
4. Label the account something that motivates you.
5. Watch the balance grow. Adjust as needed.

Final Truth: Consistency Is Sexier Than Intensity

A one-time $500 deposit is fine. But $50 a month for 5 years? That's $3,000. Plus compound interest. Plus confidence. Plus freedom.

You don't have to hustle every day to build wealth. You just have to hustle once—when you set up the system. Then you let it run. Then you flex.

You're Not Behind

You're just getting started.

Most People Don't Know This Stuff

Until they do. Now you do.

Clarity Is Confidence. And Confidence Is Sexy.

One Money Move

Set up one automatic transfer right now. Just one. Then another next week.

More to come—this chapter will continue with deep dives into specific automation tools, savings schedule examples for different incomes, how to adjust during hardship, and how automation can fuel investment accounts too.

This is your financial autopilot. And it's one of the smartest, sexiest moves you can make.

Chapter 18: Short-Term vs. Long-Term Savings Goals

Let's get something straight right now: saving money isn't about denying yourself joy. It's about creating options. It's about freedom. And freedom, darling, is sexy. You shouldn't have to choose between the beach trip next summer and your dream of retiring in peace someday. The truth is, you can have both—if you plan like a boss.

This chapter is your guide to understanding, balancing, and building both short-term and long-term savings goals without feeling like you're stuck in a scarcity mindset. Whether you want to take a solo trip to Bali, buy a house, pay off student loans, or just know you won't have a meltdown if your car breaks down—you're in the right place.

We're going to break it all down: what short-term and long-term savings goals actually mean, how to prioritize them, how to automate your savings without stressing, and how to make sure your future is just as lit as your present. Let's go.

What Are Short-Term Savings Goals?

Short-term savings goals are the things you want or need in the near future. Think 3 months to 3 years. They're the things that feel urgent, tangible, and maybe even fun:

- An emergency fund (yes, that counts!)
- A vacation to reset your soul
- Holiday gifts without credit card guilt

- A new laptop when your current one sounds like a plane taking off
- Moving expenses or security deposit for a new apartment
- Paying for a wedding, baby shower, or milestone event

The magic of short-term goals? You feel the reward quickly. That's a psychological win that builds momentum and reinforces the habit of saving.

But here's the danger: if all your focus is on short-term wins, your future self gets neglected. And that future version of you? They matter. Which is why we also need...

What Are Long-Term Savings Goals?

Long-term goals are the slow burn, the marathon, the future-you investments. These take years, sometimes decades, but they're the game changers:

- Retirement (yes, even if you're in your 20s)
- Buying a home
- Paying for your kids' college
- Starting your own business
- Reaching financial independence so you can work because you want to, not because you have to

These goals don't give you the same instant dopamine hit as buying plane tickets. But they build something even better: peace, power, and the ability to say no to things that don't serve you.

Why Both Matter

Think of your finances like a relationship. Short-term goals are the date nights, the spontaneous gifts, the spark. Long-term goals are the trust, the home you build together, the vision for the life you're growing into.

You need both to have a healthy relationship—with your money, and yourself.

If you only focus on the now, you'll never get ahead.

If you only focus on the future, you'll burn out and lose motivation.

Balance, baby. Let's build it.

How to Prioritize When You Want It All

Here's a simple 4-step formula:

1. **Secure the Foundation**: Start with your emergency fund. This is your buffer, your peace of mind, your "I'm not panicking when life gets lifey" fund. Aim for at least $1,000 to start. Then build to 3–6 months of expenses.
2. **Define Your Short-Term Desires**: Pick one or two short-term goals that excite you. Don't overload yourself. Saving for a vacation *and* a new couch *and* a new phone might feel overwhelming. Choose what matters most.
3. **Name Your Long-Term Priorities**: What do you want your life to look like in 10, 20, 30 years? Retirement? Owning a house? Having options? Set it, write it down, and don't let go.
4. **Divide and Conquer**: Based on your income, decide what percent goes to each bucket. It might be 10% short-term, 10% long-term. Or maybe you start with 5% short-term and 2% long-term. Whatever you do, make it realistic and consistent.

Tools That Make Saving Easy AF

- **High-Yield Savings Accounts**: Use one for each goal. Name them. "Future Home." "Bali Trip." "Peace of Mind." It's psychological magic.
- **Budgeting Apps**: Tools like YNAB, Mint, or Rocket Money help you track progress.
- **Bank Automations**: Set up auto-transfers the day your paycheck hits. Out of sight, out of temptation.
- **Round-Ups**: Apps like Acorns round up your purchases and invest the spare change.

Common Mistakes to Avoid

- **Treating savings like leftovers**: You won't have anything left if you don't pay yourself first.

- **Putting everything into one account**: It's confusing and demotivating.
- **Using savings as a checking account**: That's not saving—that's delaying spending.
- **Thinking small savings don't matter**: $25 a week is $1,300 a year. That's a flight, a fund, a flex.

Real-Life Story: "The Vacation That Didn't Ruin My Credit Score"

Three years ago, Monica used a credit card to go on a girl's trip to Tulum. She didn't budget. She didn't save. She just went. And she was paying it off 18 months later.

Now? She sets aside $100 a month into her "Vacation Vibes" account. This year she went to Portugal—paid in full, guilt-free, and came back with a tan *and* a high credit score. That's power.

Real-Life Story: "The Future Dad Who Started Small"

Jordan was 28 and had never thought about saving for his kid's future. Then he found out his wife was pregnant. He opened a 529 college savings plan and started with just $50 a month.

Today, his daughter is five, and the account has over $4,000—and that's just the beginning.

Short-Term vs. Long-Term Goals: At-a-Glance

Goal Type Time frame Examples Account Type

Short-Term

0–3 years

Emergency fund, travel, big purchases

High-yield savings account

Long-Term

3+ years

Retirement, home, education

401(k), IRA, investment acct

Action Steps You Can Take Tonight

- Write down 2 short-term and 2 long-term goals
- Open a high-yield savings account (Ally, Marcus, Capital One, etc.)
- Set up an auto-transfer—even if it's just $10 a week
- Talk to your partner or best friend about your goals. Say them out loud. Claim them.
- Rename your savings accounts with something fun and motivating

You're Not Behind. You're Just Getting Started.

Most people don't learn this stuff until they're knee-deep in debt, overwhelmed, or burnt out. But you? You're learning now. That's power.

And here's the truth: having money set aside for your goals—both big and small—isn't boring. It's hot. It means you're not just surviving. You're thriving.

You're not behind. You're just getting started.

Clarity is confidence. And confidence is sexy.

Make one money move before bed tonight. Just one. Then do another next week. That's how you build a glow-up that lasts.

Your future self? They're going to be blown away.

Chapter 19: Sinking Funds: The Secret to Stress-Free Spending

Chapter: Sinking Funds – The Sexiest Financial Tool You've Never Used

Let's talk about one of the most underrated, underutilized, and undeniably sexy tools in personal finance: the sinking fund.

No, it's not some outdated accounting term. It's not boring. It's not restrictive. And it's definitely not just for people who love spreadsheets.

Sinking funds are a power move. They let you say yes to the things that matter—without wrecking your monthly budget or going into debt. They're how you plan for joy, protect your peace, and stop having your finances hijacked by surprise expenses and spontaneous events.

This chapter is your step-by-step, shame-free invitation to:

- Learn what sinking funds are
- Set up your first five (tonight!)
- And use them to give yourself permission to spend with power and pride

You're not behind. You're just getting started. Let's begin.

What Is a Sinking Fund?

A sinking fund is a stash of money you set aside little by little for a specific, predictable expense.

It's not the same as your emergency fund (which is for the unpredictable). This is for stuff you *know* is coming—like holidays, car repairs, vacations, birthdays, insurance premiums, back-to-school shopping, or your best friend's wedding in Tulum.

It's your financial runway.

It's your stress-free zone.

It's your internal flex that says, "I've got this covered."

Real-Life Sinking Fund Examples

- **Holidays:** Gifts, travel, decorations—you name it. The holidays happen *every single year*. Why act surprised?
- **Car Repairs:** Your ride won't last forever. Oil changes, new tires, and "oops, I hit a pothole" moments are all part of it.
- **Girls' Trips / Bachelorette Weekends:** Just say it—you want to go and look good doing it.
- **Back-to-School:** Supplies, clothes, fees. Whether for your kids or your own continuing education.
- **Annual Subscriptions:** Amazon Prime, Costco, Spotify, that planner you love.
- **Self-Care Splurges:** Botox, spa days, hair appointments. Yes, plan for them.

How to Calculate Your Monthly Amount

Let's say you want $1,200 for a vacation next summer.

Divide it by the number of months until then. If you have 10 months, that's $120/month.

Boom. Done.

Apply that same math to every sinking fund you want.
Fund Total Needed Months Monthly Amount

Fund: Vacation
Total Needed: $1,200
Months: 10
Monthly Amount: $120

Fund: Holidays
Total Needed: $1,000
Months: 12
Monthly Amount: $83.33

Fund: Car Repairs
Total Needed: $600
Months: 6
Monthly Amount: $100

Fund: Girls' Trip
Total Needed: $800
Months: 8
Monthly Amount: $100

Fund: Annual Subscriptions
Total Needed: $300
Months: 12
Monthly Amount: $25
Total monthly sinking fund allocation = $428.33
You can adjust based on your budget. Start small if you need to.

Where to Keep Your Sinking Funds

You want them **separate** from your everyday spending money. Otherwise? You'll spend them.

Options:

- A high-yield savings account with separate buckets or nicknamed sub-accounts
- A budgeting app that lets you assign dollars to categories (YNAB, Monarch, etc.)
- A physical envelope system (if you're old school and love cash)

Pro Tip: **Name them in a way that gets you excited.**

Not "vacation fund."

Try: *Bali or Bust.*

Not "car maintenance."

Try: *Keep My Lexus Sexy.*

Not "gifts."

Try: *Slay Santa.*

The Psychology of Planned Spending

You know what's sexy? Spending money you planned for—without stress.

You're not "being bad."

You're not "breaking the budget."

You're simply cashing in on a goal you already accounted for.

Planned spending turns guilt into pride. It turns chaos into calm. It helps you say yes to joy *without* sabotaging your future self.

Action Steps: Set Up Your First Five Sinking Funds Tonight

1. Write down five expenses you know are coming in the next 6–12 months.
2. Estimate how much each one will cost.
3. Divide by the number of months until the expense hits.
4. Set up transfers or allocate those amounts manually.
5. Rename each sinking fund in a way that makes you smile.

Do that, and you're five steps closer to financial confidence.

Tools and Tech That Make It Easy

- **Capital One 360:** Lets you create nicknamed sub-savings accounts
- **Ally Bank:** Great for organizing multiple savings buckets
- **YNAB:** A budgeting app that's basically sinking fund heaven
- **Monarch Money:** Beautiful interface, user-friendly, sinking-fund friendly
- **Google Sheets / Excel:** Classic, customizable, and free

FAQs

What if an emergency hits?

That's what your emergency fund is for. Don't drain your sinking funds unless it's urgent *and* unavoidable.

What if I skip a month?

Life happens. Resume next month. Or adjust the timeline and amount.

What if I forget what a fund is for?

Label clearly. Set calendar reminders. Use one account per goal if needed.

Real Stories: Confidence on Deck

- *"I used to panic every December. Now I cruise into Christmas with $1,500 already saved."*
- *"I never thought I could travel without debt. Now my girls' trip is prepaid before I even pack."*
- *"I used to feel guilty buying skincare. Now I fund it every month and call it 'Glow Money.'"

Final Word

Sinking funds aren't about saying no.

They're about saying *"Hell yes"* without debt, guilt, or chaos.

It's not boring. It's not restrictive.

It's financial self-care.

And you?

You're not just saving. You're designing your life.

Now go glow up your budget. Let your money match your energy.

Because planned joy?

That's sexy.

Part V: Investing Is the New Aphrodisiac

Welcome to the part of your financial glow-up where your money stops just sitting around and starts seducing your future. Part V is about power moves, long games, and getting your money to work for you while you sleep, eat, date, dream, and live your damn life.

Investing isn't just for Wall Street bros or tech billionaires. It's for teachers, creatives, entrepreneurs, single parents, newlyweds, and anyone who wants to stop hustling paycheck to paycheck. It's for people who are done being scared of money and ready to start building real wealth.

This section breaks it all down—from index funds and IRAs to stocks, compound interest, and why time in the market beats trying to time it. You'll learn how to set up accounts that make sense for your goals, dodge the common traps that keep folks stuck, and build confidence one smart move at a time.

By the time you're done with this part, you'll understand that investing isn't a gamble—it's a strategy. And done right? It's the ultimate aphrodisiac: powerful, long-lasting, and sexy as hell.

Ready to turn your money on? Let's invest like grownups.

Chapter 20: Banking Basics That Feel Like a Power Move

Let's be honest—walking into a bank and opening an account doesn't feel all that thrilling. But here's the truth: banking done right is a power move. It's not just where your money sits. It's how your money breathes, earns, protects, and multiplies. When you know how to work the system, you don't just bank—you build.

This chapter is your crash course in choosing and using the right accounts so you can feel powerful, not passive. We'll unpack high-yield savings accounts, online banks, credit unions, checking strategies, and the smart tech tools that make your money life simpler and sexier. Because when your money is organized, you move through the world differently. With confidence. With calm. With power.

The Foundation: Banking Isn't Boring—It's Strategic

Think of your bank accounts like your financial house. If your checking account is the kitchen—where things are constantly coming in and going out—your savings is the pantry. It holds what you're not using now, but will definitely need later. And your high-yield savings? That's your rooftop garden—quietly growing the good stuff while you handle life inside.

Banking basics are anything but basic when you use them right.

High-Yield Savings Accounts: Earn While You Chill

If your current savings account pays you 0.01% interest, congratulations—you're making pennies a year. You deserve better. High-yield savings accounts (HYSAs) pay significantly more, often 4.00% APY or higher. That means your money works while you sleep.

Why You Need One:

- Inflation is real. If your savings isn't growing, it's shrinking.
- Compound interest builds wealth without drama.
- It separates your emergency fund from your everyday money.

Where to Get One:

- Online banks often offer better rates than traditional ones. Think Ally, Marcus by Goldman Sachs, SoFi, or Discover.
- Make sure it's FDIC-insured (Federal Deposit Insurance Corporation) up to $250,000.

Pro Tip:

Don't overdraft your checking and pull from savings to cover it. Most online HYSAs don't allow easy transfers for a reason—they protect you from your impulses. That's a win.

Checking Accounts: Choose the Right One for Your Rhythm

Your checking account is your financial hub. It's where your paycheck lands, bills are paid, and your debit card pulls from.

What to Look For:

- No monthly fees.
- No minimum balance requirements.
- Mobile check deposit.
- ATM access—without surcharges.
- Easy bill pay and transfers.

Avoid:

- Banks that charge you for breathing.
- Overdraft fees that drain your wallet before your paycheck hits.

Pro Tip:

Open two checking accounts: one for bills, one for lifestyle. Send a set amount to each. That way, your "fun" money doesn't accidentally eat your rent.

Credit Unions: The Underrated Powerhouse

Credit unions are nonprofit banks owned by their members. That means they often offer:

- Lower interest rates on loans.
- Higher yields on savings.
- Fewer fees.

They might not have all the digital bells and whistles of big banks, but if you're someone who values community-based institutions and better service, don't sleep on credit unions.

Online Banks vs. Traditional Banks: What's Right for You?

Online Banks

Pros:

- Higher interest rates.
- Lower fees.
- Excellent apps and tech features.
- Cons:
- No physical branches.
- Cash deposits can be tricky.

Traditional Banks

Pros:

- In-person support.
- Cash deposits, not a problem.
- Wide ATM networks.
- Cons:

- Lower interest rates.
- More fees.
- Outdated tech.

Bottom Line:

If you're tech-savvy and prefer everything digital, go online. If you like face-to-face help and occasionally need to walk into a branch, traditional might work.

Sub-Saving Accounts: Your Budget's Best Friend

Want to save for five different things at once—vacation, wedding, holidays, new car, and emergency fund? Don't open five different banks. Open a HYSA that lets you name sub-accounts or use budgeting tools like:

- Ally Bank (allows savings buckets)
- Capital One 360
- Qapital or YNAB (You Need A Budget)

Naming your savings is powerful. "$500 for Mexico Trip" feels way more real than "Savings #245." Clarity breeds discipline.

Automate Like a Boss

If it's not automatic, it's emotional. That's the truth.

Set up auto-transfers to your savings right after payday hits. Don't wait to "see what's left." Move money like a CEO—intentionally and without hesitation.

Frequency matters:

- Weekly is better than monthly.
- Automate small amounts if big ones feel scary.

Examples:

- $50 every Friday to your Emergency Fund.
- $100 on the 1st to your Vacation Fund.

The habit is more important than the number. Build the muscle.

Hidden Fees = Financial Ick

Banks make billions off of overdraft and maintenance fees. You're too smart for that.

Check your statement for these culprits:

- Monthly maintenance fees.
- Paper statement charges.
- ATM fees (especially out-of-network).
- Overdraft fees.

Move your money if your bank is charging you to keep your money there. Loyalty is cute in relationships. In banking? Not required.

Emergency Fund = Confidence Bank

Remember: your savings account is more than a bucket. It's your parachute.

Store 3 to 6 months of expenses in an easy-access, high-yield savings account. Name it something that reminds you of your power: "Peace of Mind," "F*ck-You Fund," or "Freedom Money." Whatever makes you smile every time you see it.

This isn't money you touch casually. This is your safety net. And safety is sexy.

Banking Security: Lock It Down

Your account setup matters. So does your digital hygiene.

To protect your accounts:

- Use 2-factor authentication.
- Don't use the same password for every account.
- Set up account alerts (large withdrawal, low balance, etc.).

Because financial glow-ups should never come with identity theft.

Banking Tech That Makes Life Easier

Apps and tools that help you stay in control:

- **YNAB (You Need A Budget)** – great for goal setting and zero-based budgeting.
- **Qapital** – automates savings with rules (like rounding up every purchase).
- **Mint** or **Rocket Money** – expense tracking and budgeting.
- **Zelle/Venmo/Cash App** – fast peer-to-peer payments (use responsibly).

Banking as an Act of Power

Choosing the right accounts isn't just about rates and fees. It's about building a system that reflects your priorities, protects your peace, and helps your money do more with less effort.

When your checking and savings work in sync—when your emergency fund sits strong, your bills are paid without stress, and your travel fund grows quietly in the background—you feel in control. That's not just sexy. That's revolutionary.

You're Not Behind—You're Just Getting Started

You don't need a finance degree to move like a financial grown-up. You just need structure, clarity, and the right tools. Banking basics are not beneath you. They're the bedrock.

Clarity Is Confidence. And Confidence Is Sexy.

Open the account. Move the money. Name the bucket.

Your Move Tonight:

Open a high-yield savings account. Name it something powerful. Set an auto-transfer. It's not about the amount. It's about the action.

Let's go build.

Chapter 21: Investing Isn't Just for Old Rich Guys

Let's get something straight: the idea that investing is only for old, white-haired men sipping scotch behind mahogany desks is a myth. A dated, dusty myth. The game has changed, the doors are wide open, and you've got every reason to walk through them like you own the building. Because if you play your cards right? One day, you just might.

This chapter is your wake-up call and your invitation. It's here to break down the mental barriers that have kept everyday people from becoming investors. Whether you're 23 with a side hustle, 37 with three kids, 45 and divorced, or 61 and still building your comeback—investing is your playground too. And when done right, it's one of the sexiest power moves you can make.

We'll break down the big, scary words Wall Street loves to hide behind. We'll translate the financial jargon into human language. And most importantly, we'll show you how to build real wealth—without waiting to be rich first.

Because investing isn't just about getting wealthy. It's about getting free.

Let's Start with the Mindset Shift

Investing isn't reserved for people who already have a trust fund. It's for people who want to change the trajectory of their life. It's for people who've been left out of the conversation—and are finally pulling up a chair. This chapter starts with crushing the most common lie: "I'll invest when I make more money."

No. You invest to make more money.

Even if it's $10 a week. Even if it's the change left over after your bills are paid. What matters is consistency, not complexity. The mindset you need is this: "I'm building a future. One automatic transfer at a time."

Why Investing Is the Game-Changer

Let's be real. Saving is safe, but investing is how you grow. When you leave your money sitting in a regular savings account earning 0.01% interest, you're not building wealth—you're babysitting it. Meanwhile, inflation is sneaking into your house and stealing purchasing power like a silent thief.

Investing is your way of fighting back. It's how your money works for you—while you sleep, while you work, and while you live.

Let's break it down:

- **Savings = safety net.**
- **Investing = wealth builder.**

You need both. But you can't build a legacy without investing.

Stocks, Bonds, and What the Heck Is an ETF?

Here's the simple breakdown:

- **Stocks**: You're buying a tiny slice of a company. When the company does well, your slice grows.
- **Bonds**: You're lending money to a company or government. They pay you interest. Less risky, but usually slower growth.
- **Index Funds**: A basket of stocks (like the S&P 500) you buy all at once. It's instant diversification. These are low-cost and smart for beginners.
- **ETFs**: Think of them like index funds you can trade during the day. Flexible, affordable, and powerful.

Start with what makes sense for your lifestyle. If you want to invest without constantly checking your phone, an index fund is your new best friend.

How to Actually Get Started

- Open an account: Start with a Roth IRA, a traditional IRA, or a brokerage account.
- Choose a platform: Fidelity, Vanguard, Charles Schwab, or robo-advisors like Betterment or Wealthfront.
- Automate it: Set it and forget it. Invest a fixed amount every month—no matter what.
- Ignore the noise: Don't try to time the market. Time *in* the market beats timing the market every time.

Action Steps You Can Take Today

1. Open a Roth IRA (or ask your HR department about your 401(k)).
2. Set up an automatic transfer—even if it's just $25 a paycheck.
3. Choose a low-cost index fund like VTI or FXAIX.
4. Commit to leaving it alone unless it's a real emergency.

Let's Talk Emotions: Risk, Fear, and Confidence

Investing can feel like dating. You want to trust, but you've been burned. You don't want to swipe right on the wrong stock and end up ghosted by your portfolio. But here's the thing: risk is part of the process. The goal is not to eliminate all risk—it's to manage it.

That's why diversification matters. That's why consistency matters. That's why getting started *now* matters.

Remember:

- The market will go up and down.
- You will feel tempted to pull your money out.
- Your future self will be glad you didn't.

Real-Life Glow-Up: Tasha's Story

Tasha was a 29-year-old teacher who thought investing was for people with finance degrees. She opened a Roth IRA with $50 and committed to $100 a month. Seven years later, her balance hit $14,000. She used part of it for a down payment on a condo. That money didn't just grow—it gave her options.

You don't need to be a millionaire to invest. But you do need to invest to become one.

Pros and Cons—Real Talk

Pros:

- Builds wealth faster than savings
- Beats inflation over time
- Can create passive income
- Gives you financial independence

Cons:

- Market volatility can be stressful
- Requires a long-term mindset
- You may lose money in the short term
- Emotional investing can lead to bad decisions

Keep your eyes on the prize. Wealth-building isn't a straight line—it's a marathon with a few plot twists.

You've Got This

Investing is a declaration. A flex. A commitment to your future self. It's how you stop working for every dollar—and start making your dollars work for you.

So don't wait until you're "ready."

Start small.

Start smart.

Start now.

You're not behind. You're just getting started.

Most people don't know this stuff—until they do. Now you do.

Clarity is confidence. And confidence is sexy.

Make one money move before you go to bed tonight. Just one. And then do another next week.

Your mirror will thank you.

Your bank account will thank you.

And your future self?

They'll be blown away.

Chapter 22: Your Sexy Starter Pack: Roth IRA, 401(k), Brokerage

Let's be real—most of us didn't grow up having deep, illuminating conversations about Roth IRAs over dinner. Nobody sat you down and said, "Let's unpack your 401(k) strategy and analyze your brokerage diversification." But that doesn't mean you're behind. It means the system kept things confusing on purpose. Intimidation and jargon are how people stay disempowered. Not anymore. You're here. You're ready. And we're breaking it all down without shame, fear, or financial fog.

This chapter is your money glow-up kit. It's where you ditch the mystery and get intimate with three of the most powerful tools in your wealth-building toolbox: the Roth IRA, the 401(k), and the brokerage account. Think of them as your sexy starter pack for long-term freedom. They're not just accounts—they're the engines that turn your income into independence.

We're going to walk through:

- What each account actually is
- Who it's for
- Why it matters
- How to open it
- How to use it smartly
- What mistakes to avoid
- And how to feel like a boss while doing it

You don't need a finance degree to use these tools—you just need some clarity, some action steps, and a little swagger. This chapter will give you all three. Whether you're working a W-2 job, freelancing, parenting full-time, or rebuilding from scratch, these accounts can work for you.

Because investing isn't just for old rich guys—it's for you. And these accounts? They're your entry point.

Let's break it down:

Part I: Roth IRA – The Underdog with Superpowers

The Roth IRA might be the most underrated player in your financial playbook. It's flexible, tax-efficient, and quietly powerful. Here's why it deserves your attention.

What It Is

A Roth IRA (Individual Retirement Account) is a retirement savings account where you contribute after-tax dollars. The trade-off? Your money grows tax-free, and you can withdraw it in retirement without paying a dime in taxes.

Why It's Sexy

- Tax-free growth and withdrawals
- You can contribute even if you already have a 401(k)
- You can withdraw your *contributions* (not earnings) anytime without penalty
- Great for younger earners or anyone who thinks their taxes will be higher in retirement

How to Open It

- Choose a brokerage: Fidelity, Vanguard, Schwab, or a robo-advisor like Betterment
- Link your bank account
- Set up automatic monthly contributions
- Choose your investments: index funds, ETFs, or target-date funds

Rules to Know

- Contribution limit: $7,000/year (or $8,000 if you're 50+)
- Income phase-outs apply (starts phasing out around $146,000 for single filers)
- Earnings can't be withdrawn before age 59½ without penalty (unless you qualify for an exception)

Common Mistakes

- Not investing the money after contributing (it'll just sit in cash)
- Ignoring income limits and overcontributing
- Thinking you have to pick stocks (you don't—broad index funds are your friend)

Part II: 401(k) – The Workplace Workhorse

This one's a classic. If you have access to a 401(k) through your job, you're sitting on one of the best wealth-building tools available.

What It Is

A 401(k) is an employer-sponsored retirement plan that lets you contribute pre-tax (traditional) or post-tax (Roth) dollars. Many employers also offer a match—a bonus contribution when you invest.

Why It's Sexy

- High contribution limit ($23,000/year for 2025)
- Employer match = free money
- Reduces your taxable income (for traditional 401(k))
- Automatic deductions from your paycheck make saving consistent

How to Use It

- Log into your HR portal
- Choose your contribution percentage (start with 10%, aim for 15–20%

if possible)
- Pick a target-date fund or index fund to start

Rules to Know

- You must start taking Required Minimum Distributions (RMDs) at age 73 (for traditional 401(k))
- Loans and early withdrawals often come with penalties
- You can roll over your 401(k) if you leave your job

Common Mistakes

- Not investing aggressively enough early in your career
- Cashing out when changing jobs
- Not taking full advantage of the match

Part III: Brokerage Account – The Freestyle Flex Account

This is the account with the fewest rules. It's not for retirement—it's for anything and everything. This is where you invest money you want to grow but need access to before age 59½.

What It Is

A brokerage account lets you buy and sell stocks, ETFs, mutual funds, and other investments. There are no contribution limits or income restrictions. You pay taxes on dividends and capital gains.

Why It's Sexy

- Full flexibility: withdraw any time
- Great for building wealth outside of retirement
- Can be used for goals like home buying, travel, or early retirement

How to Use It

- Open one through a platform like Fidelity, Schwab, Robinhood, or

E*TRADE

- Set up regular transfers
- Choose a mix of low-cost ETFs or index funds

Pros and Cons

- Pro: Total flexibility
- Pro: No contribution limits
- Con: No tax shelter—gains are taxable
- Con: Easy to overtrade or chase hot stocks

Common Mistakes

- Day trading without a plan
- Not accounting for taxes on gains
- Panic selling in a market dip

The Power Combo: How They Work Together

Start with your 401(k) if your employer offers a match. That's free money and consistent savings. Next, open a Roth IRA for long-term tax-free growth. Then, as your income and savings grow, build out your brokerage for medium- and long-term goals.

Use each account for what it does best:

- 401(k) = employer leverage and retirement base
- Roth IRA = tax-free growth and flexibility
- Brokerage = accessible growth and lifestyle goals

Let's Get You Moving

You don't have to be perfect. You just have to start.

- Log into your HR system and increase your 401(k) contribution
- Open a Roth IRA today and schedule monthly transfers

- Transfer $50 a week to a brokerage and let it grow

Give every dollar a job—and every account a purpose. That's what powerful people do.

You're not behind. You're just getting started.

Most people don't know this stuff—until they do. Now you do.

Clarity is confidence. And confidence is sexy.

Make one money move before you go to bed tonight. Just one. And then do another next week.

Own your financial life. Own your options. Own your damn power.

Let's make it effortless. Let's make it bold. Let's make it sexy.

Chapter 23: Compound Interest = Money Making Money

Let's talk about seduction—the slow, powerful, magnetic kind. The kind that doesn't just happen overnight but builds over time. That's compound interest. It's not flashy at first. It's not sexy in the way a viral meme or a fresh pair of sneakers is. But give it time, and compound interest becomes the most attractive force in your financial life. It's money making money—while you sleep, while you work, while you live. It's financial intimacy on autopilot.

And once you understand it—not just the math, but the mindset—you'll never see saving or investing the same way again.

This chapter is going to seduce you into understanding:

- What compound interest actually is (plain and simple)
- Why it's the ultimate reward for patience
- How to use it to build wealth even if you don't earn six figures
- Where to apply it: savings accounts, IRAs, 401(k)s, brokerage accounts, custodial accounts for your kids
- How it works with time, consistency, and realistic contributions
- The mental trap of short-term thinking (and how to escape it)
- Real-world examples that make the magic undeniable
- The power of starting early—but also the power of starting now

Let's start with this truth: You don't need a big salary to build big wealth.

You need time and discipline. You need a plan that honors your future self.

Because compound interest doesn't just reward the rich. It rewards the consistent. The intentional. The patient.

You're not behind. You're right on time. And if you're ready to flirt with financial freedom, compound interest is your perfect partner.

This chapter is where you stop hustling just to stay afloat—and start stacking effortlessly for the long game.

(Full 10,000-word breakdown to follow: We'll walk through exact definitions, formulas in plain language, comparisons between simple vs. compound interest, how monthly contributions grow over 10, 20, 30 years, and how to apply this to your Roth IRA, 401(k), savings plan, child's education fund, or retirement dream fund. Plus mindset shifts, emotional resilience, and examples like "Would you rather have $1 million today or a penny doubled for 30 days?")

Let's get into the seduction of time. And why your money deserves to grow while you live.

Because wealth isn't about working harder. It's about working smarter—and letting your money join the party.

Let's break it down.

What Is Compound Interest? (Without the Boring)

Compound interest is interest earned on both your original money and on the interest that money has already earned. It's a snowball effect. Picture your cash growing muscles at the gym. At first, those gains are small. But over time? That compounding growth adds up to something jaw-dropping.

Here's the deal in real talk: Compound interest is the reason you don't need to be rich to get rich. You just need to get started and be consistent. Time does the heavy lifting.

Let's say you invest $200 a month starting at age 25, earning an average of 8% annually. By the time you're 65, you'd have nearly $700,000. Only about $96,000 of that came from your own pocket. The rest? Pure growth. Pure seduction.

Start at 35 instead? You'll have around $300,000. That 10-year delay cost you nearly $400,000. That's what compound interest means. Time isn't just money—it's the sexiest wealth multiplier in the game.

Simple vs. Compound: Why It Matters

Simple interest only earns interest on your original deposit. Compound interest earns on everything—your deposit AND your previous earnings. That's why compounding over time beats everything else. It's wealth building in the background.

If simple interest is a one-night stand, compound interest is a relationship that gets better with time.

How It Actually Works (Plain Language Version)

The formula is $A = P(1 + r/n)^{(nt)}$, but we're not here to talk algebra. Here's what that means:

- A = the amount you'll have
- P = the amount you start with
- r = the annual interest rate (as a decimal)
- n = how many times it's compounded per year
- t = the number of years

You don't need to memorize this. You just need to understand that compounding means the earlier and more often you add money, the faster it grows.

Where to Put Your Compound Interest to Work

High-yield savings accounts (for short-term needs)

- Not super sexy returns, but it's a start. Great for emergency funds.

Roth IRAs and 401(k)s

- Tax advantages + compound growth = long-term wealth magic

Brokerage accounts

- More flexibility, more growth potential. Use for goals 5+ years away.

529 plans or custodial accounts

- Start small for your kid's future and watch it stack over time.

Your Real-Life Compound Interest Glow-Up

Let's play out a few scenarios:

Scenario 1: You're 22, just out of college. You put $100/month into a Roth IRA. By 65, you could have over $500K.

Scenario 2: You're 38 and just getting started. You invest $300/month. You'll still have over $300K by 65. Starting later is okay. Starting matters more.

Scenario 3: You're 50 and feel like you missed the boat. Nope. If you invest $600/month until 70, that's 20 years of compound growth—enough to make real waves.

The key? Don't wait. Don't wish you started earlier. Start now.

The Mental Side of Compounding

Here's the truth: Compounding isn't always emotionally satisfying at first. Early on, it can feel slow. But just like fitness, results stack over time. And then one day, you wake up and realize your money has been doing pushups in the background.

Delayed gratification isn't sexy until you realize you've bought yourself freedom, choice, and peace of mind.

What Not to Do

- Don't pull out early. Let that money ride.
- Don't pause your investing for small splurges.
- Don't obsess over market dips. Long-term beats short-term every time.

Action Steps

1. Pick one account to invest in consistently (Roth IRA, 401(k), brokerage).
2. Set up auto-contributions—monthly is fine.

3. Choose a simple index fund to start.
4. Leave it alone. Seriously.
5. Watch it grow once a year—not daily.

A Reality Check (With Love)

Most people don't get rich fast. They get rich slow—by leveraging time. That's what compound interest gives you. And it's available to everyone.

A Sexy Takeaway

Compound interest is money working harder than you ever could. It's the financial equivalent of working out once and seeing abs forever. (Okay, not quite—but you get the idea.)

One Prompt Before You Close This Chapter

Make one money move tonight. Open that Roth IRA. Set up that auto-transfer. Choose that index fund.

Clarity is confidence. And confidence is sexy.

You're not behind. You're just getting started.

And your money? It's ready to go to work for you.

Chapter 24: How to Pick Stocks Without Guessing

Let's be real: picking stocks sounds sexy. It's the financial equivalent of picking the winning horse, the next big app, the IPO that's about to blow up. But in reality? Guessing your way through the market is like dating based only on someone's Instagram—deceptive, high-risk, and often disappointing.

This chapter is about shifting that mindset. Because smart investing isn't guessing—it's strategy. It's clarity. It's confidence wrapped in compound returns. Whether you're just starting out or trying to upgrade from a Robinhood roulette habit, you're about to learn how to invest with intention, not impulse.

What the Stock Market Actually Is

The stock market is a marketplace where people buy and sell ownership in businesses. When you own a stock, you own a slice of that business. The market exists to connect businesses that need capital with investors who want to grow their money. It's not a casino—even though it sometimes feels like one. It's a system built on long-term economic growth, business fundamentals, and supply and demand.

Stocks vs. Funds: Know the Difference

- **Individual Stocks**: Buying one company's stock. High risk, high reward, and often high anxiety.
- **ETFs (Exchange-Traded Funds)**: Baskets of stocks you can buy and sell like individual stocks.
- **Index Funds**: These are the goats. They passively track an entire market index like the S&P 500.
- **Mutual Funds**: Actively or passively managed collections of stocks, often with higher fees.

Why Index Funds Are the Beyoncé of Investing

They're reliable. Consistent. Widely admired. Index funds give you exposure to hundreds of companies at once, reducing your risk and increasing your odds of solid long-term growth. You're not betting on one performer—you're backing the whole stage.

ETFs: Your Flexible, Low-Fee Bestie

Like index funds, but with a bit more flexibility. Lower expense ratios, real-time trading, and built-in diversification. For most people, a total market ETF is a great place to start.

Why Most People Shouldn't Pick Stocks Solo

Unless you want to make investing your part-time job, stock picking is a tough gig. It takes research, discipline, and the emotional resilience to watch your favorite pick drop 30% without panic-selling. Most people lack the time, tools, and temperament. That's not a flaw. That's a sign to stick with diversified funds.

Emotional Traps to Avoid

- **Timing the Market**: Trying to buy low and sell high sounds good, but it's nearly impossible to do consistently.
- **Chasing Hype**: If your cousin, barber, or favorite influencer is hyping a stock—you're already too late.
- **Panic Selling**: Markets go down. If you sell every time they dip, you lock in your losses.

Building a Portfolio That Matches You

- **Risk Tolerance**: Can you stomach a 20% drop? If not, dial down the volatility.
- **Timeline**: If you need the money soon, you shouldn't be heavily in stocks.
- **Goals**: Are you investing for a house in 3 years or retirement in 30?

Real-World Example

Janelle, 28, a graphic designer, invested $200/month into a total market index fund. She avoided stock-picking stress and stayed consistent. By age 35, she had over $40,000. No spreadsheets. No drama. Just steady growth.

Advanced Tools to Know

- **Sector ETFs**: Want to bet on tech, green energy, or healthcare? These let you focus without putting all your eggs in one company.
- **Target-Date Funds**: Adjust risk automatically as you age. Ideal for retirement.
- **Dividend Stocks/ETFs**: Get paid while your investments grow.
- **Dollar-Cost Averaging**: Invest the same amount monthly, smoothing your buying price over time.

Where to Start

- **Roth IRA**: Grow and withdraw tax-free. Very sexy.
- **401(k)**: Especially if there's a match. That's free money.
- **Brokerage Account**: For money you might need before retirement.

Tax-Aware Moves

- Max your Roth first if eligible.
- Use pre-tax options (401(k)) to lower taxable income.
- Tax-loss harvest if investing in taxable accounts.

Action Steps

1. Open a Roth IRA or brokerage account today.
2. Set up auto-deposits ($25, $100—whatever works).
3. Choose a low-cost total market index fund or ETF.
4. Stick to the plan.

Remember

This is a long game. The goal isn't to beat the market—it's to build your wealth over time with less stress and more intention. You're not here to gamble. You're here to grow.

Final Word

Clarity is confidence. Confidence is sexy. And consistency? That's how you win.

Make one money move before you go to bed tonight. Just one. Then do another next week.

That's how wealth gets built—one smart move at a time.

Chapter 25: Real Estate Romance – Buying Property for Income and Lifestyle

Let's talk about real estate—not in the HGTV, fixer-upper fantasy way. Let's talk about it in the way that actually matters: how buying property can transform your financial future, anchor your lifestyle, and give you leverage most people never tap into.

This chapter isn't about just owning a home because that's what your parents did. It's about owning smart. Owning with clarity. Owning with power.

Because real estate, when done right, is more than just a roof over your head. It's a relationship. And if you play it smart, it can be one of the most rewarding, stable, long-term relationships you'll ever have. We're talking rent checks, tax breaks, appreciation, and that sweet, subtle flex of owning something that grows in value while you sleep.

Let's be real: real estate isn't for everyone, and it isn't always a fairytale. But it can be an incredible wealth-building vehicle when it fits your goals, your budget, and your risk tolerance. Whether you're dreaming of your first condo, eyeing that duplex with rental potential, or thinking of buying property in a different state altogether—this chapter is your roadmap.

We're going to unpack:

- How to decide if real estate is right for you (and when it's not)
- Renting vs. buying with real math, not myths

- Understanding primary homes, rentals, vacation properties, and house hacking
- What cash flow really means (and why "passive income" is often a lie)
- Red flags that can turn a good property into a financial mess
- What makes a location "investment-worthy"
- How to run the numbers like an investor, not a romantic
- Financing options: conventional, FHA, VA, DSCR, and creative strategies
- Pros and cons of short-term rentals (Airbnb) vs. long-term tenants
- How to avoid rookie mistakes like overleveraging, underestimating maintenance, or skipping inspections
- How real estate fits into your whole financial picture—not just your ego

If you're not ready to buy yet, that's fine. You're not behind. This chapter will help you prepare, plan, and make your move when the time is right. Because in real estate, timing isn't everything—but preparation is.

And if you already own property, we'll talk about:

- How to make that property work harder for you
- Using HELOCs (Home Equity Lines of Credit) as a financial tool
- When to refinance, when to renovate, and when to sell
- What it means to own rental property across state lines (or internationally)
- Building your real estate team: agents, property managers, contractors, CPAs, and lawyers

We'll break down the lingo: cap rates, cash-on-cash returns, amortization, depreciation, appreciation, 1031 exchanges, and more—so you don't just sound smart, you are smart.

Because real estate isn't just a move—it's a mindset.

Real estate romance doesn't mean you need to marry the first property you meet. It means being intentional. It means knowing your numbers. It means walking into a showing with confidence, not confusion.

By the end of this chapter, you'll know how to:

- Decide if owning is better than renting for your stage of life
- Spot good deals—and walk away from bad ones
- Use real estate to generate income, tax savings, and long-term wealth
- Ask the right questions (about neighborhoods, comps, HOAs, taxes, zoning)
- Start small and scale strategically

Real estate can be sexy when you're not just buying a home—you're buying freedom, leverage, and lifestyle design. And the best part? You don't have to wait until you're "rich" to start. You can start now, wherever you are, with strategy.

So let's ditch the Pinterest boards for a moment. Let's stop obsessing over backsplash and start thinking equity. Let's build a financial relationship that grows with you, pays you, and protects you.

Remember:

You're not behind. You're just getting started.

Most people don't know this stuff—until they do. Now you do.

Clarity is confidence. And confidence is sexy.

Make one money move before you go to bed tonight. Just one. And then do another next week.

You don't need to buy real estate tomorrow. But you do need to know how the game works. So when the time comes? You play to win.

Let's make real estate part of your wealth story—not just a line item in your debt column.

Your future self will thank you. Your bank account will wink at you. And your mirror?

It'll say, "Damn, we did that."

Now let's go build equity with intention.

Chapter 26: Crypto: Flashy or Foolish?

Let's get one thing out of the way: crypto isn't just a buzzword. It's a full-blown cultural moment. Whether you're hearing about someone who made millions overnight—or lost everything in a crash—crypto has a way of grabbing attention.

But here's what this chapter is really about: separating the heat from the hype. Because crypto can be thrilling, sure. But we're not here for adrenaline. We're here for wealth—the kind that lasts, the kind you build with intention, not speculation.

So let's unpack crypto, block by block.

What Even Is Crypto, Really?

Crypto is short for cryptocurrency. It's a digital currency that uses cryptography for security and operates on a decentralized network—meaning no bank, no central government, no middleman. Bitcoin was the first and is still the most famous. Since then, thousands of cryptocurrencies have followed: Ethereum, Solana, Cardano, Dogecoin (yes, that Dogecoin), and more.

The backbone of most cryptocurrencies is *blockchain technology*—a decentralized digital ledger that records transactions across many computers. It's transparent, secure, and designed to be tamper-resistant.

But let's be honest: that's not why people get into crypto.

People get in for the money.

The gains. The potential to turn $500 into $50,000. The idea that you, the everyday investor, can outpace Wall Street.

Let's talk about what's real—and what's risky.

The Pros: Why Crypto Has Sex Appeal

1. **Accessibility**

- You don't need to be accredited. You don't need a broker. You can invest from your phone with as little as $1.

1. **Decentralization = Freedom**

- No central bank controlling the money. No government inflating your savings. It's peer-to-peer, baby.

1. **Innovation**

- Blockchain has uses beyond currency—like smart contracts, decentralized finance (DeFi), and NFTs. This isn't just money. It's infrastructure.

1. **Potential for High Returns**

- Volatility cuts both ways. Crypto has produced overnight millionaires. (It's also wrecked some bank accounts, but we'll get there.)

1. **Transparency**

- Transactions on the blockchain are public. You can see wallet addresses, transactions, and more. No hidden fees. No fine print.

The Cons: What They Don't Always Tell You

1. **Extreme Volatility**

- A coin that's up 300% today could crash 80% tomorrow. Crypto isn't for the faint of heart.

1. **Security Risks**

- Crypto wallets can be hacked. Exchanges can shut down. If you lose your password or key, your funds are *gone*.

1. **Lack of Regulation**

- That freedom you love? It also means fewer protections. There's no FDIC. No do-overs. No call center to cry to.

1. **Scams Are Everywhere**

- From fake coins to pump-and-dumps, crypto attracts fraudsters like moths to a flame. Do your due diligence or get burned.

1. **Unclear Tax Rules**

- Yes, the IRS wants to know about your crypto gains. And yes, that can get messy—fast.

What Crypto Isn't

Let's be clear: Crypto is not a retirement plan. It's not a magic wand. It's not a replacement for your emergency fund, your 401(k), or your Roth IRA.

If your financial foundation isn't solid—crypto will not save you.

You can't build a castle on sand.

How to Approach Crypto Like a Boss (Not a Gambler)

1. **Treat It Like Spice, Not the Main Course**

- Crypto can be 1-5% of your portfolio. It's seasoning, not the steak.

1. **Use Trusted Exchanges**

- Coinbase, Gemini, Kraken—stick to platforms with security protocols, insurance protections, and good reputations.

1. **Understand Cold Wallets vs. Hot Wallets**

- Hot = connected to the internet, easier to use, more vulnerable.
- Cold = offline, secure, less convenient. Think of it as a vault.

1. **Know Your Coin**

- Don't just buy something because it's trending on TikTok. Research the tech, the team, the use case.

1. **Avoid FOMO Investing**

- If you're buying because someone else "made a killing," you're already too late. Buy based on strategy, not fear of missing out.

Common Crypto Strategies

- **HODLing**: Buy and hold long-term, through the dips and the hype.
- **Dollar-Cost Averaging**: Invest a set amount regularly (weekly or monthly). This smooths out volatility.
- **Diversification**: Don't go all-in on one coin. Diversify across multiple tokens—or better yet, consider crypto ETFs if available.

Real Talk: Should You Buy Crypto at All?

Ask yourself:

- Do I understand the tech enough to explain it to a friend?
- Do I have an emergency fund in place?
- Am I contributing to retirement accounts?
- Can I afford to lose 100% of what I'm about to invest?

If the answer to any of those is no—you're not ready.

And that's okay. Crypto will still be here.

You don't need to be first. You need to be smart.

Crypto and Identity: The Seduction of Feeling "In the Know"

Crypto isn't just a currency. For many, it's a culture. A rebellion. A flex.

But here's the truth: real wealth isn't loud.

It doesn't have to be flashy. It doesn't need to be trending. It needs to be consistent, protected, and built on solid ground.

Investing in crypto can be part of your journey—but it's not the destination.

Deep Dive: Ethereum and Smart Contracts

If Bitcoin is digital gold, Ethereum is digital infrastructure. Ethereum is a programmable blockchain—meaning you can build things on it. Enter *smart contracts.*

A smart contract is code that runs on the blockchain. It executes automatically when conditions are met. Think of it as an agreement written in code—no lawyers, no middlemen.

Smart contracts power everything from:

- NFT transactions
- Decentralized finance (DeFi)
- Blockchain-based games
- Token swaps on decentralized exchanges

Ethereum introduced the idea that blockchain isn't just about currency—it's about capability.

DeFi: Decentralized Finance Demystified

DeFi refers to financial applications built on the blockchain that eliminate intermediaries. You can lend, borrow, earn interest, and trade—without a bank.

Popular DeFi platforms include Aave, Compound, and Uniswap.

But be warned: DeFi isn't foolproof. Bugs in code, liquidity issues, and rug pulls (where developers vanish with the funds) happen. If you're diving into DeFi, treat it like venture capital—high risk, high reward.

NFTs: Not Just Monkey Pictures

NFT stands for non-fungible token. It represents ownership of something unique—art, music, even real estate deeds.

NFTs exploded into pop culture, but the real power lies in:

- Authenticating digital ownership
- Creating new income streams for creators
- Unlocking digital scarcity in a copy-paste world

You don't need to mint an NFT today. But know this: the technology is bigger than the memes.

The Future of Crypto: Regulation and Reality

Governments are catching up. Crypto tax laws are tightening. Countries are exploring central bank digital currencies (CBDCs). Regulation is coming—and that's not a bad thing.

Clear rules mean more trust. More protection. And more room for legitimate innovation.

Watch for:

- U.S. and global tax policy changes
- Stablecoin oversight
- Crypto ETFs and broader institutional adoption
- AI and blockchain integrations

Sexy Takeaways

- Crypto is *not* a guaranteed way to get rich. It's a speculative asset class.
- Don't invest money you can't afford to lose.
- Diversify. Protect. Stay curious, not careless.
- Strategy always beats hype.

You're not behind. You're just getting started.

Most people don't know this stuff—until they do. Now you do.

Clarity is confidence. And confidence is sexy.

Make one money move before you go to bed tonight. Just one. And then do another next week.

Chapter 27: Investing Myths That Keep You Broke

Let's be honest—money myths are powerful. Especially when it comes to investing. Some were passed down at the kitchen table. Others were learned the hard way. But here's the truth: most of the beliefs that keep people from investing have nothing to do with logic—and everything to do with fear, shame, and misunderstanding.

This chapter is about busting those myths wide open.

You ready?

Let's go myth-busting—and mindset-lifting.

Myth #1: "Investing Is Only for Rich People"

You've heard it. Maybe you've even said it.

But let's be real: this belief is outdated, classist, and just flat-out false.

In the past, you needed a broker, a big account balance, or even special status to invest. But today? If you've got a phone, internet, and $5—you can invest.

Apps like Fidelity, Schwab, SoFi, Acorns, and Robinhood have made it possible for anyone to become an investor. Index funds let you buy slices of the entire market. And fractional shares? That's like buying one bite of the steak instead of the whole thing.

Investing isn't just for the rich. It's how you get rich.

Action Step:

- Open an investment account today—even if you only fund it with $10.

Do it just to see how it works. The act of starting is more important than the amount.

Myth #2: "I Don't Know Enough to Start"

Guess what? No one knows everything when they start.

You don't need to be a finance genius to invest. You don't need a master's degree in economics. You need a system. A plan. And the courage to begin.

Investing doesn't have to be complicated. In fact, the simplest strategies often outperform the fanciest ones.

Warren Buffett himself recommends the average investor stick to low-cost index funds. That's it. No stock picking. No market timing. No obsessing over the news.

Plain-Language Breakdown:

- An index fund is like buying the entire fruit stand, not guessing which apple will sell best. Safer, smoother, smarter.

Action Step:

- Research a target date fund or total market index fund. These are built for beginners. You set it, automate contributions, and let it grow.

Myth #3: "It's Too Risky"

Let's unpack this.

Yes, investing has risks. But so does not investing. Inflation eats your savings. Your cash loses power sitting in a low-yield account. Retirement creeps closer.

And here's the real twist: not investing is the riskiest move of all.

Markets go up and down—that's normal. But historically, they trend upward. Over the long term, the stock market has returned about 7–10% annually, adjusted for inflation.

You don't need to day-trade. You need to play the long game.

Action Step:

- Look at a chart of the S&P 500 over the past 30 years. See those dips? Every time, it came back stronger. That's how compound growth works.

Myth #4: "I'll Start Investing Later"

Here's the brutal truth: waiting costs you more than you think.

Let's say two people invest $100/month. One starts at 25, the other at 35. Both stop investing at 65.

The one who started at 25 will have nearly double the money—even though they both invested the same amount.

Why?

Because compound interest is a time-sensitive miracle. The earlier you start, the more your money works for you.

Sexy Takeaway:

- Time is your superpower. Use it. Don't wait to be perfect. Start while you're still messy.

Myth #5: "You Have to Pick the Right Stock"

This one causes a lot of anxiety—and it's unnecessary.

You do *not* need to guess the next Tesla. You do *not* need to become a chart-reading, trend-following, news-addicted trader.

You can build wealth by investing in the market as a whole. ETFs. Index funds. Broad diversification.

Picking one stock is like betting on one player to win the game. Index investing is betting on the whole team—and history says the team usually wins.

Action Step:

- If you're still on the fence, read up on VTSAX or VTI. These total market funds are some of the simplest and strongest wealth-building tools available.

Myth #6: "I Don't Make Enough Money to Invest"

Here's what most people get wrong:

You don't start investing *after* you're rich. You start investing to *become* rich.

Even small amounts grow over time. Even if it's $20 a week. It adds up. It compounds.

Waiting until you "have more" is a trap. It's like saying you'll start working out after you lose weight.

Real Talk:

- Investing is a habit, not a one-time event. Start where you are, with what you have.

Action Step:

- Set up an automatic investment of $25/month. Make it invisible. Let it build.

Myth #7: "The Market Is Going to Crash—So Why Bother?"

Yes, markets crash. That's part of the deal. But guess what else they do? Recover.

Every. Single. Time.

If you're young and investing consistently, a crash is actually good news—it means stocks are on sale.

Don't run from the market when it drops. That's when wealth is built.

Plain-Language Reminder:

- Timing the market is a losing game. Time *in* the market is where the magic happens.

Action Step:

- Create a "Stay Calm" note in your phone for the next time the market drops. Remind yourself that downturns are temporary.

Myth #8: "Investing Is for Men / Finance Bros / People Who Wear Suits"

This one makes us mad.

Investing isn't about gender. Or status. Or how loud someone is on YouTube.

It's about ownership. Agency. Power.

It's about building a life you control—on your terms.

More women, BIPOC investors, single parents, creatives, and everyday people are claiming their seat at the investing table than ever before.

And if that seat doesn't exist yet? Build your own damn table.

Action Step:

- Find one podcast, YouTube channel, or book that speaks to *you*—not just Wall Street. (Try "Her First $100K" or "Brown Ambition.")

Myth #9: "I Can't Invest Until I'm Debt-Free"

This is a big one—and it's complicated.

Yes, you should aggressively tackle high-interest debt (like credit cards).

But not all debt is created equal. Student loans at 3% interest? That's different from a 22% credit card balance.

You can invest *and* pay off debt.

It's not either/or. It's both/and.

Action Step:

- If you have debt under 7%, consider splitting your focus: 70% to debt, 30% to investing. Or vice versa. Just don't ignore investing forever.

Myth #10: "I'll Never Understand This Stuff"

That lie is loud.

And you know what? It benefits the gatekeepers. The ones who profit off your confusion.

But you're here. Reading. Asking. Learning.

You're already proving that myth wrong.

Financial literacy isn't about knowing *everything*. It's about taking the next right step. One at a time. Over and over.

Sexy Truth:

- Confidence isn't the result of perfection. It's the result of progress.

Action Step:

- Choose one financial term you didn't understand last year. Learn it today. Google it. Ask ChatGPT. Read an article. Just start.

Closing Truths

Most of the myths you believe about money aren't really about money. They're about fear. About identity. About shame and stories passed down like family recipes.

But those stories don't have to define you.

You get to choose your new financial narrative.

And that new story? It starts with action.

You're not behind. You're just getting started.

Most people don't know this stuff—until they do. Now you do.

Clarity is confidence. And confidence is sexy.

Make one money move before you go to bed tonight. Just one. And then do another next week.

Part VI: Protecting Your Sexy Assets

You've been building your financial glow-up—now it's time to guard it like a boss. Part VI is all about protection, not paranoia. We're talking insurance, estate planning, identity theft, and other unsexy-sounding topics that actually scream confidence when done right.

Because what's the point of building wealth if you don't shield it? This section flips the script on fear and shows you how protection equals power. You'll learn how to keep what's yours, prepare for the unexpected, and design a financial future that holds up under pressure—whether that's a medical emergency, job loss, lawsuit, or market downturn.

You'll walk away knowing:

- What types of insurance you *actually* need (and which ones you don't)
- Why a will and a living trust are acts of love, not gloom
- How to lock down your digital life and credit like a pro
- When and how to hire the right pros to protect your empire

This isn't about bubble-wrapping your life—it's about securing your assets so you can keep leveling up with swagger and clarity. Because confidence isn't just in the *building*—it's in the *defending*. And that's sexy.

Chapter 28: Insurance is Self-Love

Let's get this straight from the top: insurance is not boring. It's not just paperwork, fine print, and premiums. It's protection. It's power. It's peace of mind when life throws its inevitable punches. And most of all?

It's self-love.

Because when you insure your life, your health, your home, your ride, your future—what you're really doing is telling the world: *I matter enough to be protected.*

So let's ditch the eye rolls and start looking at insurance the way grown, sexy, confident people do: as armor. The invisible kind that lets you walk through life taller, stronger, and unbothered.

Why Most People Avoid Insurance (And Why That Stops Here)

Insurance isn't glam. Nobody posts about upping their auto liability limits on Instagram. It doesn't have the thrill of buying crypto or the instant joy of booking a vacation.

But let me tell you what's not sexy: being financially devastated by something you could've insured for $20 a month.

People avoid insurance because:

- It feels complicated
- It feels expensive
- It feels like gambling on fear
- It doesn't give immediate rewards

But here's the shift: insurance is not about betting on disaster. It's about protecting your peace.

It's about designing a financial plan that can handle a car crash, a fire, a hospital bill, a lost paycheck—without your entire life crumbling.

This chapter will walk you through the essentials:

- Health insurance
- Auto insurance
- Homeowners and renters insurance
- Life insurance
- Disability insurance
- Umbrella policies

And we'll break it down with clarity, honesty, and zero judgment.

Health Insurance: Protecting Your Body and Your Bank Account

No matter how healthy you are, one accident, one surgery, one diagnosis can cost tens or even hundreds of thousands of dollars.

Health insurance is not just about doctor visits. It's about:

- Avoiding medical bankruptcy
- Getting access to preventive care
- Managing chronic conditions affordably

What to look for:

- Deductible (what you pay before insurance kicks in)
- Copays and coinsurance (your share of costs)
- Out-of-pocket maximum (your annual cap)
- In-network providers
- Prescription coverage

If you're under 26:

- Stay on your parent's plan if you can. It's often the most affordable option.

If you're self-employed or in between jobs:

- Look into ACA marketplace plans
- Consider short-term insurance for gaps
- Check eligibility for Medicaid or subsidies

Why it's self-love:

Getting insured says, "I plan to be here for a while, and I want to take care of myself when I'm not at 100%."

Auto Insurance: It's Not Just About the Car

If you drive, you need insurance. Period. Even if you're the world's safest driver, you're not alone on the road.

There are two big reasons people get this wrong:

- They go for the cheapest policy possible
- They don't understand what their coverage actually does

Types of auto insurance coverage:

- **Liability**: Pays for other people's injuries and damage if you're at fault
- **Collision**: Pays for damage to your car from accidents
- **Comprehensive**: Covers non-collision stuff like theft, hail, fire
- **Uninsured/Underinsured motorist**: Covers you if the other driver doesn't have enough insurance
- **Personal Injury Protection (PIP)**: Helps with medical bills regardless of fault

Pro tip:

Get liability coverage beyond the legal minimum. It's usually not that much more expensive, and it protects you from lawsuits.

Why it's self-love:

You're not just protecting your car. You're protecting your *income, your time, your freedom*. A totaled car without coverage can derail your life.

Homeowners and Renters Insurance: Covering Your Space and Stuff

Whether you own your home or rent an apartment, you need insurance.

Homeowners insurance covers:

- The structure of your home
- Your personal belongings
- Liability if someone gets hurt on your property
- Living expenses if you can't stay in your home after damage

Renters insurance covers:

- Your personal belongings
- Liability
- Temporary housing if your rental becomes unlivable

Common mistake:

Thinking your landlord's policy covers you. It doesn't. Their insurance only covers the building, not your stuff.

Pro tip:

Do a home inventory. Take a video of your space and stuff. Store it in the cloud.

Why it's self-love:

Imagine losing everything in a fire and knowing your financial world doesn't collapse. That's peace of mind.

Life Insurance: Love Letters in Policy Form

Life insurance isn't about you. It's about who you leave behind.

If anyone relies on your income—a partner, a child, a parent—you need life insurance.

Two main types:

- **Term life**: Covers you for a set period (e.g., 20 years). Affordable. Great for most people.
- **Whole life**: Lasts your whole life. Has a savings component. More expensive.

How much do you need?

Rule of thumb: 10x your annual income. But it depends on your debts, dependents, and goals.

Who needs it most:

- Parents of young kids
- Couples with shared debt
- Breadwinners
- Business owners

Who might not need it:

- Single people with no dependents or debt

Why it's self-love:

Life insurance says, "Even if I'm not here, I took care of you. I made sure love turned into security."

Disability Insurance: Income Protection = Sanity Protection

You are more likely to become temporarily disabled than to die before retirement.

Disability insurance replaces a portion of your income if you can't work due to illness or injury.

Types:

- **Short-term disability**: Covers you for a few months
- **Long-term disability**: Kicks in after a waiting period and can last for years

Why it's overlooked:

- People think workers' comp covers them (it usually doesn't unless the injury is job-related)
- They underestimate how long recovery can take

Pro tip:

Check if your employer offers it. If not, consider a private policy.

Why it's self-love:

Your income is your greatest asset. Protect it like your future depends on it—because it does.

Umbrella Insurance: The Backup Plan for Your Backup Plan

If you have significant assets (home, savings, investments), consider an umbrella policy.

It kicks in when your regular insurance maxes out—like if you're sued for a car accident and owe more than your auto coverage allows.

Why it matters:

- Lawsuits can wipe out your net worth
- It's usually cheap (a few hundred a year for $1M in coverage)

Why it's self-love:

You didn't work this hard to have it taken in one lawsuit. Umbrella insurance protects your legacy.

Let's Bust Some Insurance Myths

- "I'm young and healthy, I don't need it."
- Emergencies don't ask for your birth certificate.
- "It's too expensive."
- Being uninsured is often more expensive.
- "I'll just deal with it if something happens."
- That's not a plan. That's financial roulette.
- "I don't understand it, so I'll ignore it."

- Not knowing isn't protection. Learn. Ask questions. Get help.

Action Steps

1. **Review what you already have**
2. Pull out your policies. Know your deductibles. Know your coverage limits.
3. **Get what you're missing**
4. Prioritize health, auto, and renters/home first. Then life and disability if needed.
5. **Talk to a pro**
6. Use an independent agent who can shop multiple companies for you.
7. **Name your beneficiaries**
8. And update them after major life events (marriage, divorce, kids).
9. **Put it on autopilot**
10. Automate payments. Set calendar reminders for annual reviews.

You're not behind. You're just getting started.

Most people don't know this stuff—until they do. Now you do.

Clarity is confidence. And confidence is sexy.

Make one money move before you go to bed tonight. Just one. And then do another next week.

Final Word: Insurance Is More Than Paperwork

It's your safety net. Your back-up plan. Your invisible army.

It's what makes your wealth journey sustainable.

And when you take the time to get your insurance game tight, you're not just protecting stuff. You're protecting your peace, your people, and your possibility.

That's not boring.

That's bold.

That's love in action.

Chapter 29: Disability and Umbrella Coverage – Planning for the Unexpected

Let's talk about the unsexy side of sexy.

Because what good is building wealth if it's all vulnerable?

What's the point of having a beautifully crafted financial plan if one bad fall, one car accident, one lawsuit can wipe out everything you've built?

This chapter is your bodyguard.

This is the chapter that says: you're strong, yes. But real strength means knowing how to protect yourself when life throws a left hook you didn't see coming.

Because here's the real flex:

You protect your income.

You protect your future.

You protect your peace.

That's what disability and umbrella insurance do. And it's time we talked about them without the fluff, the fear, or the fine print.

Why This Chapter Matters

Most people think insurance is just a drag on their paycheck. Something they pay for and hopefully never use.

But real talk?

Disability insurance and umbrella insurance are some of the most powerful, underrated tools in your entire financial toolkit.

They aren't exciting.

They're not flashy.

They won't make you money.

But they will *save* you money—and your dignity—when things go sideways.

And here's the kicker:

Disability is *way* more common than you think.

Lawsuits are *way* more expensive than you imagine.

Let's break it down.

Part One: Disability Insurance — Income Protection Is Self-Respect

Imagine this:

You're 32. You make $80,000 a year. You're healthy. Fit. Ambitious.

Then you get in a car accident. You can't work for 18 months.

What happens to your income?

What happens to your rent?

Your student loans?

Your kid's daycare?

Disability insurance says: I got you.

What Is Disability Insurance?

It replaces a portion of your income if you get hurt or sick and can't work.

Two Main Types:

1. **Short-Term Disability**: Usually kicks in after a week or two. Covers a few months.
2. **Long-Term Disability**: Covers you for years. Sometimes until retirement age.

Most people need **long-term disability insurance.** Because the stuff that can derail your income? It's rarely just a sprained ankle.

Think:

- Cancer

- Car accidents
- Severe depression
- Surgery complications

What Does It Cover?

A percentage of your income. Usually 50% to 70%.

Where Do You Get It?

- Through your job (check your benefits!)
- Individually from an insurance company

Why It's Sexy

You're not just planning for success.

You're protecting it.

You're refusing to let one unexpected health moment bankrupt your future.

That's what CEOs do.

That's what grown-ups do.

Common Misconceptions

- "I'll rely on workers' comp." → Only if you're injured on the job. Most disabilities are *not* work-related.
- "I have savings." → Will it last 18 months? Two years? Ten years?
- "I'm healthy." → So were millions of people until they weren't.

How Much Does It Cost?

Usually 1% to 3% of your annual income.

If you make $100K, expect to pay $1,000 to $3,000 per year.

Not cheap. But *not optional.*

If You Do Nothing Else Today...

- Find out what your employer offers
- Get a quote for an individual policy

- Know what "own occupation" coverage is (hint: you want it)

Part Two: Umbrella Insurance — Cover Your Assets (Literally)

Let's say you get into a car accident.

It's your fault.

You get sued.

The judgment is $500,000.

Your auto insurance only covers $100,000.

Where does the other $400,000 come from?

Your pocket.

Your savings.

Your house.

Your wages, garnished for years.

Unless you have **umbrella insurance**.

What Is Umbrella Insurance?

It's extra liability coverage that kicks in *after* your other insurance maxes out.

It covers:

- Car accidents
- Home accidents
- Dog bites
- Rental property incidents
- Libel and slander lawsuits

Basically, it's your legal shield.

Why You Need It

Because we live in a litigious society.

Because people sue.

Because judgments can ruin you.

Who Needs It Most?

- Homeowners

- Landlords
- High-income earners
- Public figures
- Dog owners (yes, really)
- Anyone with assets to protect

How Much Coverage Should You Get?

Start with $1 million. Most policies go up to $5 or $10 million.

How Much Does It Cost?

It's shockingly affordable.

- $1 million in coverage can cost as little as $150 to $300 per year.

Yes. For the whole year.

That's not a typo.

How to Buy It

- Usually added on top of your existing home and auto policies
- Offered by most major insurance carriers

Why It's Sexy

Because wealth is not just what you *earn*.

It's what you *keep*.

Umbrella insurance makes sure your financial glow-up doesn't turn into a financial meltdown.

Scenarios That Make the Case

- Your teen driver causes a multi-car pileup
- Your guest slips on your icy driveway
- You get into a social media feud and someone sues for defamation

Are they rare? Yes.

But rare doesn't mean impossible.

And if they happen?

They're devastating.

Final Thoughts: Protection Is Power

You hustle to earn money.

You learn to grow money.

Now it's time to protect it.

Disability and umbrella insurance aren't just about fear.

They're about *freedom*.

They say:

"Even if something goes wrong, I'm still okay."

"Even if life surprises me, I'm not starting from zero."

You deserve that peace.

You deserve that protection.

You deserve to move through life knowing your finances are fireproofed.

That's self-love.

That's strategy.

That's sexy.

Action Steps

1. **Review Your Employer Benefits**

- Do you have disability insurance? What kind?
- What's the waiting period? How long is it in force?

1. **Get a Quote for Individual Disability Insurance**

- Especially if you're self-employed or your employer coverage is weak

1. **Review Your Auto and Home Coverage Limits**

- What are your liability limits?
- Are they enough?

1. **Add Umbrella Insurance**

- Ask your agent today
- $1 million is the baseline

1. **Talk to Your Financial Advisor**

- Make protection part of your overall financial plan

You're not behind. You're just getting started.

Most people don't know this stuff—until they do. Now you do.

Clarity is confidence. And confidence is sexy.

Make one money move before you go to bed tonight. Just one. And then do another next week.

Chapter 30: Estate Planning Without the Grim Reaper Vibe

Let's start here: estate planning is not about dying.

It's about living.

It's about making choices now, while you're fully alive, conscious, and clear-minded—so the people you love aren't stuck making impossible decisions when you're gone.

This isn't about fear.

It's about love.

It's not about obsessing over death.

It's about designing your legacy.

And that? That's sexy.

Because nothing says "I love you" like removing chaos from your family's future. Nothing screams maturity like knowing where your money, property, or even your Spotify password will go.

So let's strip estate planning of the grim reaper costume and dress it in what it really is: dignity, love, order, control.

This chapter is your power move.

What Is Estate Planning, Really?

It's a plan for your stuff, your wishes, your people, and your peace.

Estate planning covers:

- Who gets your assets when you die (a.k.a. your *beneficiaries*)
- Who handles your affairs (a.k.a. your *executor*)

- What happens if you're alive but can't speak for yourself (a.k.a. *power of attorney* or *healthcare directives*)
- How your money, property, and personal items are distributed (a.k.a. *your will or trust*)

It's like programming your financial GPS for the people who love you. Clear routes. Fewer detours. No legal gridlock.

Let's break it down like you're sitting across from someone who cares about you.

Why Most People Avoid Estate Planning

1. **It sounds morbid.**

- Death talk is uncomfortable. We get it. But not talking about it won't prevent it.

1. **It feels complicated.**

- Wills. Trusts. Legal jargon. It's a lot. But we're here to untangle it.

1. **People think they don't have enough money.**

- If you have a car, a bank account, a pet, or a favorite ring? You have an estate.

1. **It feels like something only old, rich people do.**

- Wrong. Estate planning is for anyone with people they love or things they value.

1. **Procrastination.**

- "I'll get to it later." Until later becomes never. Don't do that.

The Core Components of a Sexy Estate Plan

Let's break them down with plain language and real-life clarity.

1. The Will

This is your instruction manual.

It says who gets what, names guardians for your children, and appoints your executor.

Without a will? The state decides. And they don't know your family drama, your favorite nephew, or who you trust with your jewelry.

2. The Trust

A trust is like a container. You put stuff inside (money, property, etc.) and set rules for how it's handled.

Why people love trusts:

- They avoid probate (the long, public court process that happens when there's just a will).
- They add privacy and control.
- They help with tax planning.

Revocable trusts (can be changed) vs. irrevocable trusts (can't be touched).

Choose your adventure.

3. Power of Attorney (POA)

If you're alive but incapacitated, someone needs legal access to your accounts, bills, and decisions.

This person is your financial quarterback. Choose wisely.

4. Healthcare Proxy / Advance Directive

Who makes medical decisions if you can't?

Do you want life support? What about organ donation?

These documents lay it all out—so your loved ones aren't forced to guess.

5. Beneficiary Designations

Your 401(k), life insurance, and IRAs all let you name beneficiaries. These designations override your will.

Review them regularly. Because your ex-spouse is probably not who you want cashing in.

6. Letter of Intent

This one's not legally binding, but powerful.

It's a love letter, a guide, a "here's what I want you to know." It can include funeral wishes, passwords, or just a final message of love.

Common Myths That Keep You Unprotected

1. **"I'm too young to need an estate plan."**

- If you're old enough to legally own something, you're old enough to plan for it.

1. **"I don't have enough assets for this."**

- If you have a bank account, a car, a pet, or a favorite niece—you have an estate.

1. **"I did a will 15 years ago. I'm good."**

- Divorce? Kids? New job? Moved states? Update it.

1. **"My family knows what I want."**

- That's cute. But the court doesn't.

Pros and Cons of Estate Planning Tools

Will

Pros:

- Simple
- Affordable
- Good for basic planning

Cons:

- Goes through probate
- Public record
- Doesn't help if you become incapacitated

Trust

Pros:

- Avoids probate
- Private
- More control

Cons:

- Costs more to set up
- Requires maintenance

Power of Attorney

Pros:

- Protects your finances if you're unable to

Cons:

- Can be misused if the wrong person is chosen

Healthcare Directive

Pros:

- Protects your medical wishes

Cons:

- Needs to be kept updated and accessible

Real-Life Scenarios: The Good, The Bad, The Avoidable

The "Oops" Story

A single mom didn't update her will after her second child. Only one kid was named. The other got tied up in court for over a year.

The "Hero" Story

A man set up a trust and funded it properly. When he passed, his family got their inheritance in weeks, not years. No probate. No fights.

The "I Never Thought This Would Happen" Story

A 27-year-old had a stroke. Because he had a POA and healthcare directive, his girlfriend (not his estranged dad) made the medical decisions he wanted.

Sexy Action Steps: Your Estate Planning To-Do List

1. Make a will
2. Consider a trust
3. Assign POA and healthcare proxy
4. Update beneficiary forms
5. Write a letter of intent
6. Review everything every 2-3 years (or when life changes)

Estate Planning for Every Life Stage

20s:

- Set up a will, POA, and healthcare directive.
- If you have a 401(k) or life insurance, name beneficiaries.

30s-40s:

- Add guardianship clauses if you have kids.
- Set up or revisit a trust.

50s-60s:

- Check estate tax strategies.
- Start having legacy conversations with your kids.

70s+:

- Update documents for clarity.
- Talk about funeral wishes.
- Review elder care and Medicaid planning.

Estate Planning = Love Letter + Strategy + Adulting Gold Star

Think of this chapter not as preparing for death, but planning for dignity.

This is your backstage pass to peace of mind. Your way of saying, "I got you," to the people you love.

You're not behind. You're just getting started.

Most people don't know this stuff—until they do. Now you do.

Clarity is confidence. And confidence is sexy.

Make one money move before you go to bed tonight. Just one. And then do another next week.

Chapter 31: Passwords, Paperwork, and Privacy

Let's talk about the unsexy stuff that keeps your sexy life running. Because what's the point of building wealth, love, a business, a family, or a life you're proud of—if it's vulnerable to digital pickpockets, identity thieves, or a simple lost document?

This chapter is about protection—not just in the obvious financial sense, but in the daily practical ways you shield your money, your identity, your future, and the people who matter most. It's not glamorous, but it's vital.

And once you realize how much control you *actually* have here—it gets powerful. Even sexy.

Why This Chapter Matters

You don't need a cyber attack or a tragic accident to make this stuff urgent. Every single day, your personal info is floating in the cloud. Your credit is tied to online logins. Your money is moved by keystrokes.

You wouldn't leave your front door unlocked while you sleep. So why leave your digital and financial doors wide open?

This isn't paranoia—it's preparation. And preparation is power.

Let's Start With Passwords (Yes, Really)

Because this is your digital gatekeeper. And most of us treat it like an afterthought. You don't need to be a hacker to break into someone's financial world. You just need a lazy password.

Here's your new golden rule: If you can remember your password, it's probably not strong enough.

- Use a password manager (like LastPass, Bitwarden, or 1Password). These generate complex, unique passwords for every account and store them securely.
- Turn on two-factor authentication (2FA) for your bank, email, investment platforms, and anywhere else you'd cry if you got locked out.
- Change your email password regularly. Your email is the skeleton key to your digital life.

Real Talk: If you've reused the same 3 passwords across 27 accounts? You're not alone—but it's time for a glow-up.

Paperwork: The Unsexy but Necessary Archive

No one wants to talk about paperwork. But if you've ever watched a family scramble after a sudden illness, accident, or death—you know how devastating it is not to have documents in place.

This is how you love yourself *and* the people around you.

Here's what you need, where to keep it, and how to share it:

1. **Vital Records**

- Birth certificates, passports, marriage licenses, social security cards
- Keep hard copies in a fireproof safe or safety deposit box
- Scan and save encrypted digital versions in secure cloud storage

1. **Financial Info**

- List of bank accounts, investment accounts, insurance policies, and loans
- Include account numbers, login info (stored via password manager), and contact names

1. **Legal Docs**

- Will, trust, power of attorney, healthcare directives

- If you don't have them, set a date to meet with an estate planning attorney

1. **Insurance Details**

- Policies for health, home, auto, life, disability, and umbrella coverage
- Contact info for each provider and renewal dates

1. **A "When I Die" File**

- Yes, it sounds morbid. But it's actually an act of love.
- Write down funeral preferences, legacy wishes, online accounts to be closed, and how to access your password manager.

Privacy: Keeping Your Money Moves Quiet

It's not just about keeping nosy cousins out of your business. It's about reducing your digital footprint and increasing your resilience.

Tips for protecting your privacy:

- **Freeze your credit** with all three bureaus (Experian, TransUnion, Equifax). It's free and stops identity thieves from opening accounts in your name.
- **Be mindful on social media.** Don't post about expensive purchases, investments, or travel in real time.
- **Use a VPN** when using public Wi-Fi.
- **Don't overshare with your bank.** They don't need your full life story to open an account.
- **Opt out of data brokers.** Sites like Spokeo, Whitepages, and BeenVerified collect and publish your info. You can request removal.

Digital Assets Deserve a Plan, Too

If you've got a blog, YouTube channel, crypto wallet, digital art portfolio, or even a Venmo account—congrats, you've got digital assets.

- Make a list of all your digital platforms and who should inherit/control them if something happens to you.
- Include monetized platforms (Patreon, Substack, affiliate links, etc.)
- Some platforms let you name a legacy contact (e.g. Facebook and Apple ID).

If you're earning money online in any form, don't let those earnings disappear just because no one can access the password.

Keeping Track: Build Your Financial Vault

This is your command center. Your base camp. Your brain on paper.

You can use:

- A physical binder (fireproof and labeled)
- A cloud-based secure vault (like Google Drive with encryption or Everplans)
- A shared folder with your spouse, sibling, or adult child

What to include:

- Net worth statement
- Account list
- Insurance policies
- Estate docs
- Key contacts (CPA, financial advisor, attorney)
- Copy of ID and passwords (in encrypted format or with clear instructions on where to find them)

Action Steps for the Week

1. Choose a password manager and set it up.
2. Write down your essential accounts and where they're held.
3. Schedule a "paperwork power hour" on your calendar.
4. Start a "When I Die" file. Keep it simple for now.

5. Freeze your credit—it takes 20 minutes and protects you for life.

Common Excuses (and Why They're Weak)

- "I don't have time."
- You don't have time *not* to.
- "It's overwhelming."
- Start small. One task at a time.
- "Nothing's happened to me yet."
- And that's why you're still in control.
- "My partner handles that."
- Shared knowledge is security. Don't leave them—or yourself—in the dark.

Why This Is the Opposite of Paranoia

Protecting your privacy and organizing your financial life isn't living in fear.

It's living in freedom. The kind where you sleep better at night.

The kind where you can take bigger risks because the foundation is solid.

It's not just about the stuff—it's about your peace.

Sexy Takeaways

- A weak password can wreck a strong portfolio. Fix that first.
- Organizing your paperwork is an act of love.
- Privacy isn't about secrecy—it's about security.
- You don't need to do it all at once. You just need to start.

You're not behind. You're just getting started.

Most people don't know this stuff—until they do. Now you do.

Clarity is confidence. And confidence is sexy.

Make one money move before you go to bed tonight. Just one. And then do another next week.

Chapter 32: Healthcare Costs and Retirement: The Truth Hurts

Let's not sugarcoat it: healthcare in retirement can be the silent thief of your financial peace. You plan, you save, you invest—and then, out of nowhere, a $4,000 hospital bill shows up, or you find out your prescription will cost more than your monthly car payment. It can feel like a betrayal. You did everything "right," and yet here you are, shelling out thousands when you thought you were set.

This chapter isn't here to scare you. It's here to prepare you. Because when it comes to healthcare and retirement, ignorance is not bliss. It's expensive.

We're going to talk about how much healthcare *really* costs after 65, what Medicare does and doesn't cover, and how to set yourself up so medical expenses don't hijack your golden years.

Let's get brutally honest and beautifully proactive.

Why This Chapter Matters

Here's the hard truth most retirement calculators don't tell you: a couple retiring at age 65 today could need $300,000 or more just to cover healthcare expenses in retirement. And that's not including long-term care.

Healthcare is the one line item that often gets left out of retirement planning—or seriously underestimated. And yet, it's often the biggest wildcard. You can budget your lifestyle, you can predict your mortgage, but healthcare? It changes with age, policy, and your body.

So let's dig into the details.

The Basics: What Happens at Age 65?

At age 65, you qualify for Medicare. Sounds like a relief, right? And in many ways, it is. But Medicare isn't free, and it's not all-inclusive.

Let's break it down simply:

- **Medicare Part A (Hospital Insurance)**: Usually free if you paid into Social Security. Covers inpatient hospital stays, hospice, and some skilled nursing care.
- **Medicare Part B (Medical Insurance)**: You pay a monthly premium. Covers doctor visits, outpatient care, preventive services, and some home health care.
- **Medicare Part D (Prescription Drug Coverage)**: Optional but crucial. You pay a premium. Covers prescriptions but with gaps.
- **Medicare Advantage (Part C)**: An all-in-one plan offered by private insurers that may include Parts A, B, and D with extra benefits (like dental and vision). But it also often comes with restricted networks.
- **Medicare Supplement (Medigap)**: Helps pay the out-of-pocket costs that Medicare doesn't. There are several plans (Plan G is one of the most popular).

The Real Costs You Might Face

Even with Medicare, you'll still pay:

- Monthly premiums for Part B and D (and maybe Advantage or Medigap)
- Deductibles and copays
- Out-of-pocket drug costs
- Dental, vision, and hearing (mostly not covered by traditional Medicare)
- Long-term care (almost never covered by Medicare)

Over time, these add up.

Long-Term Care: The Elephant in the Room

This is the expense no one wants to talk about. But if you live long enough, the odds are high you'll need some form of long-term care—whether it's in-home help, assisted living, or a nursing facility.

The average annual cost of a private nursing home room? Over $100,000. And Medicare doesn't cover custodial care (like bathing, dressing, or eating assistance) unless it's short-term and medically necessary.

This is where long-term care insurance, hybrid life insurance policies, or setting aside specific savings for this risk come into play. We'll talk strategy soon.

Health Savings Accounts (HSAs): Your Secret Weapon

If you're under 65 and have a high-deductible health plan (HDHP), you can contribute to an HSA. It's triple tax-advantaged:

- Contributions are pre-tax
- Growth is tax-deferred
- Withdrawals for qualified medical expenses are tax-free

After age 65, you can even use it for *non-medical* expenses (though you'll pay income tax, like a traditional IRA).

Action step: If you qualify, max out your HSA and treat it like a retirement healthcare fund.

Estimating Your Healthcare Costs in Retirement

Use these questions to start calculating:

- Do you plan to retire before age 65? (You'll need coverage before Medicare.)
- Will you choose traditional Medicare with a supplement or Medicare Advantage?
- Do you have chronic conditions or high medication costs?
- Do you plan to relocate? (Costs and coverage vary by state.)
- Are you setting aside money for long-term care?

There's no one-size-fits-all, but you can create a realistic estimate.

Strategies to Protect Yourself

1. **Start Early**: Include healthcare in your retirement budget today. Don't wait until 64.5.
2. **Use Roth Accounts**: Tax-free withdrawals help cover unpredictable costs without tax hits.
3. **Diversify Income Sources**: Include Roth, HSA, taxable, and traditional accounts.
4. **Consider LTC Coverage**: Traditional or hybrid insurance. Don't wait too long—the earlier you apply, the cheaper it is.
5. **Work Part-Time in Retirement**: Many jobs offer health coverage or HSA eligibility.
6. **Talk to a Medicare Specialist**: Annual plan reviews can save thousands.

Myths That Keep People Unprepared

- "Medicare covers everything."
- "I'll be healthy forever."
- "I don't need to plan for long-term care."
- "I'll just work until I die."
- "It won't happen to me."

Every one of these myths has left someone broke, scared, and scrambling. Don't let that be you.

Sexy Takeaways

- Healthcare isn't a luxury. It's a guarantee. Plan like it.
- Medicare is a start, not a solution.
- HSAs are the Beyoncé of retirement tools. Bow down.
- LTC costs are real. Insure the risk or plan to self-fund.
- Awareness is protection. Structure is peace. And that's sexy as hell.

You're not behind. You're just getting started.

Most people don't know this stuff—until they do. Now you do.

Clarity is confidence. And confidence is sexy.

Make one money move before you go to bed tonight. Just one. And then do another next week.

Chapter 33: Sexy Doesn't Skip Medicare Planning

Let's be honest—no one wakes up excited to talk about Medicare. But let's flip the script: there's nothing sexier than power, and Medicare planning is one of the most powerful things you can do for your future self. Think of it as protecting your peace, your wallet, and your dignity—all in one move.

This chapter isn't here to bore you with red tape. It's here to help you step into age 65 with swagger and clarity.

Medicare 101: Let's Break It Down Without the Bureaucratic B.S.

When you turn 65, Medicare is the federal health insurance program that you become eligible for—regardless of your income or health status.

There are four main parts:

- **Part A:** Hospital insurance (think: inpatient care, skilled nursing facilities, hospice).
- **Part B:** Medical insurance (doctor visits, outpatient care, durable medical equipment).
- **Part C:** Also known as **Medicare Advantage**—private plans that bundle Parts A and B (and often Part D too).
- **Part D:** Prescription drug coverage (also run by private insurers).

In addition, you've got **Medigap**, aka **Medicare Supplement** plans. These are separate from Medicare Advantage. We'll explain the difference shortly.

Original Medicare vs. Medicare Advantage: Pick Your Flavor of Coverage

Original Medicare (Part A + Part B) is straightforward. It gives you the freedom to go to almost any doctor or hospital in the U.S. that accepts Medicare. But it doesn't cover everything. There are deductibles, coinsurance, and no limit on your out-of-pocket costs.

That's where *Medigap* comes in—it fills in the "gaps" in Original Medicare. It's a separate plan that pays for things like copayments, deductibles, and coinsurance.

Medicare Advantage (Part C) is an all-in-one alternative to Original Medicare. Offered by private insurers, these plans usually include Part D and may offer extra benefits like dental, vision, and gym memberships. The trade-off? You're typically limited to a network of providers and may need referrals for specialists.

Costs: What You'll Actually Pay

Medicare isn't free. You paid into it while working, but there are monthly premiums, deductibles, and coinsurance.

- **Part A:** Free if you worked 10+ years. If not, you'll pay up to $505/month (2024 rate).
- **Part B:** Premiums start at $174.70/month (2024), but this can increase if you earn more (IRMAA—we'll get into that).
- **Part D:** Varies by plan, usually $10–$70/month. Higher-income folks also pay IRMAA here.
- **Medigap:** Varies by age, location, plan letter, and insurer. Plans typically range from $100–$300/month.
- **Medicare Advantage:** Many plans advertise $0 premiums, but don't be fooled—it's a trade-off. You'll pay copays and may face tighter networks and formularies.

IRMAA: The Extra Cost for High-Income Earners

IRMAA stands for Income-Related Monthly Adjustment Amount. Translation? If your modified adjusted gross income (MAGI) from two years ago is above a certain threshold, you'll pay extra for Part B and Part D.

2024 thresholds start at $103,000 for individuals or $206,000 for couples. The surcharge can add hundreds per month. And yes—this is why tax planning and Roth conversions *before* 65 can save you thousands later.

Enrollment Periods: Mark Your Calendar (Seriously)

- **Initial Enrollment Period (IEP):** Starts 3 months before you turn 65 and lasts 7 months total. Miss it, and you might pay penalties.
- **General Enrollment Period (GEP):** Jan 1 – Mar 31 each year, if you missed IEP.
- **Annual Enrollment Period (AEP):** Oct 15 – Dec 7. You can switch from Original Medicare to Advantage, or change Advantage/Part D plans.
- **Medicare Advantage Open Enrollment Period:** Jan 1 – Mar 31. Switch Advantage plans or drop one to return to Original Medicare.

Real Talk: What Plan Should You Pick?

There's no one-size-fits-all. Here are some prompts to guide you:

- Do you travel frequently or live in multiple states? Original Medicare + Medigap may give you more flexibility.
- Want dental, vision, and extra perks? Advantage plans might appeal—but vet the network.
- On a tighter budget and healthy? A $0-premium Advantage plan could work, but know the fine print.
- Prefer predictability and fewer copays? Medigap might be worth the extra premium.

Medigap Plans: A-G Isn't Just for Grades

Medigap plans are standardized—Plan G from one company covers the same as Plan G from another. The difference? Price and customer service.

- **Plan G** is the most popular (covers everything except the Part B deductible).

- **Plan N** is cheaper, with small copays.
- **Plan F** used to be the gold standard but is only available if you were eligible for Medicare before 2020.

Pro tip: Premiums often rise as you age. Buying a policy earlier can lock in lower rates.

How to Actually Sign Up

- Visit www.medicare.gov
- Call Social Security at 1-800-772-1213
- Or work with a licensed Medicare agent (like the one who wrote this sexy chapter).

Just don't wait. Late enrollment = penalties that never go away.

Don't Forget These Decisions

- **Dental/Vision/Hearing:** Not covered by Original Medicare. You'll need separate plans or an Advantage plan with those benefits.
- **Long-Term Care:** Not covered. Medicare covers short-term rehab only. Consider a hybrid long-term care policy if you want to protect your retirement savings.
- **Prescription Drugs:** If you skip Part D and don't have creditable coverage, you'll face lifelong penalties.

Medicare Planning is Wealth Planning

Medicare decisions ripple across your financial life:

- A bad plan can cost you thousands in out-of-pocket costs.
- A good plan can protect your retirement income.
- IRMAA planning can save six figures over your lifetime.
- The right timing on retirement withdrawals can reduce your Medicare premiums.

This isn't just paperwork. It's legacy work.

Medicare and Employer Coverage: When the Transition Gets Tricky

If you're still working at 65 or covered under a spouse's employer plan, timing matters.

- If the employer has 20+ employees, you can delay Part B and Part D without penalty—as long as the coverage is "creditable."
- Once that coverage ends, you'll get a Special Enrollment Period (SEP) to enroll in Part B and Part D without penalties.
- If you retire and go on COBRA, COBRA is *not* creditable coverage for delaying Part B. You must enroll in Medicare at 65, or you'll face penalties and gaps.

Pro Tip: Sign up for Part A at 65 even if you're still working—it's free if you qualify and can act as secondary hospital insurance.

Spousal Coordination

If your spouse is younger and still covered under your plan—or vice versa—you'll want to:

- Talk to HR about how your Medicare enrollment affects your family coverage.
- Plan for a potential gap in their coverage.
- Consider ACA marketplace plans or a short-term bridge policy if needed.

Sexy Takeaways

- Don't let confusion delay your Medicare decisions.
- Use the 3 P's: **Plan early**, **Protect your income**, **Pick wisely**.
- Make sure your doctors, prescriptions, and lifestyle fit the plan you choose.
- Review your plan annually during open enrollment. What worked last

year might not this year.
- Coordinate with employer coverage and your spouse's benefits to avoid costly gaps.

You're not behind. You're just getting started.

Most people don't know this stuff—until they do. Now you do.

Clarity is confidence. And confidence is sexy.

Make one Medicare move before you go to bed tonight. Just one. And then do another next week.

Chapter 34: Couples, Coverage & Confusion

Let's get this out of the way: love is beautiful. Retirement can be, too. But combining the two with health coverage? That's where the confusion creeps in. If you're navigating Medicare, employer plans, or retirement health options *as a couple,* things can get messy fast. And yet, getting this right could save you tens of thousands over your lifetime—not to mention emotional stress, missed coverage, and awkward arguments at the kitchen table.

This chapter is for couples who want to move through this with clarity, confidence, and coordination. Because what's sexier than being on the same page financially *and* medically?

When One of You Turns 65 and the Other Doesn't

This is one of the most common situations couples face. One partner hits 65 and becomes eligible for Medicare. The other is still covered by an employer plan or buying insurance on the ACA marketplace.

Here's the deal:

- The partner turning 65 should enroll in Medicare Part A (it's free if you worked enough).
- If the *other* partner is still working and has a credible group health plan, the Medicare-eligible partner may delay Part B (doctor/outpatient coverage) without penalty.
- If the employer has fewer than 20 employees, Medicare becomes

primary, and you *must* sign up for Part B or risk gaps.

Action step: Confirm with HR whether your employer plan counts as "creditable coverage" for Medicare.

What If You're Both Turning 65 Around the Same Time?

Double enrollment time! You both get your own Medicare accounts. There are no family plans. Medicare is individual. But you can coordinate together:

- Choose whether to go the Original Medicare + Medigap route or the Medicare Advantage route.
- Coordinate your Part D plans if using Original Medicare.
- Compare Advantage plans to see if you can be on the same plan (if networks and doctors align).

Pro tip: Just because you're married doesn't mean your Medicare plan has to match. What works for one of you may not work for the other.

Still Working Past 65? One or Both of You?

If one spouse is still working and has employer coverage, that may cover both spouses—but you have options:

- The Medicare-eligible partner can delay Part B (and Part D) if they're covered by the working spouse's employer plan.
- But if the employer has fewer than 20 employees, Medicare usually becomes primary for the Medicare-eligible partner. Ignoring this could mean *big* penalties.

Strategy tip: If the employer plan is expensive or has a high deductible, the Medicare-eligible spouse may be better off jumping into Medicare and finding a great standalone plan.

What If You're Retired and One of You Is Younger?

This happens *a lot*. You retire together at 65, but one spouse is 62.

That younger spouse isn't eligible for Medicare yet.

Options:

- Use COBRA for up to 36 months (expensive, but keeps coverage consistent).
- Enroll in an ACA plan until Medicare kicks in.
- Consider part-time work for the younger spouse that offers benefits.

Remember: Medicare doesn't offer family coverage. You each need your own plan.

Medicare Advantage vs. Medigap as a Couple

Some couples assume they should both do the same thing. That's not always true.

- One of you may want the flexibility of Original Medicare + Medigap (especially if you travel).
- The other may be fine with a local Medicare Advantage plan that offers dental and vision.

Ask these:

- Are you okay with provider networks?
- Do you take different medications?
- What are your chronic conditions?
- What's your monthly budget?

Run the math *together*. Compare premiums, out-of-pocket costs, and networks.

Spousal Benefits and Coordination

Let's bust a few myths:

- There are **no spousal plans in Medicare**. You each enroll separately.
- You **can qualify for premium-free Part A** based on your spouse's work history (if you didn't work 10 years).

- You **can't add your spouse to your Medicare Advantage or Medigap plan**.

So what can you coordinate?

- Enrollment timing
- Financial strategy (e.g., IRMAA planning for high-income couples)
- Long-term care planning
- Annual plan reviews

IRMAA for Couples: The Double Whammy

Remember IRMAA—the extra charge high earners pay for Part B and Part D? It hits couples *harder* because it's based on joint income.

2024 thresholds start at $206,000 for couples. If you're retired but had high income two years ago, you may still pay more.

Smart move: Use Roth conversions and withdrawal strategies pre-retirement to keep your income below the IRMAA thresholds.

Annual Reviews: The Sexy Medicare Date Night

You and your boo should review your plans *every year* during Medicare Open Enrollment (Oct 15 – Dec 7).

Ask:

- Are our doctors still in-network?
- Did our meds change?
- Are premiums increasing?
- Should we switch from Advantage to Medigap or vice versa?

Yes, it might feel tedious. But so is a $1,200 surprise bill.

Real Couple Scenarios

Lisa (67) and Brian (63)

Lisa is on Medicare. Brian is still working. They keep Brian on his employer plan and Lisa on Medicare + Medigap. They plan to switch Brian to Medicare + Advantage when he retires.

Carla (65) and Jasmine (65)

Both retired. Jasmine travels a lot and wants Medigap. Carla wants dental and doesn't mind the network, so she chooses Medicare Advantage. Both are happy and covered.

Questions to Ask Each Other

- What doctors do we want to keep?
- Are we traveling a lot?
- Do we want predictable costs or lower premiums?
- Do we need vision or dental coverage?
- What medications are we on?
- How does this fit into our broader retirement income plan?

Sexy Takeaways

- Medicare isn't just about turning 65. It's about *coordinating as a couple.*
- You need separate plans, but you can make decisions together.
- Income, age gaps, and lifestyle all affect your ideal coverage.
- Review your coverage every year—not just once.
- Don't assume what worked last year (or for your neighbor) is right for you.

You're not behind. You're just getting started.

Most couples don't know this stuff—until they do. Now you do.

Clarity is confidence. And confidence is sexy.

Make one Medicare move together before you go to bed tonight. Just one. And then do another next week.

Part VII: Income is Attractive, But Wealth is Irresistible

A six-figure salary might turn heads—but lasting wealth? That's what builds legacies, buys freedom, and lets you sleep like a boss at night. In this part of the book, we shift the focus from making money to keeping it, growing it, and protecting it. Because flashy income without strategy is just noise—and true wealth whispers.

You'll learn how to turn your paycheck into a portfolio, how to break the cycle of living for the next deposit, and how to build financial systems that work even when you're not grinding. We'll cover investment strategies, asset allocation, wealth preservation, tax efficiency, and mindset shifts that separate earners from builders.

Whether you're climbing the corporate ladder, running your own business, or entering the next phase of life, this section gives you the tools to move from income-based identity to wealth-rooted confidence.

Because once you understand how money *works*—not just how to earn it—you'll never settle for anything less than financial power.

Chapter 35: Multiple Streams Are the New Monogamy

Let's say it out loud: depending on one income stream is risky. It doesn't matter if that one stream is six figures, comes with a title, or even if you love it. In today's world, putting all your financial eggs in one paycheck basket is like dating someone who swears they'll never leave but hasn't introduced you to their friends yet. It might feel stable, but it's not secure.

This chapter isn't about hustling 24/7 or turning your every hobby into a revenue source. It's about strategy, structure, and options. Because freedom isn't just about money—it's about having choices. And the more streams you build, the more powerful and protected you become.

The Psychology of a Single Paycheck: Comfort That Keeps You Stuck

For most people, the idea of living off one income feels normal. That's how we were raised. One job, one salary, one employer, and maybe a 401(k) if we're lucky. But times have changed. Companies restructure overnight. Industries evolve. Technology replaces roles. And life, as we know, doesn't always go as planned.

Relying on one job for your entire livelihood means your whole life is one HR meeting away from crisis. It creates fear around change, and fear shrinks your financial power.

Multiple streams of income aren't just about more money. They're about confidence, optionality, and never letting one person, job, or client control your peace.

What Counts as a Stream? Let's Redefine It

A stream doesn't have to be massive. It doesn't have to be passive. It doesn't even have to be sexy.

Here's what counts:

- Your paycheck
- Side hustle income
- Rental property cash flow
- Dividends from stocks
- Royalties from a book or course
- Affiliate marketing revenue
- A monthly retainer from a consulting client
- Income from a monetized YouTube channel or podcast
- High-yield savings account or CD interest
- Retirement income or pensions

Each stream adds a layer. You don't need ten overnight. But starting with two or three can completely change your energy around money.

The Core Categories of Income Streams

Let's break them down into three core categories:

1. **Earned Income**: This is what you make from actively working—your job, freelance work, contracts. You trade time and skill for money.
2. **Investment Income**: Money that works while you don't. Dividends, interest, capital gains. It takes time to build but becomes the foundation of long-term wealth.
3. **Business or Royalties**: Assets you create that pay you over time. A digital course, a rental property, a YouTube channel, even licensing a design or software.

You want to diversify across these. Earned income builds your foundation. Investment income gives you leverage. Royalties or business income create freedom.

How to Start a Second Stream Without Burning Out

You don't have to turn your life upside down to create another stream. But you do need to be intentional.

Start with this:

- **Inventory your skills**: What do people always ask you for help with?
- **Look at your calendar**: Where can you free up 5 hours a week?
- **Test the waters**: Offer a simple service or product. You're not launching a Fortune 500. You're exploring.
- **Automate or outsource early**: Use platforms, tools, and people to help you scale. Don't try to do it all alone.

Remember: It's not just about income. It's about independence.

Real-Life Scenarios: What It Can Look Like

- *Jasmine,* a high school counselor, starts tutoring online on weekends. That extra $400/month goes straight into her Roth IRA.
- *DeShawn,* a data analyst, builds a simple spreadsheet tool for realtors and sells it for $29 online. One tool becomes $10K in annual side income.
- *Maya and Chris,* a married couple, buy a duplex. They live in one unit and rent the other. The rent covers their mortgage.
- *Luis,* a retired firefighter, records audio books from home and earns royalties monthly.

These aren't unicorns. These are people who started small and stayed consistent.

The Sexy Math of Multiple Streams

Let's say you add just $500/month from a side gig and invest it in an index fund averaging 7% annually. Over 20 years, that turns into over $260,000. That's one small stream. One move. One choice. Compound interest is the quiet superhero behind financial freedom.

Now imagine three streams. Five. Ten. Suddenly your entire life shifts from "How do I stretch this paycheck?" to "How do I manage my opportunities?"

Pros and Cons (Because We Keep It Real)

Pros:

- More financial stability
- Greater freedom and autonomy
- Faster debt payoff and savings growth
- Creative and professional fulfillment

Cons:

- Time management is key
- Some income streams take time to grow
- Risk of burnout if you're not strategic
- Taxes get more complicated (but manageable)

Bottom line? The pros win. Especially if you build smart, sustainable systems.

Building Streams With Strategy, Not Stress

Here's a framework:

1. **Start With What You Know**: It's faster and cheaper to build from skills you already have.
2. **Keep It Low-Risk at First**: Don't pour thousands into something untested.
3. **Automate Everything You Can**: Invoicing, scheduling, content—let tech do the heavy lifting.
4. **Reinvest Earnings**: Use profits to buy better tools, outsource tasks, or build the next stream.
5. **Audit Quarterly**: Is it still worth your time? Could you increase pricing or efficiency?

This is how you grow without grinding yourself into dust.

Myths to Let Go Of

- "I'm not entrepreneurial." False. You're resourceful.
- "It's too late for me." False. People start income streams at 25, 45, 75.
- "I don't have time." False. You have 168 hours a week. Reallocate 5.
- "It has to be passive." False. Start active, build toward passive.

Let those excuses go. They're keeping you broke and boxed in.

Sexy Takeaways

- Dependence on one income is financial vulnerability, not loyalty.
- Small streams become rivers. Rivers become oceans.
- You don't have to hustle forever. You just have to start.
- Confidence comes from knowing you can generate income in more than one way.

You're not behind. You're just getting started.

Most people don't know this stuff—until they do. Now you do.

Clarity is confidence. And confidence is sexy.

Make one move to create a second income stream before you go to bed tonight. Just one. And then do another next week.

Don't rely on one income.

There was a time when having one steady paycheck felt like the American dream. But that dream is outdated—and honestly, it never worked equally for everyone anyway. In today's world, relying on one stream of income is like trying to sail across the ocean with one paddle. You might move forward, but you're going to work harder than you need to, and you'll be off balance the whole time.

We don't build wealth by working ourselves into exhaustion at one job. We build wealth by letting money come in from different places—some that require our time, and some that don't.

Let's unpack why multiple income streams are sexy, smart, and absolutely essential.

The Truth About Income

Let's get one thing straight: income and wealth are not the same thing. Income is what you earn. Wealth is what you keep, grow, and protect.

That high-paying job? Great. But if you get laid off, get sick, or get burned out—that income stops. Now imagine you had income from a rental property, a digital course, a dividend-paying stock portfolio, and maybe a side hustle you love. Now imagine if two of those streams still flowed even while you were on vacation.

That's the difference between hustle and strategy. Hustle burns out. Strategy builds freedom.

Types of Income Streams

1. **Earned Income:** Your job, business, or side hustle—where you trade time for money.
2. **Investment Income:** Dividends, interest, and capital gains from stocks, bonds, or ETFs.
3. **Rental Income:** Payments from tenants in properties you own.
4. **Royalty Income:** Money from books, music, intellectual property.
5. **Business Income:** Profit from a business that doesn't require your constant presence.
6. **Affiliate/Referral Income:** Commission from promoting products or services.
7. **Digital Product Income:** E-books, templates, courses.

The real flex? Income that continues even when you're asleep.

How to Get Started Without Overwhelm

You don't need to launch five businesses tomorrow. Start with your next best move:

- Look at your skills. What could you offer as a freelance service?
- Got a topic you know well? Create a simple digital guide.

- Love a product? See if they have an affiliate program.
- Own a home? Could you rent a room or space occasionally?
- Got an IRA or 401(k)? Make sure you're investing, not just saving.

Turning Your Income Stream into a Scalable Brand

Once you've tested your side hustle or passive income idea, it's time to think bigger. If it's working—don't stop there. Build a brand around it.

- **Give it a name.** Something clear, memorable, and aligned with your vibe.
- **Claim your digital real estate.** Buy the domain, start the socials.
- **Systematize.** Automate emails, use schedulers, build templates.
- **Expand your offerings.** If your ebook is selling, can you turn it into a course? A coaching package?
- **Ask for feedback.** Your customers will tell you what else they want—if you listen.

When your brand speaks clearly, consistently, and solves a problem, it becomes a magnet. That's how you move from one extra stream to a full ecosystem of abundance.

Build Systems That Run While You Sleep

The goal isn't to work 24/7—it's to create systems that make money while you do other things. Systems give your ideas legs.

- **Automate where possible.** Use email funnels, autoresponders, and scheduled content.
- **Outsource small tasks.** Hire a virtual assistant to help with admin.
- **Use tools that scale.** Sell digital products on platforms like Gumroad or Teachable.
- **Create once, earn repeatedly.** A well-designed digital product can earn for years.

We're not chasing hustle culture here. We're building lifestyle freedom.

Sexy Takeaways

- Relying on one income source is risky. Diversifying is powerful.
- Start where you are. Build one extra stream first. Then add more.
- A small digital product can turn into a six-figure business with the right systems.
- Passive income is not magic—it's math, marketing, and mindset.

You're not behind. You're just getting started.

Most people don't know this stuff—until they do. Now you do.

Clarity is confidence. And confidence is sexy.

Make one move tonight—whether it's buying a domain, outlining a guide, or brainstorming with your partner.

Build a life where the money doesn't stop when you log off.

Let your streams flow.

Chapter 36: Side Hustles That Don't Burn You Out

Let's get something straight: hustle culture doesn't mean exhaustion. Burnout isn't a badge of honor. You weren't put on this earth to grind yourself into the ground. The real flex? Earning extra income *without* giving up your peace, your joy, or your evenings. Because financial freedom isn't just about stacking cash—it's about designing a life that doesn't leave you drained.

So welcome to the sexiest corner of the money conversation: side hustles that *don't* wreck your nervous system.

The Truth About Side Hustles

Let's talk about why side hustles became so glorified in the first place.

We're living in an economy where one paycheck doesn't always cut it—even if that paycheck is technically "good." Rent, childcare, student loans, health insurance, groceries, unexpected car repairs... it adds up. Quickly.

Side hustles became the go-to answer. And in some ways, they've helped a lot of people:

- Pay down debt
- Save for big goals
- Fund a passion project
- Build a business
- Create financial breathing room

But here's the problem: if your side hustle feels like a second job you hate, you're not gaining freedom—you're losing time.

You need side income, but it better be *sustainable*. Let's break down how to make that happen.

Step One: Know Your Energy, Not Just Your Interests

Before you jump into any hustle, ask yourself:

- What time of day do I have energy?
- Do I need flexibility or structure?
- Do I want to work with people, or alone?
- What do I already do that others ask me for help with?

This is about alignment. You might love photography, but hate editing. You might enjoy tutoring, but only in short sprints. Knowing yourself helps you pick something that won't start to feel like a burden three weeks in.

Categories of Sustainable Side Hustles

Let's break this into three buckets:

1. **Low-Lift, High-Flexibility**
2. **Skill-Based, Scalable**
3. **Creative and Legacy-Building**

1. Low-Lift, High-Flexibility

These are hustles that don't require a huge upfront investment of time or energy. They fit around your life, not the other way around.

- **User Testing**: Sites like UserTesting.com pay you to test apps and websites. 20 minutes can earn you $10-$60.
- **Surveys + Focus Groups**: Sign up for sites like Respondent.io or UserInterviews.com. You might earn $50-$200 for sharing your opinion.
- **Pet Sitting / Dog Walking**: Love animals? Apps like Rover make it easy to get started.

- **Task Apps**: TaskRabbit, Handy, or Nextdoor gigs. Move a couch, build a shelf, get paid.
- **Reselling**: Got an eye for vintage or deals? Resell on Poshmark, Mercari, or eBay.

Pros:

- Low barrier to entry
- Instant earnings
- Flexible hours

Cons:

- Not scalable long-term
- Often active income (you trade time for money)

2. Skill-Based, Scalable

This is where it starts to get powerful. You have skills—don't sleep on them.

- **Freelancing**: Writing, graphic design, coding, social media, virtual assistance.
- **Tutoring**: Math, music, test prep. Sites like Wyzant or VIPKid.
- **Consulting**: Package your experience. If you've done HR, marketing, operations—people will pay for that wisdom.
- **Online Courses**: Teach what you know. Use platforms like Teachable, Thinkific, or Gumroad.
- **Coaching**: Life, career, fitness, mindset. If people ask you how you did it—you might have a coaching niche.

Pros:

- Higher income potential

- Can build into a full business
- Creates reputation equity

Cons:

- Requires consistent delivery
- May need marketing effort upfront

3. Creative and Legacy-Building

These side hustles feed your soul *and* your pockets.

- **Self-Publishing**: Write and sell ebooks. Amazon KDP makes it accessible.
- **Podcasting / YouTube**: Long game, but can create passive income via sponsorships or ad revenue.
- **Art + Merch**: Sell prints, shirts, digital downloads on Etsy, Redbubble, or Shopify.
- **Writing + Blogging**: Monetize via affiliate links, sponsorships, or subscriptions (Substack, Medium).
- **Music + Audio Work**: Beat-making, voiceover work, mixing tracks.

Pros:

- Deep personal fulfillment
- Passive income potential
- Builds a body of work

Cons:

- Slower monetization
- Can feel vulnerable at first

The Burnout Test

Ask yourself regularly:

- Does this hustle energize me or drain me?
- Is this helping my long-term goals or just patching a short-term hole?
- Do I still feel like "me" when I'm doing this work?

If your side hustle is wrecking your sleep, killing your relationships, or giving you Sunday Scaries—something needs to shift. Remember: sustainable > sensational.

Stacking Your Streams

Here's a sexy little idea: you don't need ONE perfect side hustle. You can stack TWO or THREE small ones that fit different moods and energies.

- Monday night: 2 surveys = $40
- Saturday morning: Pet sitting = $50
- Ongoing: Blog earns $30/week in affiliate revenue

Boom. That's $500/month on the side *without* burning out.

Making It Official: Legal, Tax, and Boundary Basics

- **Track Your Income**: Use apps like QuickBooks Self-Employed, Wave, or a Google Sheet.
- **Set Up a Business Entity**: If you earn consistently, look into an LLC.
- **Open a Separate Bank Account**: Keep hustle money separate.
- **Pay Estimated Taxes**: Side income isn't taxed automatically. Don't get caught off guard.
- **Set Hustle Hours**: Protect your personal time.

Real-Life Scenario: Meet Jordan

Jordan is a 38-year-old mom of two. Works full-time in healthcare. Loves baking.

Instead of trying to launch a full-time bakery, she sells decorated cookies for holidays and birthdays through Instagram. Keeps it to 4 orders/month max.

She also tutors high school biology 2x/month and takes paid online surveys during her kids' soccer practice.

Jordan's earning ~$600/month. But more importantly, she doesn't feel fried. That's the win.

Sexy Takeaways

- Not all side hustles are created equal. Know your energy, not just your skill.
- Aim for sustainable, not sensational. You don't have to "go viral" to make money.
- Diversify your hustle life the same way you diversify your investments.
- Start small. Test. Adjust. You don't need a 10-year plan—you need a weekend experiment.
- Don't build a second job. Build a second *freedom stream.*

You're not behind. You're just getting started.

Most people don't know this stuff—until they do. Now you do.

Clarity is confidence. And confidence is sexy.

Make one money move before you go to bed tonight. Just one. And then do another next week.

Let's get one thing straight: you don't need to hustle yourself into exhaustion to get ahead financially. The era of glorifying 24/7 hustle is over. Burnout is not a badge of honor—it's a red flag. And if you're working yourself to the bone just to add a few bucks to your bank account, you're missing the point.

Financial freedom is sexy, but it's also sustainable. Side income should support your life, not take it over. In this chapter, we're diving deep into how to create multiple streams of income that enhance your life, not hijack it.

This isn't about grinding until 2 a.m. or juggling five jobs. It's about building smart, sustainable, soul-aligned streams of money that help you breathe easier, sleep better, and build real wealth.

Why This Chapter Matters

Let's be real: relying on one paycheck is risky. Jobs end. Companies restructure. Economies shift. And if 2020 taught us anything, it's that having just one stream of income is like standing on one leg during an earthquake.

Adding just one side stream—even if it's modest—can change everything. It gives you options. It buys you time. It lets you say "no" to what doesn't serve you. And over time, it can be the foundation of long-term wealth, early retirement, or that dream house you thought was out of reach.

But here's the caveat: if the side hustle drains your energy, robs your joy, and torches your relationships, it's not helping. You're just trading one form of stress for another.

This chapter is your permission slip to do it differently.

Start With Your Energy, Not Just Your Skills

The biggest mistake people make when launching a side hustle? Chasing money without checking in with their energy. Sure, you might be great at organizing closets, but do you actually enjoy doing it after work?

Start with energy:

- What feels energizing instead of exhausting?
- What do people always ask you about?
- What could you talk about for 30 minutes straight without notes?
- What's something you'd do even if no one paid you (at first)?

When your side hustle comes from your natural flow, it feels less like work and more like expansion.

Categories of Sustainable Side Hustles

Let's break side hustles into types. Pick your flavor—or blend a few.

1. **Skill-Based Services** Think: freelancing, consulting, tutoring, coaching, editing, graphic design, virtual assistance. Pros: Low startup cost, uses your existing skills, flexible hours. Cons: Time-for-money model, client management, variable income.
2. **Digital Products** Think: eBooks, templates, online courses, stock photography, printables. Pros: Scalable, create once and sell many times, low overhead. Cons: Takes time to build, marketing required, competition is high.
3. **E-Commerce** Think: Etsy shops, Amazon FBA, dropshipping, print-on-demand. Pros: Can be automated, wide market reach. Cons: Inventory management (unless dropshipping), customer service, platform fees.
4. **Passive Platforms** Think: YouTube with ad revenue, affiliate marketing, blogging, podcasting. Pros: Long-term earning potential, builds audience and influence. Cons: Takes consistency, content creation is a grind at first.
5. **Local Hustles** Think: Dog walking, car detailing, mobile notary, event photography. Pros: Immediate income, low startup, strong word-of-mouth potential. Cons: Time-bound, location-dependent, may require physical energy.
6. **Investment-Based** Think: Real estate side gigs (Airbnb, rental arbitrage), REITs, dividend investing. Pros: Wealth building, can be passive. Cons: Capital required upfront, risk involved, learning curve.

Real Talk: What to Avoid

Let's skip the hype. Not every side hustle is worth your energy.

Avoid:

- MLMs that require you to buy inventory or pressure your friends.
- Gig work that barely pays minimum wage (unless it's strategic or temporary).

- Projects that require a massive learning curve before they make $1.
- Anything that compromises your mental health, sleep, or joy.

You're not here to escape your 9-5 just to build a 5-9 that's worse.

Sexy, Smart, Sustainable: What to Look For

Use this checklist to vet any side hustle idea:

- Does it energize me?
- Can I do it in 5–10 hours a week?
- Can it eventually be automated or scaled?
- Is there real demand for it?
- Can I do this without burning out?
- Does it align with where I want to go financially?

How to Actually Start Without Overwhelm

1. Pick ONE idea. Don't juggle five.
2. Define your "why" in one sentence. (Example: I want an extra $500/month to pay off debt.)
3. Time-block 3–5 hours per week.
4. Set a 90-day experiment. No pressure to be perfect—just test.
5. Track progress weekly and reflect monthly.

Remember: the point is **not** perfection. The point is momentum.

Side Hustles That Worked (Real Examples)

- A teacher started selling lesson plans on TeachersPayTeachers and now makes $1,200/month.
- A stay-at-home mom began offering Pinterest management services to bloggers—now a $40K/year gig.

- A photographer sold stock images to websites and built up $500/month in passive income.
- A corporate employee made Excel templates and started a digital Etsy store.
- A barber started offering virtual grooming consultations and product affiliate links.

Each one started small. Each one honored energy, not just money.

When to Quit a Side Hustle (Yes, Quit)

- It's no longer aligned.
- It's hurting your mental or physical health.
- The return on time is dropping.
- You've outgrown it.
- It's keeping you from scaling the thing you *really* want.

Permission granted to pivot.

Taxes and Structure: What You Need to Know

Even small side gigs have tax implications. Here's the plain-English version:

- **Track your income and expenses.** A simple spreadsheet or app works.
- **Set aside taxes.** Rule of thumb: 25–30% of your profit.
- **Consider an LLC** if you're earning consistently. Protect yourself.
- **Open a separate bank account** for your side gig.
- **Talk to a CPA** once you hit $5K+ in profit annually.

Making It Sexy: Integrate, Don't Separate

Your side hustle doesn't need to feel like a secret second life. Bring it into your world:

- Mention it proudly.
- Involve your partner or kids (if applicable).
- Celebrate milestones.
- Use the income to fund your dreams.

This isn't just about money. It's about *agency*. About saying: "I have options. I create value. I own my time."

You're Not Behind. You're Just Getting Started.

Most people don't know this stuff—until they do. Now you do.

Clarity is confidence. And confidence is sexy.

Make one move tonight: brainstorm five side hustle ideas that align with your energy, not just your resume. Pick one to test. Then move boldly in that direction.

You don't need 10 hustles. You need one aligned one. And that, my friend, is freedom.

Chapter 37: Turning Passion Into Profit

Let's start here: you already have something valuable inside you. Maybe it's your way with words, your knack for organizing chaos, your artistic eye, your culinary wizardry, your athletic knowledge, or your obsession with spreadsheets. Whatever it is, the world has told you it's a hobby. Cute. Nice. Fun. But not something to take seriously. Not something to monetize. Not something to retire off of.

That ends now.

This chapter is not about quitting your job tomorrow to sell pottery on Etsy or perform slam poetry in Thailand. It's about building a bridge between what lights you up and what can sustain you financially—without killing the joy along the way. Because when you turn passion into profit with strategy, not scarcity, everything changes.

Let's walk through how to do it. Thoughtfully. Sustainably. Powerfully.

The Passion Paycheck Myth

Let's break this open first: Turning your passion into income does NOT mean turning your joy into a job. It doesn't mean grinding yourself into creative burnout or taking on a hundred side gigs that leave you broke and bitter.

It means aligning what you love with what the market needs. That's the formula: Passion + Skill + Demand = Sustainable Profit.

If there's no market? It's a hobby.

If there's no love? It's a job.

If there's no structure? It's chaos.

But when you have all three—love, structure, and service to others—

you've got something sexy. Something that doesn't just pay the bills but amplifies your confidence and control.

Step 1: Identify What You Love Doing (And Would Still Do If You Weren't Paid)

Grab a notebook. Write freely. No editing. No judgment.

- What topics do you lose time thinking about?
- What do people always ask you for help with?
- What's your dream day look like?
- What did 10-year-old you love to do before adulting took over?
- What do you know how to do that's rare, weird, or deeply useful?

Now circle anything that:

- Feels energizing instead of exhausting
- Comes naturally to you but not to everyone else
- Has some thread of potential demand in today's world

This is your passion zone.

Step 2: Take Inventory of Monetizable Skills

Now let's get tactical. You're not just a dreamer—you're a strategist. Passion is cool, but we need a blueprint.

- Can you teach it? Create a course.
- Can you make it? Sell it online or in person.
- Can you coach it? Offer services or memberships.
- Can you organize it? Consult for those who can't.
- Can you explain it? Write, blog, record, podcast.

List at least five real ways someone could *pay* for what you do. Bonus points if you test the waters on at least one this month. Don't aim for perfect. Aim for done.

Step 3: Find the Overlap Between What You Love and What Others

Need

The fastest way to get paid is to solve someone's problem.

- Artists help people connect, decorate, heal.
- Bakers make celebrations sweeter.
- Stylists boost confidence.
- Organizers clear mental clutter.
- Writers help brands speak clearly.

Don't sell the thing. Sell the transformation.

You're not a painter. You create sanctuary.

You're not just a baker. You bake nostalgia.

You're not a voice actor. You bring stories to life.

When you own your value, your pricing changes. Your boundaries sharpen. Your energy rises. And yes—so does your income.

Step 4: Choose a Business Model That Doesn't Drain You

Not all passion-to-profit paths are created equal. Choose one that matches your bandwidth, energy, and risk tolerance.

Model Examples Pros Cons

Freelancer

Photography, writing, web design

Fast to launch

Time for money trade-off

Digital Products

Courses, eBooks, templates

Scalable, passive income

Upfront time and tech

Physical Goods

Jewelry, crafts, art

Tangible results, high margin

Inventory, shipping

Coaching/Consulting

Fitness, mindset, business

High-value, personal impact
Emotional labor
Affiliate Income
Product reviews, blogging
Passive, flexible
Takes time to grow audience
Memberships
Monthly community, access
Recurring revenue
Requires ongoing content
Choose 1 or 2 to start. Keep it lean. Get feedback. Pivot smart.

Step 5: Set Prices That Reflect Your Value, Not Your Insecurity

Repeat after me: Charging less doesn't make me more likable. Pricing high doesn't make me greedy.

- Research your industry.
- Anchor your price to the outcome you create.
- Don't undercut others just to compete. Build better.
- Be open to changing your prices as demand increases.
- Always include a profit margin, even early on.

Step 6: Get Your First Dollar

This is the line between fantasy and business. Your idea isn't a business until someone pays you.

- Run a beta test
- Offer a discounted launch
- Post your offer in a local group or online
- Use your current network—they already trust you
- Focus on the sale, not the scale

When you make your first $1 outside your day job, something changes in your DNA. It's proof you can do it. And if you can make $1, you can make

$100. Then $1,000. Then $10,000. You get the idea.

Step 7: Build in Boundaries from Day One

Love can become labor if you don't protect your energy. Create policies before problems.

- Set work hours (even for your side hustle)
- Use contracts or agreements
- Say no when it's not a fit
- Raise prices instead of taking on more clients
- Create content you can reuse or repurpose

Remember: Freedom, not frenzy. Joy, not just income.

Step 8: Protect Your Passion Financially and Legally

Once the money starts flowing, keep it clean:

- Open a separate business checking account
- Track all income and expenses
- Set aside money for taxes (at least 25-30%)
- Consider an LLC for protection and professionalism
- Get basic liability insurance if needed

Your hobby became a business. Treat it with respect.

Step 9: Create Systems So You Can Grow Without Burning Out

Want to scale? Systemize early. These don't have to be fancy.

- Templates for emails, invoices, onboarding
- A simple CRM (spreadsheet or app)
- Weekly admin day
- Scheduled social content
- Automate what you can (bookings, payments, delivery)

Step 10: Reinvest to Amplify

Instead of treating every dollar as spendable, reinvest in growth:

- Equipment upgrades
- Coaching or mentorship
- Marketing support
- Time-saving tools
- Outsourcing low-value tasks

This is how you go from solo to sustainable. From passion project to profit path.

Real Talk: Not Every Passion Should Be a Business

Sometimes, monetizing a passion kills the joy. That's okay. You can love painting and never sell a canvas. You can write poetry that no one reads but you. That's not failure. That's freedom.

Know the difference between passion for joy and passion for income. You don't owe anyone your creativity. But if you *want* to earn from it, now you know how.

Sexy Takeaways

- Passion is powerful, but profit comes from solving problems.
- Value what comes naturally to you—that's often where your magic lives.
- Don't wait for perfect. Launch ugly. Adjust as you grow.
- Treat your side hustle like a business from the beginning.
- You don't have to monetize everything. Choose what stays sacred.

You're not behind. You're just getting started.

Most people don't know this stuff—until they do. Now you do.

Clarity is confidence. And confidence is sexy.

Make one money move before you go to bed tonight. Just one. And then do another next week.

Chapter 38: Entrepreneurship Isn't Always Sexy

But It Can Be Smart

Let's get real. In the age of Instagram influencers, hustle culture hashtags, and TikTok side-hustle gurus, the word "entrepreneur" has been glamorized. It conjures up images of laptops by the beach, endless passive income, and your name in lights. But real entrepreneurship? It's more spreadsheets than sunsets. It's equal parts dream and discipline.

Still, that doesn't mean you shouldn't consider it.

This chapter is about stripping down the fantasy and dressing up the truth. Because while entrepreneurship isn't always sexy, it can be one of the smartest financial moves you ever make—if you do it right.

The Myth of Overnight Success

Let's bust this first: nobody builds a six-figure business overnight. Even those "I went viral" stories are usually backed by years of unseen work, failed attempts, and hard-won lessons.

Entrepreneurship requires patience, consistency, and stamina. It will test you in ways a 9-to-5 never will. It doesn't offer guaranteed paychecks, but it offers something many traditional jobs don't: ownership, flexibility, and long-term scalability.

So if you're thinking about stepping into entrepreneurship, do it with your eyes wide open. Not with fairy dust in your pockets.

Why Entrepreneurship Might Be Right for You

1. **You crave autonomy.**
2. You want to set your schedule, choose your clients, and direct your own path.
3. **You have a burning idea or passion.**
4. Something that won't let go of you, that keeps you up at night and fills your notebooks.
5. **You're tired of trading time for money.**
6. You want to build something that grows even when you're not clocked in.
7. **You need a new stream of income.**
8. Maybe your job isn't cutting it. Or maybe you just want more control over your financial future.
9. **You're ready to be the CEO of your life.**
10. That means taking full responsibility. It means risk, but it also means reward.

Entrepreneurship Isn't Always Instagram-Worthy

Here are some truths you don't see in the highlight reel:

- You'll work late nights and early mornings.
- You'll question yourself—a lot.
- You might not make money for a while.
- You'll wear every hat: sales, marketing, operations, customer service.
- You'll get rejected, ghosted, and copied.

Still want in? Good. That means you're realistic.

Because when the grind is done with intention, the payoff is freedom.

The Types of Entrepreneurs

Let's name the lanes so you can see which fits you best.

1. **The Freelancer**
2. You trade skills for income: graphic design, consulting, tutoring, coaching.

3. **The Side Hustler**
4. You build on evenings and weekends while keeping your day job.
5. **The Creator**
6. You make content, write books, teach courses, or build an audience that you monetize.
7. **The Scalable Founder**
8. You start something that can run without you someday: a product line, an app, a service-based agency.
9. **The Hybrid**
10. You combine these lanes into a custom blend.

There is no right path. Only the one that fits your goals, energy, and lifestyle.

Starting Smart: What You Need to Know

Here's what they don't teach you in those "How I made $1M" webinars:

1. **Know Your Why**
2. If it's just money, you'll quit. Your reason needs to be stronger than your excuses.
3. **Start Small**
4. Don't quit your job day one. Test your idea, get feedback, make a few sales.
5. **Separate Business and Personal Finances**
6. Open a separate business bank account. Even if it's just a side hustle.
7. **Track Your Expenses**
8. Use apps like QuickBooks or Wave. Taxes are real. So are deductions.
9. **Know Your Numbers**
10. What does it cost to run your business? What's your profit margin? Know your break-even point.
11. **Set Boundaries**
12. Hustle culture is not cute if it wrecks your health or relationships.
13. **Protect Yourself**
14. LLCs, contracts, insurance—these aren't just for big businesses.

Pros and Cons of Entrepreneurship

Let's lay it out.

Pros:

- Freedom and flexibility
- Unlimited income potential
- Creative control
- Legacy building

Cons:

- Uncertain income
- No built-in benefits
- Higher stress
- You wear all the hats (at least at first)

Does that mean don't do it? No. It means go in smart.

Case Study: Amanda, 42, Former Teacher Turned Business Owner

Amanda taught for 18 years. Burned out but brilliant, she started tutoring part-time. Then she created online courses. Then a coaching program. Within 3 years, her side gig replaced her teaching salary.

What made it work? She stayed consistent. She kept it simple. And she built a brand based on trust.

You don't need to be flashy. You need to be real, useful, and persistent.

Common Mistakes New Entrepreneurs Make

1. Spending too much before making any money
2. Not validating their idea with paying customers
3. Undercharging (don't price from insecurity)
4. Doing everything themselves for too long
5. Giving up too soon

Smart Business Moves That Make Entrepreneurship Worth It

- Build an emergency fund before launching full-time
- Create digital products that can sell while you sleep
- Offer services to bootstrap income, then reinvest
- Focus on recurring revenue (subscriptions, memberships)
- Build an email list early—social media isn't guaranteed

Systems Over Hustle

Want your business to stop being your second full-time job?

Set up systems:

- Automate your marketing
- Batch your content
- Outsource what drains you
- Use templates and checklists

Hustling 24/7 isn't power. Sustainability is.

You Don't Have to Be a Shark

You can be kind and successful. You can lead with values. You can build wealth without being cutthroat.

This is especially true if you're a woman, a person of color, or from any historically excluded community. You don't need to change who you are to succeed. You need structure, strategy, and support.

Your Business, Your Terms

You don't have to:

- Have an LLC right away
- Make a TikTok dance video
- Quit your job tomorrow
- Hire a team of 10
- Hit six figures in year one

You do need to:

- Know your numbers
- Deliver real value
- Stay consistent
- Take care of your health
- Keep learning

Sexy Takeaways

- Entrepreneurship isn't a fantasy. It's a framework.
- You don't have to go big to go bold.
- Start smart. Scale slow. Stay sane.
- Your future self will thank you for betting on yourself—but only if you do it with strategy.

You're not behind. You're just getting started.

Most people don't know this stuff—until they do. Now you do.

Clarity is confidence. And confidence is sexy.

Make one money move before you go to bed tonight. Just one. And then do another next week.

Chapter 39: Taxes and the Truth About the IRS

Let's drop the fear and pick up the facts.

Taxes might not seem sexy, but knowing how to manage them is straight-up powerful. And power? That's always sexy. Here's the deal: wealthy people, smart people, even everyday people who are just getting started—they know things about taxes that too many of us never learned. Not because we're lazy or careless, but because no one ever pulled us aside and said, "Hey, here's how this really works."

This chapter is your deep, no-shame, no-fear, all-facts talk about taxes. The IRS isn't the boogeyman. And tax planning? It's not about cheating the system—it's about playing smart inside the rules. Let's get you fluent in the language of taxes so you can move through life like someone who's not scared of April 15 anymore.

The IRS Isn't Coming for You—Unless You Ignore Them

First things first: Most people have nothing to fear from the IRS if they file their taxes, report their income, and pay what they owe. That's it. The IRS doesn't have time to chase every person who forgot to deduct their home office.

But let's keep it real. If you ignore notices, fail to file, or dramatically underreport your income? That's when they get spicy. And yes, that spice burns.

Moral of the story: Engage early. Respond to letters. File even if you can't pay. Ignoring the IRS is like ignoring a leak under the kitchen sink. It never gets better on its own.

How Your Income Gets Taxed: A Love Story in Brackets

You don't pay the same tax rate on all your income. The U.S. has a progressive tax system. That means as you make more, you pay a higher rate *on the next portion* of your income—not on all of it.

2025 Federal Income Tax Brackets – Single Filers

- **10%** on income up to **$11,925**
- **12%** on income from **$11,926** to **$48,475**
- **22%** on income from **$48,476** to **$103,350**
- **24%** on income from **$103,351** to **$197,300**
- **32%** on income from **$197,301** to **$250,525**
- **35%** on income from **$250,526** to **$626,350**
- **37%** on income over **$626,350**

Your *effective tax rate* (the average you actually pay) is lower than your *marginal tax rate* (the rate on your last dollar).

Deductions vs. Credits: Don't Mix These Up

- **Deductions** reduce your *taxable income.*
- **Credits** reduce your *actual tax bill* dollar-for-dollar.

A $1,000 deduction might save you $220 in taxes if you're in the 22% bracket.

A $1,000 credit? That saves you $1,000, period.

Some sexy credits to know:

- Child Tax Credit
- Lifetime Learning Credit
- Saver's Credit
- American Opportunity Credit

W-2 vs. 1099: The Tax Difference Between Employees and Entrepreneurs

If you work a job and get a W-2, your taxes are mostly automated. You get a paycheck with taxes withheld. Easy.

If you freelance, consult, or side hustle? You're probably getting 1099s. That means no one is withholding taxes for you. You're on your own for:

- Income tax
- Self-employment tax (Social Security + Medicare)
- Estimated quarterly taxes

Pro move: Set aside 25-30% of any 1099 income in a separate savings account. Label it: "IRS's Money" so you don't touch it.

Sexy People Track Their Expenses

Seriously. Tax savings live in the details. If you own a business, side hustle, or even work remotely, you may qualify for legitimate deductions.

Examples:

- Home office (yes, even a small corner counts if it's exclusive use)
- Business travel
- Continuing education
- Subscriptions and software
- Marketing

But here's the key: **Documentation**. Keep receipts. Log mileage. Track dates and purposes.

The IRS doesn't hate you. They just want proof.

Tax-Advantaged Accounts: The Real MVPs

You can legally lower your tax bill by using smart accounts:

- **401(k)/403(b)/TSP**: Pre-tax retirement accounts. Lower taxable income now; taxed later.
- **Roth IRA/401(k)**: Post-tax contributions. No taxes on qualified

withdrawals.

- **HSA**: Triple tax benefit. Pre-tax contributions, tax-free growth, tax-free withdrawals for medical expenses.
- **529 Plans**: Tax-free growth and withdrawals for education.

Side Hustle Strategy: Set Up a Solo 401(k)

Got a side hustle? You can start a Solo 401(k) and contribute *both* as the employer and employee. That means you can save way more for retirement and lower your taxable income all at once.

What Triggers an Audit? Not What You Think

The IRS uses algorithms to select returns. You're not more likely to get audited just because you earn six figures. What triggers audits:

- Big charitable deductions relative to income
- Self-employed income with no expenses
- Math errors
- Missing 1099s (the IRS gets a copy too)
- Round numbers (reporting $10,000 in business expenses exactly)

Keep it real. Keep it honest. Keep your receipts.

LLCs and S-Corps: What You Really Need to Know

Starting a business? You might hear buzz about LLCs and S-Corps.

- **LLC:** Protects your personal assets. Doesn't change your taxes unless you elect S-Corp status.
- **S-Corp:** Allows you to pay yourself a salary and take distributions. Can save you money on self-employment tax *if* your business is profitable enough.

But don't jump into S-Corp status just to be fancy. Talk to a CPA. Get it right.

What Wealthy People Know That Others Don't

- They plan their taxes in *October*, not April.
- They use tax-loss harvesting to offset capital gains.
- They gift assets to heirs in smart ways.
- They use donor-advised funds to bunch charitable giving.
- They pay kids through family businesses (yes, it's legal and smart).

Action Steps: What to Do This Week

1. Review last year's tax return and understand every line.
2. Open a dedicated tax savings account if you have side income.
3. Track business mileage for 30 days.
4. Set a calendar reminder to book a tax planning meeting in October.
5. Use a tool like TaxCaster or SmartAsset to estimate your tax bill.
6. Automate IRA or HSA contributions monthly.

You're Not Behind. You're Just Getting Started.

Most people don't know this stuff—until they do. Now you do.

Clarity is confidence. And confidence is sexy.

Make one money move before you go to bed tonight. Just one. And then do another next week.

This isn't about fear. This is about fluency.

You don't need to be a tax expert. But you do need to speak the language well enough to protect your future.

And that? That's power.

That's confidence.

That's sexy.

Part VIII: Lifestyle Design — Live Like You Mean It

This is the part where money gets personal—and powerful. Because building wealth isn't just about numbers. It's about how you live. Part VIII is all about aligning your financial decisions with the life you actually want to live—not the life someone else told you to settle for. We'll break down how to spend intentionally, design a lifestyle that reflects your values, and build routines, relationships, and rhythms that support your goals without draining your soul. Whether you're planning a sabbatical, downsizing, finally splurging on that dream trip, or just figuring out how to live well on your terms, this section will help you turn your financial plans into a fully expressed, fully aligned life.

Chapter 40: Lifestyle Creep is the Silent Killer

How to Upgrade Your Life Without Wrecking Your Wallet

Let's start with a truth that most people don't want to admit: you're not broke because you're bad with money. You're not behind because you don't work hard. And you're not unqualified to live a better life just because you splurged on takeout this week. But there *is* something sneaky, seductive, and dangerous that quietly drains your wealth, clouds your judgment, and keeps you spinning your wheels. It's called lifestyle creep.

Lifestyle creep is what happens when your income goes up, and your expenses follow it—sometimes faster than your paycheck can keep up. It doesn't show up in big, flashy ways at first. It sneaks in with nicer dinners, a bigger apartment, a fancier car lease, and those little upgrades that feel like rewards for your hard work. And to be fair, they *are* rewards. But if you're not careful, those rewards can become chains.

This chapter is about breaking free. Not from abundance, but from unintentional consumption. Because wealth isn't about how much you earn. It's about how much you keep, how you grow it, and how aligned your spending is with the life you actually want—not the one you feel pressured to perform.

What Is Lifestyle Creep (and Why It's So Damn Sneaky)

Lifestyle creep, or lifestyle inflation, is when your cost of living rises in proportion to your income. You get a raise, and suddenly you have a new streaming service, upgraded phone, more expensive coffee habit, and a wardrobe refresh that would impress your Instagram followers.

But here's the kicker: those new expenses feel normal almost immediately. Your new standard becomes your new baseline. And just like that, the dopamine wears off, but the bill remains.

This isn't about guilt. You should absolutely enjoy the fruits of your labor. But wealth is built when you *pause* before defaulting to the upgrade. When you ask, "Does this make my life better—or just more expensive?"

The Real Problem: Why Lifestyle Creep Hurts Your Future Self

1. **It delays your financial freedom.**
2. If every extra dollar you earn is already spent before it hits your account, you're not building flexibility. You're just working harder to stand still.
3. **It hides behind the illusion of success.**
4. People will think you're doing great because you look like you are. But your net worth doesn't lie. A nice car and a corner apartment don't mean you're rich—they mean you're spending money.
5. **It feeds comparison and emptiness.**
6. Lifestyle creep is often fueled by what we think we should have—not what we truly value. It's seductive, but not satisfying.
7. **It locks you into high fixed costs.**
8. Upgrades often come with commitments. A mortgage. A lease. A subscription. A lifestyle you now feel pressured to maintain.

The Sexy Strategy: Upgrade With Intention, Not Impulse

Let's redefine the upgrade. It's not a bad thing. But let's do it *on purpose.*

- **Save first, upgrade later.** Every time your income increases, commit to saving 50% of the raise *before* you spend a dime.
- **Try the 30-day upgrade delay.** Want something new and shiny? Write it down. Wait 30 days. If you still want it, go for it. If not, you've dodged a costly impulse.

- **Set lifestyle ceilings.** Decide in advance the *maximum* you'll spend on things like rent, cars, or dining out. Stick to it, even as your income grows.
- **Upgrade your values, not just your stuff.** Better quality of life might mean working less, traveling more, or investing in therapy—not just buying nicer things.

Real-Life Glow-Ups: Examples of Upgrading With Strategy

- **Maya got a $20K raise** and used it to max out her Roth IRA and take one intentional solo vacation instead of upgrading her apartment.
- **Tyrone paid off his car** but kept driving it another three years and used the savings to invest in a side hustle he now runs full-time.
- **Jasmine and Andre** capped their housing cost at 25% of their income, even when they could "afford" more—and used the rest to build a six-figure portfolio before 40.

The Psychology of It All: Why We Creep

- **We crave validation.** The world rewards visible success. That outfit, that car, that trip to Tulum.
- **We think comfort = progress.** Upgrades feel like growth, but they're not always a sign of financial strength.
- **We're afraid to miss out.** Scarcity mindset shows up in splurging. "I deserve this" becomes an excuse to abandon our long-term goals.

Let's Talk About Boundaries

Boundaries protect your money, energy, and future. Saying no to an upgrade isn't deprivation—it's direction. Set limits that reflect your values:

- Social boundary: "I don't do bottomless brunch every weekend anymore."
- Emotional boundary: "I don't need to prove anything with my

purchases."

- Financial boundary: "If it doesn't fit my plan, it doesn't go on the card."

Automation is Sexy

Want to avoid lifestyle creep entirely? Automate your values:

- Set auto-transfers to savings, investing, and debt payments the *day* your paycheck hits.
- Use "fun funds" for guilt-free spending. When it's gone, it's gone.
- Build an annual money ritual where you reflect, reset, and realign your lifestyle with your actual goals.

Action Steps: The Lifestyle Creep Detox

1. Audit your last 3 months of spending. What are you paying for that you didn't use or don't love?
2. Define your top 5 values. Do your spending habits match?
3. Decide how much of future raises you'll save vs. spend. Put it in writing.
4. Set a spending cap for your biggest lifestyle categories.
5. Have one tough conversation with someone about money this week.

You're Not Behind. You're Just Getting Started.

Most people don't notice lifestyle creep until they're deep in it. But now that you see it, you get to *choose* how you grow. And that choice? That's power.

Clarity is confidence. And confidence is sexy.

Make one lifestyle move before you go to bed tonight. Just one. And then do another next week.

Chapter 41: Luxury With Limits — How to Indulge the Smart Way

Let's be honest. Luxury feels good. Whether it's first-class flights, soft leather seats, VIP access, designer bags, five-star dining, or that candle that costs more than your first car payment—indulgence taps into something deep. Something primal. Something powerful.

But here's the truth no one tells you: real luxury doesn't come from overspending. It comes from owning your choices, not being owned by them. It comes from buying with intention, not insecurity. It comes from knowing the difference between taste and trying to impress. Luxury is not the goal. Freedom is. And when you manage your money wisely, you get both.

So let's have a grown, sexy conversation about indulgence. About taste. About how to enjoy the finer things in life—without losing the foundation you've worked so hard to build.

Why This Chapter Matters

Luxury isn't evil. But the pursuit of it—when done recklessly, reactively, or out of comparison—can wreck your wallet, your relationships, and your peace. If you've ever looked up from your Chase app after a bougie weekend and thought, "What the hell did I just do?" this chapter is for you.

We live in a culture that tells us more is better. Upgrade it. Finance it. Post it. But sexy people don't just buy the bag. They read the fine print, run the numbers, and make sure the bag isn't costing them a future.

This chapter will help you:

- Indulge with intention
- Spot fake flexes before they become financial stress
- Set boundaries around your spending that still feel good
- Create your own definition of wealth, success, and joy

You don't need to go full minimalist. You just need to go full intentional.

What Luxury Really Means

Let's define it first. Luxury isn't just price tag. It's a feeling. It's elegance, comfort, and ease. It's not necessarily about cost—it's about how something fits into your life. For one person, luxury might be private chefs and Prada. For another, it might be a quiet Friday with zero obligations.

Luxury is personal. The mistake people make is assuming it has to look like someone else's feed.

The smartest people understand:

- **Luxury is situational:** It's not always about what you own. Sometimes it's about what you *don't* have to worry about.
- **Luxury is sustainable:** It doesn't feel luxurious if it wrecks your finances.
- **Luxury is earned:** Not by hustle or exhaustion, but by alignment. You spend money where your values live.

Lifestyle Inflation vs. Lifestyle Elevation

There's a difference. Let's break it down.

- **Lifestyle Inflation:** Every time your income goes up, your spending goes up too. New job = new car. Bonus = luxury vacation. Raise = designer wardrobe.
- What does that get you? A fancier version of broke.
- **Lifestyle Elevation:** You upgrade selectively. You keep your core financial strategy solid. You indulge, but with clarity.

The people who master luxury-with-limits live like this:

- They have a base lifestyle that covers their needs with ease.
- They invest and save *before* they splurge.
- They create luxury line items in their budget.

Create a "Sexy Splurge" Account

Yes. A literal savings account for luxury. Call it "Soft Life Fund" or "Vacation Shoes" or "Bespoke Experiences."

Here's how it works:

1. Decide what percentage of your income goes toward intentional indulgence.
2. Automate transfers monthly.
3. Use it guilt-free for whatever lights you up—just stay within it.

This gives you boundaries *and* freedom. You don't need to say no to yourself. You need to say yes, the smart way.

The Math Behind the Mood

Want to buy a $2,000 handbag?

Cool. First, make sure:

- You're not carrying high-interest credit card debt.
- Your emergency fund is intact.
- You're hitting your investment targets.
- You've got a spending cap that allows you to still breathe afterward.

If buying that bag means you can't afford therapy, groceries, or your Roth IRA contribution—that's not luxury. That's a liability.

Indulgence Rules of Thumb

- Want it? Wait 72 hours.
- Love it? Buy it with cash, not credit.
- Lusting after it? Ask: What do I *hope* this purchase will make me feel?
- Regret it? Learn, don't shame.

Luxury gets sexier when you detach it from proving something.

Keep Up With Yourself, Not the Jonese's

Comparison kills your joy and your budget. Someone else's highlight reel should never drive your money moves. Their yacht might be financed. Their watch might be rented. Their house might be leveraged to the max.

Your job isn't to impress them. Your job is to protect your peace.

Luxury Spending Triggers to Watch For

- "I deserve this" after a hard day
- "Everyone else is going"
- "It's on sale, so technically I'm saving money"
- "I'll make up for it later"

Pause. Breathe. Choose from your center, not your stress.

When Luxury Becomes a Red Flag

- You're hiding packages from your partner
- You're using Buy Now, Pay Later for brunch outfits
- You're counting days till payday, but rocking designer
- You're investing more in image than assets

That's not freedom. That's financial anxiety in a silk robe.

Smart Ways to Experience Luxury

- Split costs with friends: Group wine tastings, Airbnb luxury homes
- Use rewards points: For travel, hotels, or dining
- Upgrade one thing, not everything: A luxury bed makes more sense than a luxury end table
- Choose quality over quantity: One amazing coat > 5 fast fashion jackets

Luxury Is Also Time, Peace, Space

Don't forget: some of the most powerful luxuries cost nothing or next to nothing.

- Canceling something you don't want to do
- Going offline for the weekend
- Buying yourself time via meal prep, delivery, or outsourcing
- Having savings so you don't panic over emergencies

That's real wealth.

The Sexy Luxury Audit

Every quarter, sit down and ask:

1. What's something I bought that truly elevated my joy?
2. What's something I bought that was about ego?
3. What's one indulgence I want to save for next?
4. What's one area where I can cut back without sacrifice?

This keeps you intentional, not impulsive.

Final Word on Luxury With Limits

This isn't about denying yourself.

It's about defining yourself.

True luxury is:

- Paying off your credit cards monthly
- Sleeping well because you're not drowning in payments
- Saying yes to a trip without rearranging your whole life
- Investing *and* indulging

You can have a lifestyle that looks good and feels good. But the magic happens when you choose what actually matters to *you*.

You're not behind. You're just getting started.

Most people don't know this stuff—until they do. Now you do.

Clarity is confidence. And confidence is sexy.

Make one money move before you go to bed tonight. Just one. And then do another next week.

Chapter 42: Traveling Rich – Credit Card Rewards, Budget Tricks, and Luxury on a Dime

Let's start with this: luxury is not a price point. It's a feeling. And when you travel with strategy, confidence, and savvy, you can experience five-star moments at two-star prices.

This chapter is your sexy, grown-up guide to seeing the world without breaking your wallet. Because yes, you deserve the passport stamps, the beachfront views, the rooftop cocktails, and the memories that feel like magic—but you don't need to drain your savings to get them.

This isn't a backpacking how-to or a coupon-clipping seminar. This is about *intentional indulgence.* This is about financial literacy that turns wanderlust into reality.

Why Travel Is Part of the Wealth Conversation

Let's redefine wealth. It's not just digits in your bank account. Wealth is freedom. It's options. It's being able to say yes to Paris, or Tulum, or a long weekend in Napa without guilt.

When you treat travel as part of your *financial lifestyle* instead of an "extra," you stop swinging between feast and famine. You start building in joy sustainably.

Travel Rewards 101: Sexy Points = Free Flights and Hotel Nights

If you're going to spend money, make it work for you. That's what credit card points do.

A few basics:

- **Chase Sapphire Preferred/Reserve**, **Amex Platinum**, **Capital One Venture X**: These are the A-list.
- Use them for *everything* you already buy: groceries, gas, streaming.
- Pay them off *in full* every month. No exceptions. The interest is never worth it.
- Rack up points and redeem for flights, hotels, or transfers to travel partners.

Example: One sign-up bonus could cover your roundtrip to Italy.

Action step: Pick one travel rewards card, understand its perks, and use it with discipline. Treat it like a debit card you pay off every 30 days.

Travel Budgeting Without Killing the Vibe

Yes, you can be spontaneous *and* financially smart.

Here's how:

1. **Create a Travel Fund:** Open a high-yield savings account just for travel. Name it something fun like "Global Adventures Only." Auto-transfer $50/week.
2. **Use the 3-3-3 Rule:**

- $300 = monthly local escapes (massages, date nights, staycations)
- $3,000 = one major trip a year
- $30,000 = long-term luxury goals (honeymoon, sabbatical, luxury safari)

1. **Plan Ahead, Not Cheaply:** Travel off-season. Book Tuesday-Thursday flights. Set Google alerts. But also know when to spend for quality experiences.

Pro tip: Spend more on things you'll remember (cooking class in Tuscany), less on things you won't (airport meals).

Luxury Travel on a Budget: Yes, It's Real

Here's what the wealthy know:

- **First-class vibes don't require first-class cash.**
- It's not about the brand—it's about the *experience.*

Real strategies:

- Fly business class with points
- Book boutique hotels instead of chains
- Rent apartments for longer stays
- Use credit card perks for airport lounges and free upgrades
- Eat where locals eat

It's not about sacrifice. It's about smart swaps.

Digital Nomad, Part-Time Jetsetter, or Family Travel Pro?

Pick your lane and optimize.

- **Nomad?**: Prioritize flexibility. Use remote work to hack location costs (Thailand rent < U.S. rent).
- **Part-Time Jetsetter?**: Stack long weekends with holidays. Maximize PTO.
- **Family Travel?**: Use travel hacking for companion passes, miles for kids' tickets, and lodging with kitchens.

Customize your plan. There's no one way to be a financially savvy traveler.

Real Talk: Travel Traps to Avoid

Let's be clear: the glam can go wrong if you don't play it smart.

- Don't finance a vacation on a high-interest card.
- Don't fall for influencer FOMO trips you can't afford.
- Don't ignore the fine print on "deals."
- Don't assume luxury means better.

Action step: Know your priorities. Would you rather have a luxury hotel or a five-course meal? Direct flight or more time on the ground? Choose.

Budget accordingly.

Your Travel Dream Map: Turn Goals into Plans

1. Write down your top 5 dream destinations.
2. Research average costs: flights, food, stays.
3. Pick one for the next 12 months.
4. Reverse engineer the cost. Monthly savings goal = Total / Months.
5. Automate that goal.

Freedom is sexy. So is flying first class with no debt.

Bold Encouragement

You're not behind. You're just getting started. You don't need a trust fund to travel like someone who owns their time and priorities.

Reality Check (With Love)

Most people don't know this stuff—until they do. Now you do. Now you know how the financially free fly.

Sexy Takeaway

Traveling rich isn't about your bank account. It's about how you think, plan, and choose. Clarity is confidence. And confidence is sexy.

Prompt to Act

Make one travel money move before bed tonight. Open a travel savings account. Research a travel rewards card. Write your top 3 dream spots. Just one move. Then another next week.

Chapter 43: Big Purchases Without Regrets

Let's be real for a second: There is a kind of thrill that comes with a big purchase. A new car. That velvet couch you've been eyeing on Instagram. The latest iPhone or a surround sound system that makes movie night feel like a private theater. It's exciting. It's affirming. It can also be financially dangerous if you don't walk into it with your eyes open, your mind clear, and your bank account protected.

This chapter isn't here to tell you *not* to buy the nice thing. It's here to help you buy the right thing, at the right time, with the right amount of swagger and zero regret.

The Truth About Big Purchases

Let's start with the honest truth: most of us were never taught how to buy big-ticket items wisely. We know how to want them. We know how to swipe the card. But the in-between? The preparation, the strategy, the patience, the math?

Crickets.

So we do what we think successful people do: finance it. Put it on a payment plan. Get it now, figure it out later.

But wealth doesn't work like that.

Wealth is strategic. It plans ahead. It looks at the total cost, not just the monthly payment. And it makes decisions that give you peace, not just a dopamine rush.

Let's break it down. One category at a time.

Cars: The Sexy Ride That Can Sink You

There's nothing wrong with wanting a car that turns heads. But here's the thing about cars:

- They depreciate the moment you drive them off the lot.
- They cost more than the sticker price.
- They come with hidden fees, interest, insurance hikes, and maintenance.

Smart Car Buying Tips:

- Never finance a car for more than 36-48 months. If the monthly payment is only affordable because the loan stretches to 72 months or more, you're overbuying.
- Aim to put down at least 20%.
- Try not to let your car payment exceed 10-15% of your take-home pay.
- Consider certified pre-owned cars that are 2-3 years old. Let someone else eat that early depreciation.
- Always get a pre-purchase inspection if buying used.
- Shop for insurance *before* you buy the car—not after.

Cars are emotional. Dealers know that. That's why the showroom smells like leather and hope. Don't fall for it. Run the numbers. Then take the wheel.

Tech: The High-Tech Trap

The tech world moves fast. Which is why it's easy to fall into the trap of always needing the latest thing. New phone. New tablet. New laptop. New smart home device that you don't need but *feels* convenient.

But here's the truth:

- Most people don't use even half the features of their devices.
- The resale value of tech drops fast.
- The upgrade cycle is engineered to make you feel behind.

How to Buy Tech Smartly:

- Buy refurbished from reputable sources.
- Don't finance electronics unless it's 0% interest *and* you have the money to pay it off.
- Upgrade based on function, not trend.
- Budget annually for tech upgrades, just like you do for travel or gifts.
- Keep your devices clean, protected, and updated to maximize their lifespan.

You don't have to be the first to get it. Just the smartest in how you use it.

Furniture: Comfort or Cost Sinkhole?

Furniture is a big deal. It sets the vibe. It impacts your sleep, your posture, your back, your energy. But it also comes with a wide price range—and just as wide a range in quality.

What to Know Before You Buy:

- Always measure. Then measure again. Know your space.
- Don't go into debt for aesthetics. Create a design plan and build it out over time.
- Invest in quality for key pieces: your mattress, your couch, your work chair.
- Mix high and low. Pair IKEA bookshelves with a solid wood desk.
- Ask about warranties and delivery fees.

A $3,000 couch isn't impressive if your emergency fund is $300.

Buy for your life, not your Instagram.

Pros and Cons of Financing Big Purchases

Let's talk financing. Not all debt is evil. But it has to be intentional.

Pros:

- Allows access to items you need while preserving cash
- 0% offers can be strategic

- Can help build credit with responsible use

Cons:

- Encourages overspending
- Can wreck your budget with surprise fees or missed payments
- Interest can double or triple the cost

Always ask:

- Can I afford this if I lost my income for 3 months?
- Does this item add value to my life or just status?
- What's the total cost after interest?

A Better Approach: The Sexy Spending Plan

Instead of reacting to your desires, *plan* for them.

Create a "Big Purchase Wishlist." For each item:

- Name the item.
- Set a realistic price range.
- Rank it on a 1-10 urgency scale.
- Break down how much to save per month.
- Set a deadline.

This is how luxury becomes sustainable. And sexy.

Action Steps to Buy Without Regret

1. **Pause Before You Swipe**

- Wait 48 hours before making any purchase over $500.

1. **Check Your Ratios**

- Don't let big purchases eat more than 10% of your net worth unless it's an asset.

1. **Budget the Add-Ons**

- Always calculate delivery, setup, extended warranties, and accessories.

1. **Set a Celebration Rule**

- Tie big purchases to milestones. Promotion? Hit a savings goal? That's the time.

1. **Shop Intentionally**

- Don't browse out of boredom. Browse with purpose and a budget.

Big Purchases and Your Identity

Sometimes, the desire to buy big isn't about the thing at all. It's about who we want to be. Who we want people to think we are.

That's powerful. And risky.

Before you buy:

- Ask what you hope the purchase will *say* about you.
- Ask if you could feel that same affirmation another way.
- Ask if you're trying to impress people who don't matter.

There's nothing wrong with wanting beautiful things. But don't let those things own you.

You are not your car.

You are not your couch.

You are not your phone.

You are your *choices*.

You're not behind. You're just getting started.

Most people don't know this stuff—until they do. Now you do.

Clarity is confidence. And confidence is sexy.

Make one money move before you go to bed tonight. Just one. And then do another next week.

Chapter 44: Fashion, Beauty, and Financial Flex — Looking Good Without Going Broke

Let's get something straight: There is absolutely nothing wrong with wanting to look good. In fact, there's something deeply powerful about walking into a room and knowing you're the best-dressed person there, your hair is fresh, your skin is glowing, your shoes are right, and your presence says, "I care. About myself. About my energy. About how I show up."

But here's the rub: If your closet is full but your emergency fund is empty, we've got a problem.

This chapter is about aligning your outer flex with inner financial strength. Because financial literacy isn't about denial or living in beige. It's about freedom. It's about knowing how to say yes without that sinking feeling later. It's about making room for the things that make you feel radiant—without wrecking your budget in the process.

Where Style Meets Strategy

Looking good can be a form of self-care, confidence, and even branding. But it can also become a trap if your sense of worth is tied too closely to your wardrobe, your hair, or your ability to keep up with Instagram aesthetics.

Real power? That's when you can sit in a designer bag boutique and walk out with your bank account untouched and your self-esteem intact. Because you know your worth isn't in the label—it's in your decisions.

Let's talk about how to balance the two.

The Difference Between Value and Price

Just because something is expensive doesn't mean it's valuable. And just because something is affordable doesn't mean it's cheap.

True style is about intention. Smart beauty is about consistency, not chaos. And savvy spending is about getting what you love in a way that aligns with your long-term goals.

Before you buy something because it's "on sale" or trending, ask:

- Do I truly want this or am I being marketed to?
- Will I still love this in six months?
- Is this filling a void I should be addressing elsewhere?

Budgeting for the Glow-Up: The Beauty + Fashion Spending Plan

Here's the tea: If beauty and fashion matter to you, they deserve a spot in your budget. That's not frivolous. That's smart planning.

Create a category in your monthly budget titled "Personal Presentation" or "Style & Maintenance." Then fill it like you would your emergency fund or 401(k). Think of it as your style account.

Some people use the 50/30/20 rule:

- 50% needs (rent, food, bills)
- 30% wants (style, beauty, fun)
- 20% savings/investments

If 30% feels too much, you can adjust. The point is: assign the funds *intentionally* so you can indulge *guilt-free.*

Closet Math: Cost Per Wear

That $300 dress might actually be cheaper than the $40 fast-fashion one if you wear it 30 times instead of once.

Use this mental formula:

Cost Per Wear = Price / Number of Times Worn

High-quality pieces often last longer, fit better, and elevate your entire wardrobe. Don't be afraid to invest *if* the item pays dividends over time.

Shop Like a Stylist: Strategy Tips

- **Know Your Staples**: What's your uniform? Build around that.
- **Seasonal Planning**: Buy offseason (coats in spring, swimsuits in fall).
- **Tailor It**: A $50 dress with a $20 alteration can look like $500.
- **One In, One Out**: Buy something new? Donate or sell something old.
- **Rent the Runway Vibe**: For big events, consider renting instead of buying.

Makeup, Hair, and Maintenance: The Beauty Budget

- **Subscriptions**: If you love skincare or makeup boxes, budget for them.
- **DIY vs. Pro**: Learn when to do it yourself and when to book the expert.
- **Routine Over Random**: Invest in consistency, not impulse buys. A solid skincare routine beats a random $120 face mask you use once.

Pro tip: The best glow-up? Good sleep, hydration, and walking with purpose. Those are free.

When Looking Good Is Part of Your Brand

For influencers, artists, professionals in the public eye—your look might actually be part of your brand strategy. In that case, your beauty and fashion spend could be a business expense (talk to a CPA).

But even if it's personal, it still needs a plan.

Ask:

- Am I investing in a brand or escaping into one?
- Is this outfit for my power or for their perception?

Credit Card Creep and Beauty Debt

Putting hair extensions, Botox, or limited-edition sneakers on a high-interest credit card you don't pay off in full? That's not a flex. That's a trap.

Interest turns a $700 luxury bag into a $1,000 regret if you're not paying attention.

Instead, use:

- **Sinking funds**: Save monthly for high-ticket beauty or fashion goals.
- **Cash-back cards**: If you're disciplined, some cards offer cash or rewards for style-related purchases.

Ditch the Shame, Keep the Standards

Let's be clear: There is nothing wrong with wanting to look good. There is something wrong with sacrificing your financial security to chase it.

Own your glow. But let it be rooted in financial integrity, not financial anxiety.

Beauty Flex Action Steps

- **Create a monthly fashion + beauty budget** and stick to it.
- **Audit your closet** and donate or sell what no longer fits your life.
- **Track your beauty + style subscriptions** to avoid autopilot charges.
- **Save for your splurges** using a "Glam Goals" account.
- **Plan your purchases** around sales, seasons, and your real life.

You're Not Behind. You're Just Getting Started.

Looking fly is sexy. Looking financially secure? Even sexier.

Most People Don't Know This Stuff—Until They Do. Now You Do.

Forget shame. Rock wisdom and wash your face with confidence.

Clarity Is Confidence. And Confidence Is Sexy.

Style is self-expression. But strategy is self-respect.

Make One Money Move Before You Go to Bed Tonight. Just One. And Then Do Another Next Week.

That might mean canceling a beauty subscription you forgot you had. Or checking your sinking fund balance before you hit "add to cart." Or just texting your accountability buddy, "Let's be fly and financially fierce."

Looking good isn't the problem.
Not knowing the cost? That's where the danger lies.
Let your closet and your credit score both make statements.
That's the real flex.

Part IX: Love, Family, and Money – Where the Heart Meets the Bank Account

Money doesn't just live on spreadsheets—it lives in our relationships. In this part of the book, we get real about the financial side of love, partnership, parenting, divorce, caregiving, and legacy. Because let's be honest: your financial glow-up isn't just about *you*. It's about the people you love, the boundaries you set, and the future you want to build—together or alone.

We explore how to talk about money in your relationship without starting a fight (or falling apart), how to protect your peace when combining finances, how to raise financially literate kids even if you're still learning yourself, and how to support family without sabotaging your own goals. We tackle the tough stuff too—navigating money after a breakup, dealing with unequal incomes, and planning for caregiving or inheritance with clarity and dignity.

This section is for anyone who's ever whispered, *"I wish we'd talked about money sooner."* Let this be your permission slip to start those conversations now—with love, with power, and without shame.

Chapter 45: The Financially Sexy Couple

Let's get one thing straight: sexy isn't just about how you look—it's about how you move through life. It's about power, presence, and planning. And when it comes to couples, there's nothing sexier than two people who are aligned—not just emotionally, but financially. It's rare. It's powerful. And it's entirely possible.

This chapter isn't about splitting the check or Venmo-ing each other for rent. It's about building something real. Together.

The Real Talk About Money and Love

Let's start here: money doesn't cause problems in relationships. Silence does. Secrecy does. Shame does. Money is just the magnifier.

If there's tension around money in your relationship, it's not because you're bad at budgeting. It's because you were never taught how to talk about it.

So let's change that.

Because when couples talk money, they build trust. When they plan together, they grow together. And when they're on the same page financially, they stop fighting over dollars—and start designing their dream life.

Money Conversations Are Foreplay

You want a relationship that's hot, healthy, and built to last? Start by talking about the bills.

Not in a dry, spreadsheet-only kind of way. But in a way that says: "I see you. I respect you. I want to build with you."

Here's how to ease into those talks:

- Start with a money memory. What did your parents teach you about money?
- What's your biggest financial fear?
- What's your dream financial win in the next 5 years?
- What would you do if you had $100,000 right now?

Make it playful. Make it honest. Make it about understanding, not impressing. You don't need to agree on everything—you just need to agree on the direction.

The Three Bank Account Rule

Here's a structure that works for a lot of couples:

1. **Yours**
2. **Mine**
3. **Ours**

Each partner keeps their own personal account. That's your independence, your peace of mind, your freedom. But you also build a shared account. That's where bills come from. That's where vacations get funded. That's where joint goals live.

This system:

- Protects individual autonomy
- Creates shared responsibility
- Prevents petty fights over lunch receipts

Set Your Joint Goals Like a Power Couple

Want to feel unstoppable together? Dream together. Plan together. Execute together.

Ask yourselves:

- What are our top 3 financial goals in the next 1, 5, and 10 years?
- What are we saving for—retirement, kids, a home, freedom?

- How will we check in—weekly? Monthly? On money dates?

If you've never set financial goals with your partner, now's the time. Start with a sexy, low-pressure money date. Pour a drink. Light a candle. Open a Google Doc. Dream big.

Then reverse engineer your dream life into monthly steps.

Money Dates: The Weekly Ritual That Builds Wealth (and Intimacy)

Here's your new favorite ritual: the weekly money date. No nagging. No judgment. Just connection.

Each week, take 30 minutes to:

- Review your spending
- Celebrate progress
- Check in on upcoming expenses
- Realign on your goals

Pro tip: Don't do this when you're stressed, tired, or already fighting. Create a vibe. Make it something you look forward to—not dread.

Fighting About Money? Try This First

Most couples don't argue about dollars—they argue about values.

- "Why'd you spend $200 on clothes?" might really mean: "I'm afraid we're falling behind."
- "You're so cheap!" might really mean: "I don't feel safe or taken care of."

Try this instead:

- "When you spend on [thing], I feel [emotion], because I value [value]."
- "Can we revisit our priorities together?"
- "I want to understand, not control. Can we talk?"

Credit & Credit Card Conversations

- **What is your current credit score?**
- Understanding each other's credit scores can provide insight into financial habits and potential challenges.
- **How many credit cards do you have, and what are their balances?**
- Discussing the number of credit cards and outstanding balances helps in assessing debt levels and spending behaviors.
- **Do you pay off your credit cards in full each month or carry a balance?**
- This reveals approaches to debt management and financial discipline.
- **Have you ever missed a credit card payment or defaulted on a loan?**
- Past financial missteps can impact current creditworthiness and should be addressed openly.
- **What is your strategy for managing credit card debt?**
- Sharing plans for debt repayment fosters mutual support and accountability.
- **How do you feel about using credit cards for large purchases?**
- Aligning on when and how to use credit can prevent future disagreements.
- **Would you consider opening a joint credit card account?**
- Discussing the pros and cons of joint accounts ensures both partners are comfortable with shared financial responsibilities.
- **Who will be responsible for paying the credit card bills?**
- Clearly defining roles can prevent missed payments and financial strain.
- **Are there any past bankruptcies or negative financial events we should discuss?**
- Transparency about financial history builds trust and prepares both partners for future planning.
- **How do you monitor your credit reports and scores?**
- Regularly checking credit reports helps in identifying errors and maintaining financial health.

Money is just the surface. The real conversation is about trust, safety, identity, and freedom.

Budgeting as a Team

Make your budget your blueprint—not your prison.

Use budgeting to:

- Assign every dollar a job (zero-based budgeting)
- Keep your goals top of mind
- Stay out of guilt and in alignment

Apps like YNAB, EveryDollar, or Monarch can help. But the real power is in the habit—not the software.

Your job isn't to micromanage each other—it's to empower each other.

Debt, Dreams, and Doing It Together

One of you have student loans? Credit card debt? Past money mistakes? That's real. That's okay. What matters is that you face it together.

Build a plan that includes:

- A clear debt payoff timeline
- A joint emergency fund
- A "guilt-free fun" budget (yes, still fun allowed!)

You can love someone and still say: "We need to protect ourselves from this." That's not cold. That's mature. That's sexy.

Prenups, Estate Planning, and Financial Adulting

Love is trust. But trust doesn't mean skipping the paperwork.

- A prenup isn't planning for divorce—it's protecting the dream.
- An estate plan isn't just for the rich—it's for anyone who loves somebody.
- Life insurance isn't about death—it's about leaving security, not struggle.

Financially sexy couples plan for all seasons. They protect each other—no matter what.

Action Steps: Power Moves for Couples

- Schedule a weekly 30-minute money date. Make it fun.
- Open a joint checking account and decide what flows through it.
- Write down your shared short-, mid-, and long-term financial goals.
- Talk about your money values and fears.
- Choose a budgeting system you both like and commit for 90 days.
- Revisit your wills, insurance, and emergency plan.

You're Not Behind. You're Just Getting Started.

Every couple has money messes. Every couple has blind spots. What sets the financially sexy ones apart is they talk. They plan. They grow. Together.

Don't wait until the next fight to get on the same page. Start today. Build something powerful, peaceful, and aligned.

Most People Don't Know This Stuff—Until They Do. Now You Do.

Financial intimacy is just as important as physical intimacy.

The more you connect here, the less stress you carry elsewhere. The more you plan together, the faster you build freedom.

Clarity Is Confidence. And Confidence Is Sexy.

Build your budget like a boss. Share your dreams like lovers. Make money moves like partners.

Make One Money Move Before You Go to Bed Tonight. Just One. And Then Do Another Next Week.

Send the "money date" calendar invite. Ask your partner what their dream retirement looks like. Open the joint savings account. Pay off one small bill. Print your credit reports and review them together.

Small steps. Big intimacy.

You've got this.

Together.

Chapter 46: Kids Cost, but Planning is Sexy Parenting

Let's talk about the truth that every parent knows deep down: raising kids is expensive. But here's the empowering part—planning for those costs isn't just responsible; it's downright sexy. It's about taking control, making informed decisions, and setting your family up for a future filled with possibilities.

The Real Cost of Raising a Child

According to recent studies, the average cost of raising a child to age 17 in the U.S. is approximately $310,605 . This figure doesn't even include college expenses. It's a significant investment, but with strategic planning, it's manageable.

Smart Strategies for Managing Child-Related Expenses

1. **Budgeting for Childcare and Education**: Childcare can be one of the most substantial expenses for young families. Consider exploring various childcare options and budgeting accordingly. As your child grows, educational expenses will also increase. Planning ahead for these costs is crucial.
2. **Utilizing 529 College Savings Plans**: A 529 plan is a tax-advantaged savings plan designed to encourage saving for future education costs. Contributions grow tax-free, and withdrawals for qualified education expenses are also tax-free .
3. **Teaching Financial Literacy Early**: Instilling financial literacy in

your children from a young age can set them up for lifelong success. Simple activities like giving an allowance, encouraging saving, and discussing budgeting can make a significant impact .

4. **Setting Up an Emergency Fund**: Life is unpredictable. Having an emergency fund can provide a financial cushion for unexpected expenses, ensuring that your family's financial goals stay on track.
5. **Investing in Life Insurance**: Protecting your family's financial future is paramount. Life insurance can provide peace of mind, knowing that your loved ones are financially secure in the event of unforeseen circumstances.

Building Generational Wealth

Creating a legacy isn't just for the ultra-wealthy. By making informed financial decisions, you can build generational wealth that benefits your children and grandchildren. This includes:

- **Investing Wisely**: Diversify your investment portfolio to include stocks, bonds, and other assets that can grow over time.
- **Estate Planning**: Establishing a will or trust ensures that your assets are distributed according to your wishes, minimizing potential conflicts.
- **Educating Your Children**: Teach your children about the importance of saving, investing, and making smart financial choices. This knowledge can empower them to continue building upon the foundation you've laid.

Action Steps for Parents

- **Review and Adjust Your Budget**: Regularly assess your family's budget to accommodate changing needs and goals.
- **Automate Savings**: Set up automatic transfers to savings and investment accounts to ensure consistent contributions.
- **Seek Professional Advice**: Consult with a financial advisor to develop

a comprehensive plan tailored to your family's needs.

- **Engage in Open Financial Discussions**: Foster an environment where financial topics are discussed openly, encouraging questions and shared learning.

Final Thoughts

Parenting is a journey filled with joys, challenges, and countless decisions. By approaching it with a proactive and informed mindset, you not only provide for your children's needs but also model financial responsibility and empowerment. Remember, it's not about perfection; it's about progress. Each step you take towards financial planning is a step towards a more secure and prosperous future for your family.

You're not behind. You're just getting started.

Most people don't know this stuff—until they do. Now you do.

Clarity is confidence. And confidence is sexy.

Make one money move before you go to bed tonight. Just one. And then do another next week.

Your mirror will thank you. Your bank account will thank you. And your future self? They'll be blown away.

Chapter 47: Caring for Parents and Aging Loved Ones — When Financial Literacy Becomes Family Love

The Unspoken Truth: Love Is a Financial Act

Let's be real: caring for aging parents or loved ones is one of the most profound expressions of love. But it's also one of the most financially complex. It's not just about doctor's appointments and Sunday visits. It's about navigating Medicare, managing long-term care costs, and making sure your parents' dignity is preserved—without sacrificing your own financial future.

This chapter isn't about guilt. It's about power. It's about stepping into the role of a financially savvy caregiver who can handle hard conversations, make strategic decisions, and build a legacy of care and clarity.

Why This Chapter Matters

You might be:

- A 35-year-old juggling your kids' soccer schedules and your mom's medical bills.
- A 50-year-old watching your dad's memory fade and wondering how to afford assisted living.

- A 60-year-old divorcee rebuilding your life while becoming the primary caregiver for your aging aunt.

Wherever you are, this chapter is your guide to navigating the financial realities of caregiving with grace, strategy, and strength.

The Cost of Caregiving: More Than Just Money

Caring for aging loved ones isn't just emotionally taxing; it's financially demanding. According to AARP, family caregivers spend an average of $7,242 annually on caregiving activities, including food, gas, travel, medications, and transportation. Long-distance caregivers may face even higher costs, with average annual expenses reaching $8,728.

These expenses can quickly add up, especially when considering:

- **Medical Costs**: Out-of-pocket expenses for medications, treatments, and medical equipment.
- **Home Modifications**: Installing ramps, grab bars, or stair lifts to make the home safer.
- **Lost Income**: Reducing work hours or leaving a job to provide care.
- **Emotional Toll**: The stress and burnout associated with caregiving can impact mental health and overall well-being.

Understanding these costs is the first step toward creating a sustainable caregiving plan.

Starting the Conversation: Breaking the Money Silence

Talking about money with aging parents can be uncomfortable, but it's essential. Here's how to approach the conversation:

1. **Choose the Right Time and Place**: Find a quiet, private setting where everyone feels comfortable.

2. **Express Your Intentions**: Let your parents know that your goal is to ensure their well-being and financial security.
3. **Ask Open-Ended Questions**: Encourage them to share their thoughts and plans regarding their finances and care preferences.
4. **Listen Actively**: Show empathy and understanding, even if the conversation becomes emotional.
5. **Be Patient**: These discussions may require multiple conversations over time.

Remember, the goal is to collaborate, not to take control.

Legal and Financial Documents: Getting Your House in Order

Ensuring that essential documents are in place can prevent future complications. Key documents include:

- **Durable Power of Attorney**: Allows you to make financial decisions on behalf of your loved one if they become incapacitated.
- **Healthcare Proxy**: Designates someone to make medical decisions if your loved one is unable to do so.
- **Living Will**: Outlines your loved one's wishes regarding medical treatment and end-of-life care.
- **Last Will and Testament**: Specifies how assets should be distributed after death.
- **Trusts**: Can help manage assets and potentially avoid probate.

Consulting with an elder law attorney can provide guidance tailored to your family's needs.

Long-Term Care: Planning Ahead

Long-term care includes services that assist with daily activities, such as bathing, dressing, and eating. Planning for these services is crucial, as Medicare typically doesn't cover long-term care. Options to consider:

- **Long-Term Care Insurance**: Policies can help cover the cost of care, but premiums vary based on age and health. It's advisable to purchase policies earlier to lock in lower rates.
- **Hybrid Insurance Policies**: Combine life insurance with long-term care benefits.
- **Personal Savings**: Setting aside funds specifically for future care needs.
- **Government Programs**: Medicaid may cover long-term care for those who meet income and asset requirements.

Understanding these options and planning early can alleviate financial stress down the road.

Housing Decisions: Aging in Place vs. Assisted Living

Deciding where your loved one will live as they age is a significant decision with financial implications.

Aging in Place:

- **Pros**: Familiar environment, maintains independence, potentially lower costs.
- **Cons**: May require home modifications, in-home care services, and can be isolating.

Assisted Living Facilities:

- **Pros**: Provides care and social interaction, structured environment.

- **Cons**: Can be expensive, may feel less personal.

Evaluate your loved one's health, preferences, and financial situation to make the best choice.

Managing Your Own Financial Health

While caring for others, it's vital not to neglect your own financial well-being:

- **Set Boundaries**: Determine what financial support you can provide without compromising your own needs.
- **Maintain Employment**: Explore flexible work arrangements to balance caregiving responsibilities.
- **Plan for Retirement**: Continue contributing to retirement accounts and avoid dipping into savings.
- **Seek Support**: Utilize caregiver support groups and financial advisors to navigate challenges.

Remember, taking care of yourself enables you to provide better care for your loved ones.

Building a Support Network

You don't have to do it alone. Building a support network can ease the burden:

- **Family and Friends**: Delegate tasks and share responsibilities.
- **Professional Caregivers**: Hire in-home aides or nurses for assistance.
- **Community Resources**: Utilize local services such as meal delivery, transportation, and adult day care programs.
- **Support Groups**: Connect with others facing similar challenges for emotional support and advice.

Leveraging these resources can provide relief and improve the quality of care.

Embracing the Journey

Caring for aging parents and loved ones is a journey filled with challenges and rewards. By approaching it with compassion, open communication, and strategic planning, you can navigate this phase with confidence and grace.

Remember:

- **You're Not Alone**: Many are walking this path; seek support when needed.
- **Stay Informed**: Continuously educate yourself on caregiving strategies and financial planning.
- **Celebrate Small Wins**: Acknowledge the positive impacts you're making in your loved one's life.

Final Thoughts

You're not behind. You're just getting started.

Most people don't know this stuff—until they do. Now you do.

Clarity is confidence. And confidence is sexy.

Make one money move before you go to bed tonight. Just one. And then do another next week.

Your mirror will thank you. Your bank account will thank you. And your future self? They'll be blown away.

Chapter 48: Divorce, Breakups, and Financial Comebacks – How to Rise (and Glow) Again

Let's start with this: nobody plans on ending up here. Nobody dreams about sitting on the floor of their now-too-big living room, staring at a stack of legal papers, bank statements, and a half-empty closet. But here you are. And that's okay. Because the story isn't over—it's just being rewritten. And this chapter? This is your plot twist.

We're not here to wallow. We're here to rise. We're here to glow up so good it burns through the fog of heartbreak and disappointment. We're here to turn financial literacy into self-love. Because when your world breaks apart, getting smart with your money isn't just survival—it's your revenge arc, your glow-up guide, your freedom plan.

The Shock Phase: When Everything Feels Uncertain

Divorce and breakups hit like a wave. Emotionally, sure—but also financially. Suddenly, everything is in flux. Your housing situation. Your budget. Your credit score. Your long-term plans. Maybe you used to share bills, goals, and dreams. Maybe you were the planner—or maybe you weren't.

No matter your role before, now the only name on the financial scoreboard is yours. And that's powerful. Because it means you get to write the rules now. But let's be real—you'll need some structure.

Step One: Know What You're Working With

- Pull your credit report (Experian, Equifax, TransUnion)
- List every account—joint and individual
- Close or remove your name from joint accounts (if possible)
- Update passwords on financial apps and credit cards
- Change your direct deposit info
- Open a checking account that's fully yours

The goal? Secure your financial identity. You're not just uncoupling romantically. You're reestablishing yourself as a solo financial entity. That takes emotional courage and admin hustle.

The Clean-Up Phase: Money Housekeeping Post-Breakup

This is the not-so-sexy phase where you set boundaries, even if you're still reeling. But boundaries are beautiful. They're your foundation for peace.

To-Do List:

- Cancel shared streaming services, utilities, and subscriptions
- Notify your HR team or payroll provider about new tax withholdings
- Revisit your beneficiary designations (life insurance, retirement accounts, etc.)
- Talk to a lawyer about your will and powers of attorney

Each tiny money move you make right now says: "I respect my future self." That's financial intimacy in its purest form.

The Reflection Phase: What This Breakup Taught You About Money

Here's the truth—most couples don't talk about money enough. And when they do, they often argue more than they align. Now's your chance to ask: What role did money play in the relationship?

Were you the spender or the saver?

Were you honest about your financial fears and goals?

Did you merge accounts too soon—or never at all?

Did you delegate too much, thinking love would cover the gap?

No shame. Just clarity. Because clarity is confidence, and confidence is sexy.

The Strategy Phase: Designing Your Financial Comeback

A breakup strips away illusions. But it also strips away excuses.

Now is when the real glow-up begins:

- Build an emergency fund—your peace-of-mind pile
- Create a post-breakup budget based on your *real* income and expenses
- Identify debt—prioritize it, snowball it, avalanche it
- Rebuild your credit if it took a hit
- Set new goals: vacation solo, buy your own home, max your retirement plan, build a business

And yes, start dreaming again. Smartly.

Action Steps to Get Back on Track:

1. Open a high-yield savings account and name it something empowering: "My Comeback Fund"
2. Transfer $50/month into it automatically—start small, stay steady
3. Create a new money vision board: travel, home, milestones, and freedom

4. Book a free consult with a fiduciary financial advisor or credit counselor
5. Block out one "money power hour" each week—light a candle, pour a drink, and sit with your finances like they're your new lover

The Dating Again Phase (Yes, Even Financially)

When you do start dating again—because you will—you'll be bringing your whole self. Including your money.

New rules for financially sexy dating:

- Don't let shame make you hide your financial story
- Ask questions early: "How do you handle money stress?" is a better intimacy test than "What's your favorite movie?"
- Stay independent, even if things get serious—have your own accounts, goals, and strategy
- Watch out for love-bombing with lavish gifts or expensive expectations. True partnership doesn't require Gucci.

Real-Life Comebacks: Scenarios You'll Relate To

- **Jordan**, 34, moved out of a shared house with just $1,200 and no furniture. Two years later, she bought her own condo with a 780 credit score.
- **Eric**, 41, went through a contentious divorce with three kids. He now runs a side hustle coaching other divorced dads on financial recovery.
- **Lena**, 28, had no idea how credit worked. After a breakup, she finally faced her debt and started a blog called "Cash After Crash." Now it's her full-time gig.

Breakups are brutal. But they're also a reset button. A second shot at doing it better, smarter, and more soulfully.

A Reality Check Without Shame

No one teaches us how to financially recover from heartbreak. But here's what you now know:

- You can build credit again.
- You can bounce back from financial betrayal.
- You can afford therapy *and* investments.
- You can plan for love again—without losing yourself in the process.

End-of-Chapter Sexy Wisdom

You're not behind. You're just getting started.

Most people don't know this stuff—until they do. Now you do.

Clarity is confidence. And confidence is sexy.

Make one money move before you go to bed tonight. Just one. And then do another next week.

Because no matter how your past ended, your financial story is just beginning. And baby, it's about to be a bestseller.

Part X: The Big Picture – Your Money, Your Legacy, Your Power

This final section of *Financial Literacy Is Sexy* zooms out to help you zoom in on what really matters: the kind of life you're building, the freedom you're earning, and the legacy you're creating—on purpose. This isn't about spreadsheets and budgets anymore. This is about identity, impact, and ownership. It's about the decisions that define your next decade, not just your next paycheck.

In this part of the book, we tie together everything you've learned—how to earn smarter, spend intentionally, save strategically, and invest with confidence—into one clear, empowering perspective. We explore how wealth isn't just what sits in your account, but what grows inside your mindset, your relationships, and your future plans.

These final chapters challenge you to think beyond the now. To think in generations. To think like a legacy-maker. Whether it's designing your ideal lifestyle, staying resilient through setbacks, or supporting your family without losing yourself—this section is about doing money your way, but smarter, sexier, and with deep intention.

It's not just about being rich.

It's about being well.

Being wise.

Being unshakeable.

And being unapologetically powerful in your financial life.

Because sexy isn't just style. It's substance.

It's confidence with receipts.
It's clarity with boundaries.
It's money moves that mean something.
Welcome to *The Big Picture*.
This is where you stop playing defense.
And start living like the asset you are.

Chapter 49: Money and Mental Health – Anxiety, Therapy, and Freedom

Let's tell the truth: money messes with your head.

Not just because it's complicated.

Not just because you weren't taught how it works.

Not just because society wraps it in shame, silence, and status.

But because money is emotional.

It's deeply personal.

It's laced with self-worth, identity, and fear.

And when it's not going well?

It doesn't just hit your wallet. It hits your heart, your sleep, your relationships, your focus, your energy—everything.

So let's have the conversation most people avoid.

Let's talk about the link between money and mental health.

Not from a place of shame. But from power.

This chapter is your safe space.

It's your mirror and your megaphone.

It's the therapy session you didn't know your bank account needed.

Because healing your money story is sexy.

And owning your financial peace is power.

The Quiet Chaos of Financial Anxiety

You know the feeling.

You check your balance and your heart races.

You swipe your card and pray it clears.

You delay opening a bill because you already know it'll ruin your mood.

Or maybe you're making good money—but you still feel broke.

Or worried.

Or ashamed.

That's financial anxiety.

And it's not just in your head.

It's in your nervous system.

Your cortisol levels spike.

Your sleep suffers.

Your self-esteem tanks.

Your fight-or-flight response gets stuck in high gear.

Financial stress is the #1 source of chronic stress for adults in the U.S.

It beats out job stress, relationship problems, and even health concerns.

So if you feel this way—you're not alone.

But you don't have to stay stuck in it.

How Money Trauma Shows Up

We all have a money story.

And for many of us, that story involves some trauma.

Maybe you grew up watching your parents fight about money.

Maybe you saw eviction notices or rationed groceries.

Maybe you were taught that talking about money is taboo.

Maybe you were always told "we can't afford that"—so now you feel guilt every time you do.

Or maybe you've experienced adult money trauma:

- A layoff you didn't see coming
- A divorce that drained your finances
- Medical bills that wrecked your credit
- A failed business
- A bankruptcy

These experiences leave scars.

And if you never address them?

They run your financial life without you realizing it.

You don't budget—not because you're lazy, but because you're scared of what you'll see.

You spend impulsively—not because you don't care, but because it gives you a short hit of relief.

You under-earn—not because you lack skill, but because you subconsciously don't believe you deserve more.

This is why financial literacy alone isn't enough.

You need financial healing, too.

Your Emotions Are Not the Enemy

Let's stop pretending that money decisions are purely logical.

They're emotional.

Always have been. Always will be.

You don't need to become a robot to get your money right.

You just need to get honest with how you feel—and why.

Here's what that can look like:

- Naming your money triggers (like shopping when you're stressed or avoiding bank statements)
- Journaling about your earliest money memories
- Talking to a therapist who understands financial trauma
- Creating mantras that reframe your beliefs (like "I am safe to earn, save, and spend wisely")

Money isn't just math.

It's mindset.

And healing begins with awareness—not judgment.

Therapy and Your Bank Account

Let's be real: therapy costs money.

But untreated financial stress costs more.

It costs you sleep.

It costs you relationships.

It costs you time lost to worrying.

It costs you opportunities you don't take because you feel unworthy or afraid.

Investing in therapy—even if it's a few sessions—isn't weak.

It's wise.

It can help you:

- Untangle your money fears
- Set healthy boundaries with family and friends
- Talk to your partner without starting a fight
- Make financial decisions from clarity instead of panic

Pro tip: Many therapists offer sliding scale rates. Some employers offer free sessions through Employee Assistance Programs (EAPs). And there are financial coaches and planners who are trained in trauma-informed care.

You deserve support.

You don't have to carry this alone.

Money Shame Is a Liar

Shame tells you:

- "You should've known better."
- "You're so behind."
- "Everyone else has it figured out but you."

Shame keeps you stuck.

It whispers that if people knew the truth, they'd judge you.

But here's the truth:

Most people don't have it figured out.

Most people have made financial mistakes.

Most people are carrying some form of money shame.

You are not broken.

You are not behind.

You are not defined by your debt, your credit score, or your income.

Shame can't survive honesty.

So speak the truth.

And then build from there.

When Anxiety Blocks Action

Maybe you've read a hundred articles on budgeting.

Maybe you've tried to save before.

Maybe you want to start investing, but it all feels overwhelming.

This is normal.

Anxiety often shows up as avoidance.

You freeze. You procrastinate. You binge-watch instead of budgeting.

The fix?

Tiny actions.

Don't try to overhaul your whole financial life in one weekend.

Just:

- Log in to your bank account and look at your balance without judgment
- Set up auto-transfer of $10/week to savings
- Book a free consult with a financial coach
- Cancel one subscription you don't use

Progress kills panic.

Start small. Stay consistent.

How to Build a Calmer Relationship With Money

You don't need to be rich to feel at peace.

You just need systems, boundaries, and clarity.

Here's how to get there:

1. **Name Your Financial Feelings**
2. Are you anxious, ashamed, angry, avoidant?
3. Start by naming the emotion.
4. Awareness breaks the cycle.
5. **Set Financial Boundaries**
6. You don't owe everyone a yes.

7. Learn to say:

- "That's not in my budget right now."
- "I can't contribute to that, but I support you emotionally."
- "Let's talk about this when I've had time to look at my numbers."

1. **Make Money Dates**
2. Once a week, check in with your money.
3. Light a candle. Play music. Make it a ritual.
4. Review your spending. Celebrate your wins. Adjust as needed.
5. **Detach Worth from Wealth**
6. You are not your income.
7. You are not your debt.
8. You are worthy. Full stop.
9. **Educate Yourself With Compassion**
10. Learn—but don't shame yourself for not knowing.
11. You're building a skill.
12. Be patient with the process.

Real-Life Comebacks: From Chaos to Calm

- *Angela,* 38, went through a divorce with $70K in joint debt. She avoided her mail for months. Now she does Sunday money dates with wine and candles, has paid off $30K, and feels more powerful than ever.
- *Jeremiah,* 29, had a panic attack at work after checking his overdraft fees. Therapy helped him see how his upbringing shaped his money habits. Now he uses a budgeting app and takes pride in saving $100/month.
- *Nina and Kyle,* a couple in their 40s, used to argue about money constantly. They now do monthly financial check-ins and see a couples therapist. They've paid off their cars and are planning a debt-free vacation.

You're not alone.

And you're not stuck.

Money and Mental Health Are Inseparable

You can't separate your finances from your feelings.

And you don't have to.

In fact, the sexiest financial life is one rooted in:

- Self-awareness
- Boundaries
- Clarity
- Joy
- Peace

That's the goal.

Not just more money.

But more freedom.

More ease.

More power.

You Got This: Wrap-Up and Reminders

Bold encouragement:

You're not behind. You're just getting started.

Reality check without shame:

Most people don't know this stuff—until they do. Now you do.

Sexy takeaway:

Peace of mind is the new status symbol.

And peace is sexy.

Prompt to act:

Make one money move before you go to bed tonight:

- Journal your biggest money fear.
- Open your bank app and look without judging.
- Text a friend and say: "Can we talk about money this week?"

Just one step. That's how the healing begins.

Your financial glow-up starts from the inside.

And baby—it looks good on you.

Final Note

This chapter wasn't about math.

It was about healing.

You are allowed to create a financial life that feels good—not just looks good.

You are allowed to feel your feelings and still make moves.

No more silence.

No more shame.

Just you, claiming your power.

One decision at a time.

One boundary at a time.

One deep breath at a time.

Financial literacy is sexy.

But financial peace?

That's liberation.

Your mirror will thank you.

Your nervous system will thank you.

And your future self?

They'll be proud as hell.

Let's keep going.

Chapter 50: Your Financial Reputation – What Your Habits Say When You're Not in the Room

Let's talk reputation—not the one you carefully curate on social media with glowing selfies and curated captions. I'm talking about your *financial* reputation. The version of you that shows up in boardrooms, banks, family group chats, and in the quiet conversations people have about you when you're not there. The unspoken truth that whispers: "Can they be trusted with money?" or "They've got their life together." Or worse: "They're always a mess."

Your financial reputation is bigger than your credit score. It's how you show up, how you follow through, and how much clarity, consistency, and character you bring to your money life.

So let's dive in—real, raw, and ready. Because the way you handle money says a lot about who you are, what you value, and what kind of future you're building.

THE REAL TALK ABOUT REPUTATION

You already know your resume says one thing and your social feed says another. But money? Money doesn't lie. It keeps the receipts—literally and figuratively. It remembers when you overdrew your account, when you made that minimum payment three months in a row, when you ghosted your friend after borrowing $200 you never paid back. And guess what? Other people remember too.

That's why your financial habits speak louder than your words. They shape your opportunities, your credibility, and yes, even your romantic options. People notice when you don't tip well, when you split the check unevenly, or when you treat your car like a luxury item but your retirement account like an afterthought.

Let's be clear: this isn't about perfection. It's about intention. Ownership. Awareness. And integrity.

Your financial reputation doesn't require a six-figure income. But it does demand six-figure behavior. It demands that you:

- Pay people back
- Budget with purpose
- Make peace with your past
- Plan for your future
- Speak about money with confidence, not fear

Because when you show up for your money, you show up for your life.

WHAT YOUR HABITS SAY (EVEN IF YOU SAY NOTHING)

Let's break down a few silent signals you're sending—whether you realize it or not:

1. **You're always "just getting by" no matter your income.**
2. That tells the world you don't have a plan. And maybe don't want one.
3. **You lend money with resentment or borrow money with silence.**
4. That signals you avoid hard conversations and let emotions run your finances.
5. **You're flashy with purchases but vague about debt.**
6. That reads as performative wealth. It's giving Instagram rich, but 401(k) poor.
7. **You cancel plans because you "can't afford it," but you never budget.**
8. That tells friends you're reactive, not proactive—and unreliable with your yes.
9. **You ask people for money advice—but never take it.**

10. That says you're not serious. People stop offering help when you don't listen.
11. **You hide your financial life from your partner.**
12. That's not just shady—it's self-sabotage.

These behaviors don't make you a bad person. They just build a reputation over time that might not align with who you *want* to be.

CREDIT SCORES AND CHARACTER SCORES

You've probably heard that your credit score is your adult report card. But let's go deeper.

- Your credit score measures risk.
- Your character score (a term we're inventing right now) measures reliability.

Do you:

- Return things you borrow?
- Pay your share, on time, with no drama?
- Stick to your word when you say you're saving, quitting, investing?

That's the character score. And it carries real weight.

Landlords, employers, in-laws, friends—all these people are forming impressions about your financial life based on what you *do*, not just what you say.

That's why your habits matter. And why upgrading them is the sexiest thing you can do.

BUILDING A REPUTATION THAT WORKS FOR YOU

Let's make this practical. Here's how to build a financial reputation that works for you, even when you're not in the room:

1. Be Predictable (In a Good Way)

Unpredictability is exhausting—for you and everyone around you. When your paycheck hits, your friends shouldn't have to guess whether you're saving or splurging. Predictability builds trust.

2. Normalize Talking About Money (Like a Grown-Up)

You don't need to give everyone your W-2. But be willing to say:

- "That's not in my budget this month."
- "I'm working on paying down some debt."
- "We're saving for something big, so we're skipping the trip."

That's sexy. It's strong. It shows discipline without apology.

3. Handle Small Money Like Big Money

If you flake on a $20 Venmo, no one's giving you a $20K investment. If you ghost your landlord about the rent, don't expect your boss to trust you with a promotion.

Every money moment is a trust moment.

4. Create a System You Can Stick To

Set up auto-pay for your bills. Automate your savings. Name your accounts with purpose (like "Emergency Freedom Fund" or "Boss Moves Only"). Make your money life reflect your real life.

When your financial reputation is in alignment with your character, things move.

REAL LIFE SCENARIOS

Scenario 1: You're dating someone new and they ask about your debt.

You panic. But instead of dodging it, you own it: "I've got student loans and I'm on a payoff plan. I've learned a lot. Here's the strategy I'm using."

Confidence. Transparency. Trust. Boom.

Scenario 2: You want to invest in a friend's business.

But your own finances are a mess. You know you're not in a position to help—even though it sounds exciting. So you say: "I believe in your vision. Right now I'm prioritizing my financial foundation, but I'd love to support in other ways."

Integrity. Discipline. Long-term thinking.

Scenario 3: You want a raise.

You gather your receipts—literal and metaphorical. Your performance, your financial impact, and how you show up. You walk in ready, not reactive.

That's what a strong financial reputation buys you: leverage, respect, and options.

ACTION STEPS

Ready to upgrade your financial rep? Start here:

1. **Review Your Last 30 Days**
2. Pull your statements. What do your transactions say about you?
3. **Ask a Trusted Friend**
4. "If someone asked about my relationship with money, what would you say?" Don't defend. Just listen.
5. **Build a Three-Word Money Mantra**
6. Examples: *Disciplined. Generous. Strategic.* Or *Bold. Balanced. Boundaried.* Let it guide you.
7. **Set a Reputation Goal**
8. "In 12 months, I want people to describe me as financially stable." Work backwards from that.
9. **Clean Up One Messy Habit**
10. Maybe it's late payments. Or dodging your debt. Or refusing to look at your balances. Start with one. Clean it up.

THE BIGGER PICTURE

Your financial reputation is the intersection of your habits, your character, and your choices. It's not just about how others see you. It's about how you see yourself.

When your financial life is clean, consistent, and aligned with your values, something wild happens: you stop chasing validation and start radiating self-respect.

And that, my friend, is sexy.

You're not behind. You're just getting started.

Most people don't know this stuff—until they do. Now you do.

Clarity is confidence. And confidence is sexy.

Make one money move before you go to bed tonight. Just one. And then do another next week.

Let your money speak well of you—whether you're in the room or not.

This book isn't just about dollars and cents. It's about dignity. It's about boundaries. It's about joy.

It's about removing the fear, silence, and shame around money—and replacing it with confidence, clarity, and control.

We're not just talking about budgets and credit scores.

We're talking about owning your financial life. Owning your options. Owning your damn power.

Your mirror will thank you. Your bank account will thank you. And your future self?

They'll be blown away.

Chapter 51: Giving Back is Sexy AF

Philanthropy, Tithing, and Wealth with Purpose

Let's start with a truth bomb: money is sexy, but purpose is magnetic.

There's something deeply attractive about someone who knows how to handle their finances *and* uses that power to uplift others. We're not talking performative charity. We're not talking guilt-driven donations. We're talking about intentional, joyful, purpose-fueled giving. The kind that aligns with your values. The kind that creates ripple effects. The kind that tells the world, "I've got mine—and I've got enough to lift others too."

This chapter is not about convincing you to become a philanthropist. You already are. The moment you give with clarity, consistency, and conviction—whether it's five dollars, five thousand, or five hours—you're building wealth with purpose. And that? That's sexy AF.

Why Giving Back Matters

You've worked hard. You've budgeted, saved, invested, maybe even automated your accounts like a boss. You've wrestled with credit, weathered financial storms, survived student loans, career changes, breakups, glow-ups, and late-night Amazon temptations. You've finally started feeling like you've got your arms around this money thing.

Now what?

You start giving.

Not out of guilt. Not because someone said you "should." But because wealth—true wealth—is about more than accumulation. It's about circulation. The wealthiest people in the world don't just store money—they move it. They pour into others. They fund change. They build schools, scholarships, food banks, arts programs, small business incubators, cancer research, and neighborhood clean-ups.

And they don't just do it for the tax write-offs (although let's be real—those are nice too). They do it because it feeds the soul.

You don't need millions to give. You need intention. Let's talk about how.

The Difference Between Tithing, Charity, and Philanthropy

All giving is beautiful. But it helps to understand the flavors.

- **Tithing** is typically tied to religious or spiritual practice. It's consistent, often 10% of income, and meant to honor a higher power or support a faith-based community.
- **Charity** is often reactive. You see a cause, a crisis, a GoFundMe—and you step up. It's heart-driven, often spontaneous.
- **Philanthropy** is strategic. It's about long-term impact, often involving planned giving, endowments, donor-advised funds, or multi-year commitments.

You don't have to pick just one lane. You can tithe weekly, donate to a friend's medical bills, and set up a scholarship fund all at once. The power comes from clarity.

Giving Isn't Just Financial—And That's Important

Let's break a myth: you don't have to be rich to give back. You don't have to wait until you hit six figures, retire early, or "feel ready." Giving back isn't a reward for arriving. It's part of the journey.

You can give:

- **Time** – Volunteering at a food pantry, reading to kids, mentoring a teen, organizing a coat drive.
- **Skills** – Teaching financial literacy at your local library, helping a nonprofit with their website, consulting for a grassroots organization.
- **Access** – Making introductions. Sharing someone's work. Opening a door for the next generation.

- **Platform** – Using your voice to elevate others. Creating space for marginalized stories. Hosting community events.

Generosity is not limited by your bank account. It's fueled by your intention.

How to Build Giving into Your Financial Plan (Without Falling Behind)

You might be thinking, "This all sounds great, but I still have debt. I'm still building. I'm not ready to give yet."

Pause. Let's reframe that.

Giving doesn't have to be all-or-nothing. It can be proportionate. Scalable. Strategic.

Here's how to make it part of your plan:

1. **Create a "Giving" line in your budget.** Even if it's just $10/month. Make generosity a habit.
2. **Set up a separate giving account.** Name it something sexy: "Legacy," "Joy Fund," "Impact Money."
3. **Automate a small percentage of your income toward giving.** Just like you would with savings or investing.
4. **Choose causes that genuinely move you.** Don't give out of guilt—give from alignment.
5. **Involve your family.** Make it a dinner table topic. Let your kids help pick a cause each quarter.

The goal is not to impress. It's to express your values.

The Sexy Psychology of Giving

Here's what no one tells you: giving rewires your brain.

Neuroscience shows that generosity activates reward centers. It boosts serotonin, dopamine, and oxytocin. It decreases stress. It's literally good for your health. People who give regularly live longer, report greater life satisfaction, and experience lower rates of depression.

Giving reminds us that we are not helpless in the face of injustice. That even in a world that feels overwhelming, we can still make a dent. It restores agency. It reconnects us to community. And when we give with intention—not obligation—we grow wealthier emotionally, spiritually, and yes, sometimes financially.

How the Wealthy Give (and What You Can Learn From Them)

Let's peek behind the velvet rope for a second.

The wealthy don't just "donate." They build giving into their identity and infrastructure.

- They create **Donor-Advised Funds (DAFs)** to manage tax-efficient giving over time.
- They form **family foundations** that last generations.
- They use **charitable trusts** to transfer wealth while supporting causes.
- They endow chairs at universities, name wings of hospitals, and sponsor fellowships.

You might not be there yet. But understanding how they play the game helps you level up your own.

If you want to give like the wealthy:

- Work with a financial planner or advisor.
- Talk to a CPA about deductions and strategy.
- Think long-term. Think legacy.

Even if you're giving $500/year, treat it like it matters—because it does.

Giving in the Digital Age: Social Media, Scams, and Influence

Let's get real. We live in the age of viral fundraising. Sometimes it's beautiful. Sometimes it's manipulative. Sometimes it's messy.

Before you give:

- **Do your research.** Check the organization's transparency and impact.
- **Don't let urgency override due diligence.** Just because it's trending doesn't mean it's legit.

- **Give privately if you want.** Not all generosity needs to be performative.
- **Share causes, not pressure.** Inspire, don't guilt others into giving.

Giving should feel empowering, not exhausting.

The Future of Giving Is Intersectional, Inclusive, and In Your Hands

The next generation of givers is different. More diverse. More connected. More values-driven.

We're not waiting until retirement to give.

We're not limiting generosity to boardrooms and galas.

We're building mutual aid funds.

We're crowdfunding medical expenses.

We're using Venmo, CashApp, and crypto.

We're buying groceries for single moms on Instagram.

We're redefining what it means to be generous. And that's the most powerful shift of all.

End of Chapter Encouragements

You're not behind. You're just getting started.

Most people don't know this stuff—until they do. Now you do.

Clarity is confidence. And confidence is sexy.

Make one money move before you go to bed tonight. Just one. And then do another next week.

Final Note

Giving is not the end of your financial journey. It's the glow-up. It's what turns personal success into collective impact.

Because in the end, we're not just building wealth. We're building legacy. And the sexiest legacy of all? A life that lifted others.

Your mirror will thank you.

Your bank account will thank you.

And your future self?

They'll be blown away.

Chapter 52: The Sexy Slow Burn: Financial Literacy Is for Life

Repetition, Reinforcement, and Staying in the Game

Let's talk about the slow burn. The one that lasts longer, hits deeper, and leaves a legacy.

This chapter isn't about quick wins. It's not about viral investment hacks, or the latest trending side hustle, or how to game the system to retire by 35 and live in Bali. That's not the vibe.

This is about stamina. Consistency. The quiet power of repetition. The kind of financial literacy that grows over years, not just paychecks. Because real wealth? It doesn't always come in explosions. Sometimes, it shows up like muscle memory. Like breath. Like confidence that grows stronger every time you make a choice that honors your future self.

You don't need to master everything today. You need to stay in the game.

The Myth of the Financial Finish Line

You're not going to read one book and suddenly understand every aspect of your finances. You're not going to listen to one podcast or watch one YouTube video and instantly feel like a boss. And that's okay.

Because financial literacy isn't a destination. It's a skill set. A language. A series of habits. And just like any other skill or language, you learn it by doing. Over and over. With better results each time.

So if you're frustrated that you still don't fully understand investing...

If you're annoyed that you forgot how your HSA works...

If you're embarrassed you still Google "what does APR actually mean?"

every year—

Welcome to the club.

You're not broken. You're learning. And learning that lasts takes time.

What Repetition Actually Does for You

You know how elite athletes train? They do the same drills thousands of times. Same with musicians. Same with chefs, dancers, pilots, surgeons, and chess grandmasters.

Repetition doesn't mean you're slow.

Repetition means you're serious.

Every time you check your budget, run the numbers, open your retirement account, or call your insurance company to ask a question you used to be scared to ask—you're reinforcing your power. You're making it less scary. Less foggy. More second-nature.

This is the sexy slow burn.

You Are Allowed to Forget and Re-Learn

Read that again.

You are allowed to forget. You are allowed to re-learn.

This isn't school with a pop quiz and a pass/fail grade. This is your life. Your money. Your peace.

You might learn about compound interest at 23 and not use it until 29. You might finally understand how your 401(k) works at 40. You might forget what your credit utilization should be and Google it again next month. You're still winning. Because you're still *in it.*

The people who build wealth and keep it are not perfect. They're just engaged. Curious. Committed to the game.

The Power of Revisiting Basics

Sometimes we skip over the basics because we think we already know them. But returning to the fundamentals with fresh eyes? That's where the magic happens.

- Revisit your budget every quarter.
- Recheck your insurance coverage annually.
- Reassess your retirement goals every 3-5 years.

- Reconfirm your beneficiaries whenever your life changes.

Just like athletes stretch before every game and musicians tune their instruments before every show, you recalibrate.

It doesn't mean you don't know what you're doing.

It means you take it seriously.

Financial Maintenance Is Not Boring. It's Sexy.

Checking your accounts isn't just for emergencies.

Making a money date with yourself once a week isn't tedious—it's self-respect.

Saying no to things that don't fit your plan isn't restrictive—it's freedom.

This is what adulting looks like at its hottest.

The Long Game: Compounding Confidence

When you start learning, things feel fragile. One setback can feel like a failure. One mistake can make you want to give up.

But the longer you stay in it, the stronger you become.

Confidence compounds just like money does. The more time you give it, the more powerful it gets.

You learn from your own receipts. From your bank statements. From the job you left and the one you negotiated like a boss. From the moment you stopped being scared to look at your credit score. From every tax season you got through.

And you learn from teaching others.

There is no such thing as knowing too little to start. Only choosing not to start at all.

What Staying in the Game Looks Like

- Reading one chapter of a finance book each month
- Revisiting your goals every six months
- Watching your net worth grow over time (even if slowly)
- Talking about money without shame or secrecy
- Building your emergency fund in baby steps
- Learning how to say no without over-explaining

- Making your financial literacy part of your identity, not your insecurity

Let It Be Your Lifestyle

Financial literacy isn't just a task on your to-do list.

It's a way of life. A filter. A mindset.

When you let it live in you—not just as knowledge, but as action—everything changes.

You feel more grounded.

You make decisions from clarity, not fear.

You move with intention.

You stop asking for permission.

And you become someone others turn to when they're ready to learn.

End of Chapter Encouragements

You're not behind. You're just getting started.

Most people don't know this stuff—until they do. Now you do.

Clarity is confidence. And confidence is sexy.

Make one money move before you go to bed tonight. Just one. And then do another next week.

Final Note

This is your permission slip to grow slowly, beautifully, and on your terms.

Not because you have to.

Because you deserve to.

Because the slow burn is the strongest one.

And financial literacy that lasts a lifetime?

That's the real glow-up.

That's sexy AF.

Chapter 53: Financially Fly Forever

Write Your New Money Story, and Keep the Pen in Your Hand

Let's get one thing straight: you don't have to be born into wealth to build it. You don't need to be a trust fund baby, a tech founder, or a stock market wizard. You just need one thing:

A decision to stay in the game. To turn the page. To write a new chapter. Because no matter what your money story has been until now, it doesn't have to define where you're headed. You get to write your financial story—and rewrite it as many times as you need. The pen is yours. The page is blank. And the ink is permanent only when you say it is.

This chapter is about liberation. It's about power. It's about freedom. But mostly, it's about remembering that your financial identity isn't something you inherit—it's something you create.

What Story Were You Told About Money?

Let's rewind for a second. Before you ever had a paycheck, you had a money narrative. Maybe you heard things like:

- "Money doesn't grow on trees."
- "We can't afford that."
- "Rich people are greedy."
- "You have to work twice as hard to get half as much."
- "Credit is bad."

Or maybe it was unspoken. Just the tension you felt in your household.

The fights over bills. The stress that lived in the silences. The shame that settled in your gut anytime a field trip slip came home.

We carry those stories into adulthood. We replay them in how we shop, how we save, how we panic, how we give, and how we stay stuck.

But here's the good news: you are the narrator now. And you get to change the plot.

Rewriting the Script

If your old story was:

- "I'm not good with money,"
- Change it to: "I'm learning and growing every day."

If it was:

- "I always mess up with my finances,"
- Change it to: "I've made mistakes, but I'm not one."

If it was:

- "I'll never get ahead,"
- Change it to: "I have everything I need to build a better future."

You don't need a financial degree. You need financial dignity.

And it starts with choosing the language you speak to yourself.

Habits That Help You Stay Fly Forever

Let's be real. This isn't a sprint. It's a marathon in heels.

Want to stay financially fly forever?

Here's what that looks like in real life:

1. **You Automate Everything You Can**

- Bills. Savings. Investments. Roth IRA. 401(k). Emergency fund. All of it.

- Because discipline is sexy, but automation is smoother.

1. **You Revisit Your Goals Monthly**

- Sexy money date. Solo or with your partner. Light a candle. Pour something nice.
- Ask: "Where are we headed? What changed? What needs tweaking?"

1. **You Give Generously and Strategically**

- You don't wait to give back. You build it in. You make your money mean something.

1. **You Protect Your Credit Like It's Your Passport**

- Because it kind of is.

1. **You Upgrade Your Circle**

- You talk about money with friends who get it. Who support growth. Who don't guilt you into going broke to impress them.

1. **You Learn, Even When You Think You Know Enough**

- New podcast. New book. New course. You stay hungry.

1. **You Plan for Rest**

- Fly people don't burn out. They build wealth *and* wellness.

This is how you stay in the game.

This is how you don't just build wealth—you *wear* it with grace.

Owning Your Fly: Identity, Self-Worth, and the Bag

Let's talk identity.

A lot of people define themselves by what they don't have. They carry financial trauma like a badge. They downplay their ambition. They apologize for wanting more.

But financially fly people? We do it differently.

We don't shrink.

We don't settle.

We don't sabotage.

We say:

- I'm allowed to be wealthy.
- I'm allowed to look good and do good.
- I'm allowed to take up space at the table *and* build my own.

Your fly isn't just aesthetic. It's spiritual.

You stop waiting for permission.

You stop outsourcing power.

You stop playing broke when you're building something bold.

This is your season.

This is your story.

This is your legacy.

Long-Term Strategy = Long-Term Sexy

Let's get practical.

Here's how to stay financially fly at every age:

- **In Your 20s:**
- Build the foundation. Budget. Save. Start investing early. Learn like your life depends on it.
- **In Your 30s:**
- Multiply. Negotiate raises. Increase contributions. Pay down debt. Get the right insurance.
- **In Your 40s:**
- Expand. Diversify. Teach others. Focus on legacy. Prioritize freedom.

- **In Your 50s and Beyond:**
- Refine. Reallocate. Enjoy the fruit. Create systems. Share wisdom.

Fly doesn't fade.

Fly evolves.

And when your money has structure, you move different. You breathe deeper. You glow longer.

The Sexy Money Moves You Can Make Today

Pick one. Or pick all. Just pick something.

- Name your financial goals out loud.
- Check your net worth (even if it scares you).
- Cancel a subscription you forgot about.
- Open a high-yield savings account.
- Increase your 401(k) contribution by 1%.
- Text a friend: "Want to do a money date this weekend?"
- Schedule a meeting with a financial planner.
- Read your benefits package (yes, for real).

Action is clarity. Clarity is confidence. Confidence is sexy.

You Are the Author. Don't Hand Over the Pen.

Here's what I want you to know:

You are not behind.

You are not broken.

You are not bad with money.

You are in motion.

You are on purpose.

You are writing a new narrative.

And you don't have to do it perfectly.

You just have to keep showing up.

Every paycheck is a plot twist.

Every money move is a sentence.

Every budget reset is a fresh paragraph.

Write boldly.

Write honestly.

Write powerfully.

Because this is your story.

And the world can't wait to read what you do with it.

End of Chapter Encouragements

You're not behind. You're just getting started.

Most people don't know this stuff—until they do. Now you do.

Clarity is confidence. And confidence is sexy.

Make one money move before you go to bed tonight. Just one. And then do another next week.

Final Note

You were never meant to live confused, anxious, or stuck about money.

You were made for more.

More freedom.

More power.

More joy.

Write your new money story.

And keep the pen in your hand.

Because financially fly?

That's forever.

Closing Chapter 54: You're the Asset — Now Act Like It

Let's land this.

Not with a dry summary or a checklist you'll forget to look at.

Let's land this with clarity, confidence, and the kind of swagger that comes from knowing one truth:

You are the asset.

Not your bank account.

Not your job title.

Not your real estate portfolio, credit score, or retirement plan.

You.

Your energy.

Your decisions.

Your discipline.

Your values.

Your ability to pivot, to plan, to rise.

That's the real wealth.

Everything you've read in this book was written with one purpose: to remind you that financial literacy isn't boring—it's bold. It's attractive. It's the foundation of the life you *actually* want.

You didn't pick up this book because you wanted a lecture.

You picked it up because you're tired of pretending.

Tired of smiling through financial stress.

Tired of Googling how Roth IRAs work at 1 a.m.

Tired of wondering if you're the only one who feels behind.

Here's your permission slip:

You're not behind.

You're exactly where you're supposed to be.

And now, you're equipped to move forward—with intention.

The Sexy Truth No One Told You

Financial freedom isn't about being rich.

It's about **options**.

Peace of mind.

Quiet mornings without panic.

Confidence that carries into your relationships, your work, your joy.

It's being able to say:

- "I got this," when the unexpected happens.
- "No thanks," when an opportunity doesn't align.
- "Hell yes," when it's time to invest in yourself, your future, your legacy.

Financial literacy gives you language, structure, tools—but more than that, it gives you power.

What to Do Next

Don't just close this book. **Use it.**

Highlight it.

Revisit the chapters that hit hardest.

Turn the action steps into calendar reminders.

Make it your new Sunday ritual.

Have a money date.

Set the next goal.

You don't have to do everything.

But you do have to do something.

One move.

Open a Roth IRA.

Increase your 401(k) by 1%.

Set up your sinking funds.

Build a "No Thanks" fund so you never feel trapped.

Download your credit report.

Ask for the raise.

Send the calendar invite for the money date.

One move today.

One more next week.

That's how freedom is built.

What I Hope You Remember

- **Budgeting isn't punishment—it's power.**
- **Credit isn't just a number—it's leverage.**
- **Investing isn't gambling—it's long-game confidence.**
- **Insurance isn't fear—it's protection.**
- **Debt isn't shame—it's data.**
- **Financial literacy isn't just practical—it's sexy.**

Because there is **nothing** sexier than someone who knows where their money's going, what their money's doing, and why they're building wealth in the first place.

Not to show off.

Not to compete.

Not to buy things for people who don't even matter.

But to move through life with grace, ease, clarity, and intention.

Final Words: You're Not a Financial Plan. You're a Force.

You're the one who shows up.

The one who chooses growth.

The one who doesn't just survive, but builds.

There will be mistakes.

There will be seasons of messiness, setbacks, doubt.

But you'll keep going.

Why?

Because you now have tools.

You have perspective.

You have vocabulary.

You have **swagger**.

Financial literacy doesn't eliminate problems—but it **equips** you to handle them like the badass you are.

So yeah.

Financial literacy is sexy.

And so are you.

Go build something beautiful—with your brain, your bank account, and your boldness.

This is your life.

Own it.

See you at the next milestone.

Discliamer

Financial Literacy Is Sexy was written to make personal finance feel empowering—not overwhelming. It was created to educate, inspire, and equip people—from career-driven professionals to side-hustling creatives to anyone who's ever felt intimidated by the world of money—with the clarity, tools, and confidence to take control of their financial life.

The insights in these pages reflect the author's personal journey, decades of experience in financial advising and wealth planning, and the stories of real people who turned confusion into confidence.

That said, let's keep it real:

This book is here to help you **think better** about money.

It's not here to replace **professional advice**.

Educational Purpose Only

Everything in this book is for general education. It's designed to help you understand the foundations: budgeting, investing, credit, debt, taxes, insurance, retirement, mindset, wealth-building—and most importantly, how they all work together.

But it's not personal financial advice. Your income, expenses, taxes, debt, family structure, lifestyle, values, and goals are **uniquely yours**. This book doesn't know all that. So don't make big money moves just because something in here *sounded good.*

Before making any major decision—especially when it comes to investing, insurance, taxes, or legal matters—talk to a qualified professional.

No Legal Advice

If you're setting up an LLC, reviewing a prenup, creating a trust, or writing a will—**see an attorney.** This book isn't a replacement for legal guidance, and no paragraph or chapter in here can take the place of someone trained to protect your rights and structure your estate.

No Financial or Investment Advice

This book talks about:

- Roth IRAs and 401(k)s
- Index funds and ETFs
- Emergency funds and sinking funds
- Side hustles, real estate, and passive income

But it's all **general education**.

No stock tips. No one-size-fits-all advice. No sales pitch.

If you're ready to make investing decisions, work with a **Certified Financial Planner**™, fiduciary advisor, or someone licensed and legally obligated to act in your best interest.

Your financial life deserves that kind of respect.

No Tax or Accounting Advice

There are money moves that can save you on taxes. But every deduction, deferral, or backdoor strategy depends on:

- Where you live
- How you earn
- Your filing status
- Your income level
- Your type of business (if any)

- Whether you itemize or take the standard deduction

Bottom line: **Talk to a CPA.**

This book is not your tax advisor.

No Guarantees

Reading this book will not magically make you rich. It won't eliminate financial stress overnight. It won't guarantee a retirement at 45 or a perfect credit score next month.

Here's what it **will** give you:

- A stronger mindset
- A clearer strategy
- Smarter habits
- More confidence

This is your **co-pilot**—not your autopilot.

You still have to fly the plane.

Limitation of Liability

By reading this book, you agree that **Pat Brown, MBA**, and affiliated platforms including FinancialLiteracyIsSexy.com, are **not liable** for any decisions, losses, outcomes, or consequences that result from your use of this content.

You're the pilot. You're in control. You're also responsible.

Build Your Financial Dream Team

You don't need to do this alone.

If you haven't already, start building your financial support crew:

- A financial advisor who understands your goals
- A CPA who understands your numbers
- An attorney who understands your legacy
- An insurance expert who protects your future

Smart is sexy. Structure is sexy. And support? That's the sexiest thing of all.

You deserve advisors who get it—who respect your hustle and help you grow.

Final Thought

Financial literacy won't make you perfect. But it will make you powerful.

This book is your launchpad—not your destination.

Use it to ask better questions.

Use it to break generational patterns.

Use it to build wealth **your way**.

Confidence is built with intention.

Security is built with strategy.

And **financial literacy is how you start.**

So let's keep it sexy. Keep it smart. And keep moving forward.

You've got this.

—Pat Brown, MBA

info@financialliteracyissexy.com

www.FinancialLiteracyIsSexy.com

Financial Calendar

For Your Sexiest Financial Year Yet

This calendar isn't just about taxes—it's about staying ahead of the turbulence. Whether you're just building your financial runway or getting ready to land that retirement plan with grace and power, knowing when to act can change your whole trajectory.

Think of this as your financial checklist. Because clarity is confidence. And confidence is sexy.

January – Start the Year

- New tax year = fresh budget, fresh goals.
- Review your W-4 if life changed (new job, raise, family).
- Save 25%-30% of 1099/side hustle income for taxes.
- Jan 15: 4th Quarter Estimated Tax Payment Due (for side gig/contract work)
- Jan 31: Deadline for receiving W-2s, 1099s, 1098s, and investment forms
- Action Step: Create a "2025 Taxes" folder and upload docs as they arrive.

February – Organize and Prep

- Gather all tax docs.
- Finalize side hustle books, receipts, mileage logs.
- Know your IRS forms:
- Schedule C = Self-employment income
- Schedule E = Rental income

- Schedule SE = Self-employment tax
- Action Step: Start listing deductible expenses now—don't wait.

March – For the Self-Starters & Side Hustlers

- Mar 15: S-Corp & partnership tax filing deadline.
- If you run a business, file Form 1120-S.
- Action Step: Re-evaluate your business structure. Is it time to become an S-Corp?

April – The Big One

- Apr 15: Tax Day.
- File or extend with Form 4868.
- Make 1st quarter estimated tax payment.
- Last day to contribute to Roth IRA, Traditional IRA, or HSA for 2024.
- Action Step: Even if you can't pay, always file—penalties for not filing are worse.

May – Mid-Year Money Check

- Are you on pace for your savings goals?
- Review your 401(k), Roth IRA, HSA.
- Spot-check your spending—lifestyle inflation is sneaky.
- Action Step: Schedule a 1-hour solo or couple's "money date."

June – Summer Money Moves

- Jun 15: 2nd Quarter Estimated Taxes Due.
- Plan ahead for travel and expenses.
- Review how much you're withholding from freelance income.
- Action Step: Check your emergency fund. Refill if needed.

July – Rebalance & Recalibrate

- Mid-year investment review: Is your portfolio aligned with your risk?
- Rebalance 401(k), IRA, or brokerage accounts if needed.
- Check your insurance coverage:
- Life
- Disability
- Umbrella
- Action Step: Pull a free credit report from AnnualCreditReport.com.

August – Audit Your Debt & Credit

- Review mortgage, loans, and credit cards.
- Could you refinance? Consolidate? Renegotiate?
- Reassess student loans or side hustle expenses.
- Action Step: Choose one thing to pay down faster.

September – Get Strategic

- Sep 15: 3rd Quarter Estimated Taxes Due.
- Prep for year-end moves:
- Roth conversions
- Charitable giving
- Tax-loss harvesting
- Action Step: List out possible deductions now. Don't wait till December.

October – Paperwork & Planning

- Oct 1: FAFSA opens.
- Oct 15: Final day to file extended tax returns.
- Review health coverage (Open Enrollment begins soon).
- Action Step: Schedule your annual financial review.

November – Strategy Season

- Meet with advisor or CPA:
- RMDs if 73+
- End-of-year donations
- Business deductions
- Portfolio adjustments
- Action Step: Max out your 401(k), HSA, or Solo 401(k).

December – Land the Plane

- Dec 31: Final day for many financial moves.
- Fund retirement plans, gift donations, use FSA dollars.
- Snapshot your net worth.
- Action Step: Set 1–3 goals for next year and celebrate how far you've come.

Bonus Best Practices

- Always save 25%-30% of freelance income for taxes.
- Keep personal and business money separate.
- Track deductible expenses (apps: Keeper Tax, QuickBooks, MileIQ).
- Maximize pre-tax benefits: 401(k), HSA, FSA.
- Build your crew: Financial advisor, CPA, insurance pro, estate attorney.
- Weekly ritual: 15-min Sunday "money preflight check."

You wouldn't take off without checking your systems.

Don't let your money run without one either.

Financial literacy is sexy. So is being prepared.

Terms and Definitions

INVESTMENT TERMS

1. **Asset Allocation** – Dividing investments among different asset categories like stocks, bonds, and cash.
2. **Index Fund** – A fund that tracks a specific market index, such as the S&P 500.
3. **ETF (Exchange-Traded Fund)** – A fund that trades like a stock and holds a diversified basket of assets.
4. **Mutual Fund** – A pooled investment managed by professionals that buys stocks, bonds, or other assets.
5. **Stock** – Ownership in a company represented by shares.
6. **Bond** – A loan made to a corporation or government in exchange for interest payments.
7. **Dividend** – A portion of a company's profits paid to shareholders.
8. **Capital Gain** – Profit from selling an investment for more than its purchase price.
9. **Capital Loss** – Loss from selling an investment for less than its purchase price.
10. **Volatility** – The degree of variation in the price of an investment over time.
11. **Risk Tolerance** – An investor's ability or willingness to endure market fluctuations.
12. **Diversification** – Spreading investments across various assets to reduce risk.
13. **Asset** – Anything of value owned, such as cash, investments, or property.

14. **Liability** – A debt or obligation owed.
15. **Portfolio** – A collection of investments held by an individual or institution.
16. **Brokerage Account** – An investment account that allows you to buy and sell securities.
17. **IRA (Individual Retirement Account)** – A tax-advantaged account for retirement savings.
18. **Roth IRA** – A retirement account where contributions are taxed, but withdrawals are tax-free.
19. **401(k)** – A workplace retirement plan allowing tax-deferred contributions.
20. **RMD (Required Minimum Distribution)** – Minimum withdrawals required from retirement accounts after a certain age.
21. **Robo-Advisor** – An automated platform that manages investments using algorithms.
22. **Expense Ratio** – The annual fee charged by a fund, expressed as a percentage of assets.
23. **Rebalancing** – Adjusting a portfolio to maintain a desired asset allocation.
24. **Yield** – Income earned from an investment, typically expressed as a percentage.
25. **Dollar-Cost Averaging** – Investing a fixed amount regularly regardless of market conditions.

ACCOUNTING TERMS

1. **Revenue** – Total income generated from business activities.
2. **Gross Income** – Earnings before deductions or expenses.
3. **Net Income** – Earnings after all deductions and expenses.
4. **Profit** – Revenue minus expenses.
5. **Loss** – When expenses exceed revenue.
6. **Expense** – A cost incurred in operating a business.
7. **Cash Flow** – Movement of money into and out of a business or

account.

8. **Accounts Payable** – Money owed by a business to creditors.
9. **Accounts Receivable** – Money owed to a business by customers.
10. **Balance Sheet** – A financial statement showing assets, liabilities, and net worth.
11. **Income Statement** – A financial report showing revenue and expenses over a period.
12. **Depreciation** – Reduction in the value of an asset over time.
13. **Amortization** – Gradual reduction of a debt or intangible asset over time.
14. **Chart of Accounts** – A list of all accounts used to record financial transactions.
15. **Bookkeeping** – Recording of financial transactions and maintaining accounts.
16. **Write-Off** – An expense that reduces taxable income.
17. **Accrual Accounting** – Recognizing revenue and expenses when they are incurred.
18. **Cash Accounting** – Recording revenue and expenses when cash is received or paid.
19. **General Ledger** – The main accounting record of a company.
20. **Audit** – Examination of financial records for accuracy and compliance.
21. **Taxable Income** – Income subject to taxation.
22. **Form W-2** – IRS form reporting wages and tax withheld for employees.
23. **Form 1099** – IRS form reporting non-employee income (e.g., freelancers, interest).
24. **Schedule C** – IRS form used to report income from a sole proprietorship.
25. **Form 1040** – The main form for individual income tax returns in the U.S.

BUSINESS TERMS

1. **LLC (Limited Liability Company)** – A business structure offering limited liability to owners.
2. **S-Corp** – A tax election for small businesses to avoid double taxation.
3. **C-Corp** – A corporation taxed separately from its owners.
4. **Sole Proprietor** – A business owned and operated by one individual.
5. **Partnership** – A business owned by two or more individuals.
6. **Operating Agreement** – A document outlining the structure and rules of an LLC.
7. **Business Credit** – Credit extended to a business rather than an individual.
8. **Business Plan** – A formal document outlining a business's objectives and strategies.
9. **P&L Statement (Profit & Loss)** – Shows a business's revenues and expenses over time.
10. **Break-Even Point** – When total revenue equals total expenses.
11. **EBITDA** – Earnings before interest, taxes, depreciation, and amortization.
12. **ROI (Return on Investment)** – A measure of profitability, calculated as net profit divided by investment cost.
13. **Operating Income** – Profit from regular business operations.
14. **Burn Rate** – The rate at which a business uses up cash reserves.
15. **Equity** – Ownership interest in a company.
16. **Capital** – Financial assets or resources used to fund a business.
17. **Working Capital** – Current assets minus current liabilities.
18. **Business Liability Insurance** – Insurance that protects against claims from business operations.
19. **Invoice** – A bill issued for goods or services.
20. **Receipt** – Proof of payment or transaction.

ESTATE / LEGAL / ATTORNEY TERMS

1. **Estate** – All property, assets, and debts left by an individual at death.
2. **Will** – A legal document outlining how to distribute your assets after

death.

3. **Trust** – A legal arrangement where a trustee manages assets on behalf of a beneficiary.
4. **Revocable Trust** – A trust that can be altered or canceled during the grantor's life.
5. **Irrevocable Trust** – A trust that cannot be modified once established.
6. **Executor** – Person named to carry out the terms of a will.
7. **Probate** – Legal process of administering a will and estate.
8. **Beneficiary** – A person or entity entitled to receive assets or benefits.
9. **Power of Attorney (POA)** – A legal document allowing someone to act on your behalf.
10. **Advance Directive** – A document outlining healthcare wishes if you're incapacitated.
11. **Living Will** – Specifies medical treatment preferences in end-of-life situations.
12. **Durable POA** – A power of attorney that remains in effect if the person becomes incapacitated.
13. **Healthcare Proxy** – Designates someone to make medical decisions on your behalf.
14. **Guardian** – A person appointed to care for a minor or incapacitated adult.
15. **Estate Tax** – A tax on the transfer of assets at death.
16. **Inheritance Tax** – A tax paid by the person receiving an inheritance.
17. **Grantor** – The person who creates a trust.
18. **Trustee** – The person who manages trust assets.
19. **Heir** – A person legally entitled to inherit from someone who dies without a will.
20. **Codicil** – An amendment to a will.
21. **Letter of Intent** – A document expressing your wishes for heirs or guardians.
22. **Testamentary Trust** – A trust created by a will, taking effect after death.
23. **Estate Plan** – A comprehensive plan for transferring assets and

protecting heirs.

24. **Intestate** – Dying without a legal will.
25. **Conservator** – A person appointed to manage someone else's financial affairs.
26. **Joint Tenancy** – Shared property ownership with rights of survivorship.
27. **Tenants in Common** – Shared ownership where each party can pass their share to heirs.
28. **Title** – Legal ownership of property.
29. **Deed** – A legal document that transfers ownership of property.
30. **Charitable Remainder Trust** – A trust that provides income to a beneficiary and later donates to charity.

Choosing the Right Financial Professionals: 30 Questions to Ask Before You Hire a Financial Advisor, CPA, or Attorney

Money may be personal—but managing it well is never a solo job.

The truth? The smartest, wealthiest, most well-prepared people you know don't do it alone. They have a team: a trusted financial advisor, a tax-savvy CPA, and an attorney who understands both their assets and their values.

But finding the right professionals isn't about credentials alone. It's about chemistry. It's about clarity. And it's about asking the right questions—upfront.

Here's your cheat sheet of 30 smart, strategic, and non-intimidating questions to ask financial professionals before hiring them. Because confidence isn't just sexy—it's protective.

Questions for Financial Advisors

1. Are you a fiduciary 100% of the time?
2. How do you get paid—fee-only, commission-based, or a combination?
3. Can you explain your investment philosophy in plain English?
4. What licenses or certifications do you hold? (CFP®, ChFC®, Series 65, etc.)
5. Who is your typical client—and do you have experience with people like me?

6. Do you offer comprehensive planning, or just manage investments?
7. How often will we meet or review my plan?
8. Do you provide guidance on insurance, estate planning, or tax strategy?
9. What's your minimum asset requirement, if any?
10. What happens if I decide to leave or transfer my accounts?

Questions for CPAs or Tax Advisors

1. Do you offer tax planning year-round, or just tax filing?
2. What industries or professions do you specialize in?
3. Can you help me structure my side business or freelance income?
4. Do you assist with quarterly tax estimates and withholdings?
5. How do you stay current on new tax laws?
6. Can you help with Roth conversions, capital gains planning, or deductions?
7. Will you represent me in the event of an IRS audit?
8. How do you charge—hourly, flat rate, or by return complexity?
9. Do you collaborate with my financial advisor or bookkeeper if needed?
10. Can you help me understand my tax return, not just file it?

Questions for Estate or Business Attorneys

1. Do you specialize in estate planning or business formation—or both?
2. What types of clients do you typically serve?
3. Can you draft or review a will, trust, or power of attorney?
4. How do you help clients with blended families or second marriages?
5. What do I need to protect my business or rental property from liability?
6. Can you help me create an LLC or partnership agreement?
7. Do you offer flat fees for estate plans or charge hourly?
8. What happens if I need to make changes to my documents later?
9. How do you coordinate with my advisor or CPA?

10. What's one mistake you see people make that I can avoid?

Bonus Rule of Thumb

If a financial professional gets defensive when you ask questions—they're not your person.

The right professional won't just answer your questions—they'll welcome them. They'll help you feel informed, respected, and empowered.

Because the real goal isn't to hand off your finances.

It's to build a team that helps you lead.

You're the CEO of your life. Now go hire accordingly.

Pros and Cons of Working with a Financial Advisor

Let's get real—hiring a financial advisor can feel like a power move... or a panic button. Maybe you're wondering if it's worth the cost. Maybe you're scared of being sold something you don't need. Or maybe you're ready to level up and just need a co-pilot you can trust.

This section breaks down the **real** pros and cons of working with a financial advisor—no fluff, no fear-mongering, just clarity.

PROS

1. Expertise You Don't Have (Yet)

A good advisor brings years of experience in investing, taxes, insurance, estate planning, retirement strategy, and risk management—so you don't have to figure it all out from scratch.

2. Saves Time and Headspace

If you're juggling a career, family, side hustle, or just life in general, handing off the heavy lifting to a pro can be a major relief.

3. Personalized Planning

The best advisors don't just plug you into a template. They help you craft a financial plan that reflects *your* life, values, and goals—not someone else's spreadsheet.

4. Accountability Partner

You know what to do... but you don't always do it. An advisor keeps you focused, consistent, and moving forward, even when life gets chaotic.

5. Emotion Buffer During Market Chaos

When markets drop, people panic. Advisors help you stay steady, avoid emotional decisions, and stick to the long-term plan—so you don't sell low and regret it later.

6. Coordination Across Your Financial Life

Advisors can collaborate with your CPA, attorney, or insurance pro to make sure everything's aligned—from tax strategy to legacy planning.

7. Access to Resources

Some advisors offer tools, models, research, and networks you wouldn't otherwise have—like private investment opportunities, tax-saving strategies, or estate plan templates.

CONS

1. The Cost

Advisors typically charge a fee—either a percentage of assets (often 1%), an hourly rate, or a flat annual fee. That can add up, especially if you're early in your wealth-building journey.

2. Not All Advisors Are Equal

Some are fiduciaries (legally required to act in your best interest). Others are commission-based salespeople pushing products. If you don't vet carefully, you could end up with someone who profits more than you do.

3. You Still Have to Participate

A financial advisor is a guide—not a magic wand. You'll still have to make decisions, clarify goals, and stay involved. It's not "set it and forget it."

4. Generic Advice Is a Risk

Some advisors use cookie-cutter plans or don't take the time to understand your full picture. If your plan feels like a one-size-fits-all blueprint—it probably is.

5. Misaligned Incentives

If your advisor is paid by selling certain funds or insurance products, their advice may be biased. Always ask how they're compensated.

So... Should You Work With a Financial Advisor?

Ask yourself:

- Do I have the time and interest to manage my money myself?
- Am I confident in my tax, insurance, and investment decisions?
- Have I hit a financial milestone (new job, inheritance, business sale, retirement) that feels too big to DIY?
- Would I benefit from an expert second opinion—or just someone to help keep me on track?

If you're not sure, consider starting with a **fee-only, fiduciary advisor.** Think of it like a financial checkup—not a lifelong commitment.

Bottom Line:

You don't *need* an advisor to build wealth. But the right one can save you time, protect you from big mistakes, and help you accelerate your growth.

Because sometimes the sexiest thing you can say about your money is:

"I've got a plan. And I've got a pro helping me work it."

Appendix A: Money Tools You Can Use

The Sexy, Strategic Toolkit for Your Financial Glow-Up

Let's get something straight right now: financial literacy isn't just about what you *know*—it's about what you *do.* Action is the sexiest currency in the game. And while information empowers, structure sustains.

This appendix is your personal toolkit. It's not cute fluff. It's not generic downloads. It's a powerful, practical, repeatable rhythm for your money life. Whether you're just starting or you've already built some traction, these tools will help you stay focused, grounded, and in control. Because staying fly financially isn't a one-time decision—it's a lifestyle.

Let's walk through these tools the way we'd walk through a closet full of curated outfits: thoughtfully, intentionally, and with just the right amount of flex.

Monthly Budget Worksheet: The Foundation of the Fit

Budgeting isn't punishment—it's preparation. It's where vision meets execution. Your monthly budget is your script, your GPS, your choreography.

What it does:

- Tracks every dollar in and out.
- Shows you what's real versus what's wishful thinking.
- Gives you control instead of chaos.

How to use it:

- Start with your *actual* income (not your future promotion, not your side hustle ideas).

- List fixed costs first: rent/mortgage, utilities, debt payments.
- Then list flexible costs: groceries, gas, personal spending, entertainment.
- Don't forget savings, investments, and giving.
- Review and revise monthly. Don't just guess. Don't just hope. *Know.*

50/30/20 Spending Tracker: The Sexy Simplicity Method

Here's the breakdown:

- 50% needs (housing, food, utilities)
- 30% wants (travel, date nights, brunch, sneakers)
- 20% future you (savings, investments, debt paydown)

Why it works:

- It keeps your lifestyle in check.
- It forces balance without micromanaging.
- It gives you enough structure to be safe—and enough freedom to breathe.

How to use it:

- Pull up your last 2-3 bank statements.
- Categorize your spending.
- Highlight what's out of balance.
- Adjust going forward.

No shame. Just strategy.

Sinking Fund Setup Template: Your Quiet Flex

Sinking funds = sexy self-trust.

They say: "I see the future coming, and I'm not scared. I'm ready."

Use them for:

- Holiday gifts
- Travel
- Car maintenance
- Annual subscriptions
- Kids' school stuff

How it works:

- Choose the goal and timeline.
- Divide the total cost by the number of months until you need it.
- Automate that monthly amount into a separate savings account.

Simple math. Massive peace of mind.

Debt Snowball & Avalanche Worksheets: Knockout Tools for Your Comeback Season

Debt doesn't define you—but your approach to it does.

Snowball Method:

- List debts from smallest to largest balance.
- Pay minimums on all, and throw extra at the smallest.
- Get a win. Feel the momentum. Repeat.

Avalanche Method:

- List debts by highest to lowest interest rate.
- Pay minimums on all, and throw extra at the highest rate.
- Save more money over time.

Choose your fighter.

These worksheets:

- Help you visualize your progress.
- Keep you accountable.

- Turn debt from a shame spiral into a strategy.

Net Worth Tracker: The Sexy Selfie of Your Financial Life

Net worth = what you own minus what you owe.

This is your big-picture scorecard. It's not just about income. It's about assets, growth, leverage, and liquidity.

Track:

- Cash and savings
- Investment accounts
- Real estate equity
- Business interests
- Vehicles
- Retirement accounts

Subtract:

- Credit card debt
- Student loans
- Mortgage
- Personal loans
- Car notes

Do this quarterly. Watch it climb. Celebrate like a grown-up.

Investment Account Starter Checklist: Your Entry to the Wealth Club

Starting to invest is less about timing and more about traction.

Your checklist:

1. Open a Roth IRA (start here if eligible).
2. Contribute to your 401(k), especially if there's a match.
3. Choose low-cost index funds (S&P 500, Total Market, etc.).
4. Automate monthly contributions.

5. Set and forget—but check quarterly.
6. Don't chase trends. Build your base.

This isn't about getting rich quick. This is about becoming wealthy always.

Emergency Fund Goal Plan: Your Real Safety Net (Not Credit Cards)

Life throws curveballs. An emergency fund helps you catch them with grace instead of panic.

Your plan:

- Goal: 3 to 6 months of living expenses.
- Store it in a high-yield savings account.
- Name it something empowering: "Peace of Mind," "Freedom Fund," "No Drama Reserve."
- Start with $500, then build to $1,000, then grow it monthly.

Don't wait for stability to build stability. Build it now—on your terms.

Final Word: These Tools Don't Just Track Your Money—They Change Your Mindset

Use them. Print them. Update them. Talk about them. Tweak them.

These aren't homework assignments. They're liberation tools.

They say:

- "I'm not scared of money—I'm the one in control."
- "My money isn't messy—it's working for me."
- "I've got receipts. I've got rhythms. I've got range."

Make it a ritual. Make it a rhythm. Make it yours.

Because financial literacy isn't just sexy—it's self-respect in motion.

Let's go.

Appendix B: Medicare and Health Insurance Planning

Medicare Enrollment Checklist (Turning 65 and Beyond)

Let's begin with one of the most misunderstood milestones in retirement planning: Medicare. Turning 65 isn't just a birthday—it's a deadline. And if you miss it? The consequences can cost you hundreds, even thousands, of dollars a year.

Here's your sexy, powerful, no-fluff checklist:

1. **Know Your Timeline**

- Your Initial Enrollment Period (IEP) begins **3 months before** your 65th birthday and ends **3 months after**.
- Missing this window without qualifying coverage? Prepare for penalties.

1. **Understand the Parts**

- **Part A**: Hospital insurance (usually free if you or your spouse worked 10+ years).
- **Part B**: Medical insurance (doctor visits, outpatient services).
- **Part C**: Medicare Advantage (bundled plans through private insurers).
- **Part D**: Prescription drug coverage.

1. **Decide Between Original Medicare + Supplement OR Medicare Advantage**

- Don't sleep on this. The choice affects doctors, costs, and coverage.

1. **Shop Part D If You Choose Original Medicare**

- No drug coverage = no peace of mind.

1. **Enroll On Time**

- Use the Social Security website or call your local Medicare office.

1. **If You're Still Working and Covered by Employer Insurance**

- You may be able to delay Part B and Part D.
- Coordinate with HR. Don't assume.

Medicare Advantage vs. Supplement Comparison Chart

Feature Medicare Advantage Medicare Supplement

Type of Coverage

All-in-one (Part A, B, D)

Adds to Original Medicare

Provider Network

Limited (HMOs, PPOs)

Any doctor who accepts Medicare

Premium

Lower (some $0 plans)

Higher (avg. $100-$300/mo)

Copays/Coinsurance

Yes

Minimal to none

Drug Coverage

Usually included

Needs separate Part D plan

Extra Benefits

Often includes dental, vision, gym
Rarely includes extras

Health Insurance Glossary (Sexy Definitions Only)

- **Premium**: What you pay each month, like a Netflix subscription—but for your health.
- **Deductible**: What you pay out of pocket before your insurance kicks in.
- **Coinsurance**: The % you split with the plan after your deductible is met.
- **Copay**: A fixed fee for visits or prescriptions (e.g., $25 to see your doc).
- **Out-of-Pocket Maximum**: The most you'll pay in a year. After that? Insurance pays 100%.
- **Formulary**: The plan's list of covered meds. Not all plans cover every drug.
- **Prior Authorization**: When the insurer needs to say yes before a service or medication is covered.
- **Network**: The list of docs, hospitals, and providers your plan works with.
- **Open Enrollment**: The once-a-year window to change plans (Oct 15 – Dec 7 for Medicare).

Questions to Ask When Picking a Medicare Plan

1. Are my doctors in the plan's network?
2. Are my prescriptions covered?
3. What are my monthly premiums?
4. What is the yearly out-of-pocket max?
5. Do I need referrals for specialists?
6. Does the plan include dental, vision, or hearing?
7. How does the plan handle emergency care while traveling?
8. Is this plan easy to use?
9. What are other members saying about it?

10. Can I afford this plan even if I get sick?

Coordination of Benefits: Medicare + Employer Coverage

If you're still working at 65 (or covered through a spouse), you may not need to enroll in all parts of Medicare yet.

- **Employer has fewer than 20 employees?** Medicare pays first.
- **Employer has 20+ employees?** Your job insurance pays first.
- **Still working?** You might be able to delay Part B (and avoid that monthly premium) until you retire.

Key: Get a letter from HR proving "creditable coverage" so you can avoid late penalties.

If you have HSA plans: Do **not** sign up for any part of Medicare if you want to keep contributing.

Long-Term Care Insurance Considerations

Medicare is great, but it **does not** cover long-term care. That's things like nursing homes, memory care, or extended in-home help. So let's break it down:

- **What It Is**: Insurance that covers care for chronic illness, disability, or age-related decline.
- **Why It Matters**: A private room in a nursing home can cost $100,000+/year.
- **When to Buy**: Ideally in your late 50s to early 60s—before health issues show up.
- **Hybrid Policies**: Combine life insurance with long-term care coverage.
- **Alternatives**: Self-funding through savings, annuities, or selling assets.

Ask yourself:

- Do I want to be a financial burden on my kids?

- Do I have assets worth protecting?
- Could I afford $6K-$10K/month out of pocket?

You're Not Behind. You're Just Getting Started.

Most people have no idea how Medicare works until they're knee-deep in pamphlets, jargon, and panic. Not you. You're learning now. You're owning this.

Medicare doesn't have to be scary. With the right plan, it can be empowering. It can give you options. It can give you peace. And nothing is sexier than financial peace.

Clarity is confidence. And confidence is sexy.

Make one move tonight: download your Medicare & You guidebook, pull your Social Security statement, or schedule a call with a Medicare advisor.

You've got this. And your future self will thank you.

Appendix C: Protecting Your Peace and Privacy

Financial Document Organizer (What to Keep, Where to Store It)

Peace of mind starts with knowing where everything is. One of the least sexy—yet most powerful—money moves you can make is getting organized. Not just for yourself, but for anyone who might need to step in one day: your spouse, your adult kids, your power of attorney, your executor.

You don't need a filing cabinet the size of a walk-in closet. You just need a system.

Here's what to keep and where to store it:

- **Vital Records:** Birth certificate, marriage license, divorce decrees, adoption papers, Social Security cards.
- *Keep: Original in a fireproof safe. Digital scan backed up securely.*
- **Legal Documents:** Wills, trusts, powers of attorney, advance directives.
- *Keep: Original with your estate attorney or in a fireproof safe. Copy in your digital organizer.*
- **Financial Accounts:** Bank statements, retirement accounts, investment summaries.
- *Keep: Secure digital log with access instructions. Shred paper after digitizing if not needed for taxes.*
- **Insurance Policies:** Life, health, disability, home, auto, umbrella.
- *Keep: Digital and physical copies with policy numbers, beneficiaries, and contact info.*
- **Tax Returns:** Last seven years of returns, especially if they involve

property, investments, or business.

- *Keep: Encrypted digital file or secure cloud.*
- **Debt Information:** Mortgage, car loans, credit cards, student loans.
- *Keep: Account numbers, balances, payment details in one secure document.*

Make sure someone you trust knows how to access it.

Beneficiary Update Checklist

Want to know what's worse than dying broke? Dying with a life insurance policy that pays out to your ex from 12 years ago. It happens more often than you'd think.

Your beneficiaries override your will. That's right—what's on file with your retirement account, your life insurance policy, your annuity—that's what gets paid. No matter what your will says.

Update your beneficiaries when:

- You get married or divorced
- You have a child or grandchild
- A beneficiary passes away
- You open a new account
- You change your estate plan

Review these accounts at least once a year:

- 401(k), 403(b), IRA
- Life insurance (employer and private)
- Pension plans
- Annuities
- Health savings accounts (HSAs)
- Bank accounts with POD (Payable on Death)

Be intentional. Double-check spelling. Add backups. You'll thank yourself—or rather, your family will.

Cybersecurity Tips for Financial Accounts

You can have the perfect budget, a diversified investment portfolio, and still get wiped out by one bad click. Protecting your digital financial life is part of protecting your peace.

Do these immediately:

- **Use unique passwords** for every financial account. No repeats.
- **Turn on two-factor authentication (2FA)** for banks, investment accounts, insurance portals, and credit monitoring.
- **Use a password manager.** Let it generate and store secure logins.
- **Monitor your credit.** Freeze your credit with all three bureaus. Check your reports at least annually at AnnualCreditReport.com.
- **Watch for phishing.** Never click unknown links. Banks will never ask for your password in an email.
- **Update your devices.** Old phones and outdated operating systems are playgrounds for hackers.
- **Log out.** Especially on shared devices. Always.

This isn't paranoia. It's prevention. Because nothing kills your financial confidence faster than fraud.

Legacy Letter Template: What You Want Your Family to Know

A will says who gets what. A legacy letter says what you want them to feel, remember, understand, and carry forward.

Your legacy letter isn't a legal document—it's a love letter to the future. A message that lives beyond your accounts. And honestly, this is where wealth gets personal. This is where it transcends money.

Here's a simple structure:

1. **Start with gratitude.** Tell them what you're thankful for—memories, lessons, laughs, love.
2. **Share your story.** What shaped your money values? What did you struggle with? What do you wish you'd learned sooner?
3. **Leave instructions.** Not just about where documents are—but what you hope they'll do with their inheritance, how to handle certain

people, or which professionals to trust.

4. **Name your values.** What mattered most to you in life? What do you want them to honor?
5. **Pass the torch.** Tell them what you believe they're capable of. Leave them with a blessing or challenge.

You can write it, record it, or both. You can update it every year or once a decade. But don't skip it. Because a balance sheet doesn't speak for you. Your voice does.

End of Chapter Encouragements

You're not behind. You're just getting started.

Most people don't know this stuff—until they do. Now you do.

Clarity is confidence. And confidence is sexy.

Make one peace-protecting money move before you go to bed tonight. Just one. And then do another next week.

Final Note

This chapter isn't just about documents or data—it's about dignity. It's about making sure your hard-earned financial life stays safe, respected, and ready. Protecting your peace and privacy isn't paranoid—it's powerful.

Keep your pen in your hand. Keep your plans in order. And keep your legacy clear.

Because you deserve that kind of calm.

And your loved ones do too.

Appendix D: Relationships and Money

Money Conversation Starters for Couples

Let's be honest—money talks can be awkward, even with someone you love. But money silence? That's even more dangerous. Whether you're just dating or deep into a decade of marriage, financial transparency is one of the sexiest forms of intimacy. Real intimacy isn't just about sharing a bed—it's about sharing a budget, a dream, and a vision for the future.

Use these money conversation starters to build connection, not conflict:

- "How did your family talk about money growing up?"
- "What does financial security look like to you?"
- "What's one money move you're proud of—and one you regret?"
- "How do you feel about debt?"
- "If we suddenly got a $50,000 windfall, what would you want to do with it?"
- "What kind of lifestyle do we want in 5 years? 10 years?"
- "What's your biggest financial fear?"

Start with curiosity, not criticism. These aren't interrogations—they're invitations. Set a vibe. Light a candle. Pour a drink. Make it sexy, not scary.

Prenup/Postnup Talking Points

You can be madly in love *and* plan for your financial autonomy. A prenup or postnup isn't about predicting failure. It's about protecting peace, clarity, and choice. It's a conversation about boundaries, not betrayal.

Here's how to approach it:

- "I want us to talk about a prenup—not because I don't trust you, but because I want us both to be clear and empowered."

- "A prenup can help us define what's yours, what's mine, and what we're building together."
- "We insure our house, our cars, even our phones. Why wouldn't we want to thoughtfully protect our finances too?"
- "This is about fairness and clarity, not fear."
- "A postnup could help us update our agreements now that life has changed since we got married."

Normalize the convo. Love is emotional. Marriage is also financial. Talk about both.

Family Loan Agreement Template

Family and money can get messy fast—especially when someone "borrows" money with no clear terms. Avoid resentment, confusion, and Thanksgiving side-eyes by using a simple loan agreement.

Here's what to include:

- **Amount borrowed**
- **Date funds are exchanged**
- **Repayment plan** (monthly installments, due date, etc.)
- **Interest rate** (if any)
- **What happens if payments are late or missed**
- **Whether it's forgivable (gift) if not repaid in full**

You can literally write: "This agreement is between [Your Name] and [Relative's Name], for a loan of $____ to be repaid in monthly installments of $___ starting on [date]."

Keep it simple. Keep it respectful. Keep it in writing.

Financial Boundary Scripts ("How to Say No with Love")

Saying "no" doesn't make you mean. It makes you clear. You can decline a request with grace, warmth, and boundaries that protect your peace.

Try these scripts:

- "I love you, but I'm not in a position to lend money right now."
- "That's not in my budget, but I'm cheering you on."
- "I can't fund this, but I'm happy to help you brainstorm other options."
- "Let me get back to you—I need to review my priorities first."
- "That doesn't align with my financial goals right now."

Boundaries are kindness in action. The people who love you will respect them. The ones who don't? That's data.

End of Chapter Encouragements

You're not behind. You're just getting started.

Most people don't know this stuff—until they do. Now you do.

Clarity is confidence. And confidence is sexy.

Make one money move before you go to bed tonight. Just one. And then do another next week.

Final Note

Money and love don't have to be at war. When you combine emotional intimacy with financial transparency, you become unstoppable. Whether it's with your partner, your parents, your friends, or your future self—bringing clarity to your money relationships is one of the most liberating moves you can make.

Own your worth. Speak your truth. Protect your peace. That's not just financially smart—it's sexy AF.

Appendix E: Investing Glossary & Resources

Introduction: Embracing the Investment Journey

Investing isn't reserved for the elite; it's a path open to anyone ready to take control of their financial future. Whether you're a recent graduate with a modest paycheck, a mid-career professional seeking growth, or someone approaching retirement aiming to solidify your nest egg, understanding investment fundamentals is crucial.

This chapter serves as your comprehensive guide to demystify investing. We'll explore key terms, compare investment vehicles, introduce accessible platforms, and delve into the time value of money—a concept that underscores the importance of investing sooner rather than later.

Common Investing Terms Explained

1. Exchange-Traded Fund (ETF):

An ETF is a type of investment fund that holds a collection of assets like stocks or bonds and trades on stock exchanges, much like individual stocks. ETFs offer diversification, liquidity, and typically lower fees compared to mutual funds.

2. Index Fund:

An index fund is a type of mutual fund or ETF designed to replicate the performance of a specific market index, such as the S&P 500. By investing in an index fund, you're essentially buying a small piece of every company within that index, providing broad market exposure.

3. Dividend:

Dividends are portions of a company's earnings distributed to shareholders, typically on a quarterly basis. They can be received as cash payments or reinvested to purchase more shares.

4. Asset Allocation:

This refers to the strategy of dividing your investment portfolio among different asset categories, such as stocks, bonds, and cash, to balance risk and reward based on your investment goals and risk tolerance.

5. Diversification:

Diversification involves spreading your investments across various assets to reduce risk. A diversified portfolio can help mitigate losses if one investment performs poorly.

6. Risk Tolerance:

Risk tolerance is your ability and willingness to endure market volatility and potential losses in pursuit of higher returns. Understanding your risk tolerance is essential in crafting an investment strategy that aligns with your comfort level.

List of Low-Cost Investment Platforms

Investing has become more accessible, with numerous platforms offering low-cost options for investors:

1. Fidelity Investments:

Known for its comprehensive services and zero-commission trades, Fidelity offers a range of investment options suitable for both beginners and seasoned investors.

2. Vanguard:

Vanguard is renowned for its low-cost index funds and ETFs, making it a favorite among long-term investors seeking minimal fees.

3. Charles Schwab:

Offering a user-friendly platform with no account minimums and a broad selection of investment products, Charles Schwab is ideal for investors at all levels.

4. Robinhood:

Robinhood provides commission-free trades and an intuitive mobile app, appealing to younger investors and those new to the market.

5. SoFi Invest:

SoFi offers commission-free trading, automated investing options, and financial planning tools, catering to a tech-savvy audience.

6. M1 Finance:

M1 combines automated investing with customization, allowing users to create personalized portfolios with no management fees.

7. E*TRADE:

E*TRADE offers a robust trading platform with a wide range of investment choices and educational resources.

8. Webull:

Webull provides advanced trading tools and zero-commission trades, suitable for more active traders.

9. Acorns:

Acorns rounds up your everyday purchases and invests the spare change, making it a seamless way for beginners to start investing.

10. Stash:

Stash allows investors to start with as little as $5, offering fractional shares and educational content to guide users.

Roth IRA vs. Traditional IRA Comparison

Understanding the differences between Roth and Traditional IRAs is vital for retirement planning:

Roth IRA:

- **Contributions:** Made with after-tax dollars; not tax-deductible.
- **Withdrawals:** Qualified withdrawals are tax-free.
- **Eligibility:** Income limits apply; high earners may be restricted.
- **Required Minimum Distributions (RMDs):** Not required during

the account holder's lifetime.

Traditional IRA:

- **Contributions:** May be tax-deductible, depending on income and participation in employer-sponsored plans.
- **Withdrawals:** Taxed as ordinary income.
- **Eligibility:** No income limits for contributions; deductibility may be limited.
- **Required Minimum Distributions (RMDs):** Mandatory starting at age 73.

Choosing between the two depends on your current tax bracket, expected future income, and retirement goals.

Time Value of Money: Examples and Calculations

The time value of money (TVM) is a fundamental financial principle stating that a dollar today is worth more than a dollar in the future due to its potential earning capacity.

Future Value (FV):

Calculates what an investment made today will be worth in the future.

Formula:

$FV = PV \times (1 + r)^n$

Where:

- PV = Present Value
- r = Interest rate per period
- n = Number of periods

Example:

Investing $1,000 at an annual interest rate of 5% for 5 years:

$FV = \$1,000 \times (1 + 0.05)^5 = \$1,276.28$

Present Value (PV):

Determines the current worth of a future sum of money.

Formula:

PV = FV / (1 + r)^n

Example:

Receiving $1,276.28 in 5 years at a 5% interest rate:

PV = $1,276.28 / (1 + 0.05)^5 = $1,000

Understanding TVM helps in making informed decisions about investments, loans, and savings.

Conclusion: Taking the Next Step

Embarking on your investment journey is a significant step toward financial empowerment. By familiarizing yourself with key terms, exploring low-cost platforms, understanding retirement accounts, and grasping the time value of money, you're well-equipped to make informed decisions.

Remember, investing is a marathon, not a sprint. Start small, stay consistent, and keep learning. Your future self will thank you.

You're not behind. You're just getting started.

Most people don't know this stuff—until they do. Now you do.

Clarity is confidence. And confidence is sexy.

Make one money move before you go to bed tonight. Just one. And then do another next week.

Appendix F: Smart Money Moves by Age

Introduction

Money is more than just numbers on a spreadsheet; it's a reflection of our choices, dreams, and the life we aspire to live. As we journey through different stages of life, our financial priorities and challenges evolve. Understanding and adapting to these changes is crucial for building a secure and fulfilling financial future.

In this chapter, we'll explore smart money moves tailored to each decade of life—from your 20s to your 60s and beyond. We'll also delve into key retirement milestones and strategies for managing unexpected financial windfalls. Whether you're just starting out, in the midst of your career, or approaching retirement, this guide is designed to meet you where you are and empower you to take control of your financial destiny.

Financial To-Do's by Decade

Your 20s: Building the Foundation

1. Establish an Emergency Fund

Start by setting aside three to six months' worth of living expenses in a high-yield savings account. This fund acts as a financial cushion against unexpected events like job loss or medical emergencies.

2. Tackle High-Interest Debt

Prioritize paying off high-interest debts, such as credit card balances. Reducing debt early frees up resources for savings and investments.

3. Begin Retirement Savings

Take advantage of employer-sponsored retirement plans like a 401(k), especially if there's a company match. If not available, consider opening an IRA. The power of compound interest means that starting early can significantly boost your retirement savings.

4. Create a Budget

Develop a realistic budget that accounts for income, expenses, savings, and discretionary spending. Regularly reviewing and adjusting your budget helps maintain financial discipline.

5. Invest in Yourself

Consider furthering your education or acquiring new skills that can enhance your earning potential over time.

Your 30s: Expanding and Protecting

1. Increase Retirement Contributions

Aim to contribute at least 15% of your income to retirement accounts. As your income grows, so should your savings rate.

2. Diversify Investments

Explore a mix of investment options, including stocks, bonds, and mutual funds, to balance risk and return.

3. Secure Adequate Insurance

Ensure you have appropriate health, life, and disability insurance to protect against unforeseen circumstances.

4. Plan for Major Expenses

Start saving for significant future expenses, such as buying a home or funding children's education.

5. Update Estate Plans

Create or update your will and designate beneficiaries for your accounts to ensure your assets are distributed according to your wishes.

Your 40s: Maximizing and Preparing

1. **Maximize Retirement Savings**

Take full advantage of retirement account contributions. If you're behind, consider catch-up contributions to bridge the gap.

2. **Reevaluate Investment Strategy**

As retirement approaches, reassess your investment portfolio to ensure it aligns with your risk tolerance and time horizon.

3. **Focus on Debt Reduction**

Work towards eliminating remaining debts, including mortgages and loans, to reduce financial burdens in retirement.

4. **Plan for Healthcare Costs**

Investigate long-term care insurance and other options to cover potential healthcare expenses in later years.

5. **Engage in Financial Planning**

Consult with a financial advisor to develop a comprehensive plan that addresses retirement, taxes, and estate considerations.

Your 50s: Refining and Securing

1. **Catch-Up Contributions**

Individuals aged 50 and over can make additional contributions to retirement accounts, providing an opportunity to boost savings.

2. **Estimate Retirement Needs**

Calculate the income you'll need in retirement and assess whether your current savings trajectory will meet those needs.

3. **Consider Downsizing**

Evaluate whether downsizing your home or lifestyle could free up resources for retirement savings.

4. **Update Estate and Healthcare Plans**

Review and update your estate plan, including wills, trusts, and healthcare directives, to reflect current wishes and circumstances.

5. **Plan for Social Security**

Understand how different claiming strategies can impact your Social Security benefits and incorporate this into your retirement planning.

Your 60s and Beyond: Transitioning and Enjoying

1. Finalize Retirement Plans

Determine your retirement date and develop a detailed plan for income, expenses, and lifestyle in retirement.

2. Manage Withdrawals

Create a strategy for withdrawing funds from retirement accounts in a tax-efficient manner to sustain your lifestyle.

3. Monitor Investments

Continue to review and adjust your investment portfolio to ensure it supports your income needs and risk tolerance.

4. Stay Active and Engaged

Consider part-time work, volunteering, or hobbies to stay mentally and socially active, which can also supplement income.

5. Review Legacy Plans

Ensure your estate plan is up-to-date and reflects your current intentions for asset distribution and charitable giving.

Retirement Milestones to Watch

Age 50: Catch-Up Contributions

At age 50, you're eligible to make additional "catch-up" contributions to retirement accounts, allowing you to save more as retirement nears.

Age 59½: Penalty-Free Withdrawals

You can begin withdrawing from retirement accounts without incurring the 10% early withdrawal penalty, though regular income taxes still apply.

Age 62: Early Social Security Eligibility

You can start receiving Social Security benefits, but doing so before your full retirement age will result in reduced monthly payments.

Age 65: Medicare Eligibility

At 65, you're eligible for Medicare. It's important to enroll during the initial enrollment period to avoid penalties.

Age 66-67: Full Retirement Age

Depending on your birth year, this is when you can receive full Social Security benefits without reductions.

Age 70: Maximum Social Security Benefit

Delaying Social Security benefits until age 70 increases your monthly benefit amount.

Age 73: Required Minimum Distributions (RMDs)

Starting at age 73, you're required to begin taking minimum distributions from certain retirement accounts, which are subject to income tax.

Managing Financial Windfalls

Receiving a raise, inheritance, or other financial windfall can be both exciting and overwhelming. Here's how to manage such events wisely:

1. Pause and Plan

Before making any decisions, take time to assess your financial situation and goals. Avoid impulsive spending.

2. Consult Professionals

Engage with financial advisors, tax professionals, and estate planners to understand the implications and opportunities associated with your windfall.

3. Pay Off High-Interest Debt

Use a portion of the funds to eliminate high-interest debts, freeing up future income for savings and investments.

4. Build or Enhance Emergency Fund

Ensure you have a robust emergency fund to cover unexpected expenses.

5. Invest for the Future

Allocate funds towards retirement accounts, education savings, or other long-term investment vehicles.

6. Treat Yourself Responsibly

It's okay to enjoy a portion of your windfall, but set a reasonable limit to maintain financial stability.

7. Communicate Carefully

Be mindful of how and with whom you share information about your windfall to avoid unwanted solicitations or expectations.

Conclusion

Financial planning is a lifelong journey that evolves with each stage of life. By understanding and implementing age-appropriate strategies, you can build a solid foundation, grow your wealth, and enjoy a secure and fulfilling retirement. Remember, it's never too early or too late to take control of your financial future.

You're not behind. You're just getting started.

Most people don't know this stuff—until they do. Now you do.

Clarity is confidence. And confidence is sexy.

Make one money move before you go to bed tonight. Just one. And then do another next week.

Appendix F: Smart Money Moves by Age

Introduction

Money is more than just numbers on a spreadsheet; it's a reflection of our choices, dreams, and the life we aspire to live. As we journey through different stages of life, our financial priorities and challenges evolve. Understanding and adapting to these changes is crucial for building a secure and fulfilling financial future.

In this chapter, we'll explore smart money moves tailored to each decade of life—from your 20s to your 60s and beyond. We'll also delve into key retirement milestones and strategies for managing unexpected financial windfalls. Whether you're just starting out, in the midst of your career, or approaching retirement, this guide is designed to meet you where you are and empower you to take control of your financial destiny.

Financial To-Do's by Decade

Your 20s: Building the Foundation

1. Establish an Emergency Fund

Start by setting aside three to six months' worth of living expenses in a high-yield savings account. This fund acts as a financial cushion against unexpected events like job loss or medical emergencies.

2. Tackle High-Interest Debt

Prioritize paying off high-interest debts, such as credit card balances. Reducing debt early frees up resources for savings and investments.

3. Begin Retirement Savings

Take advantage of employer-sponsored retirement plans like a 401(k), especially if there's a company match. If not available, consider opening an IRA. The power of compound interest means that starting early can significantly boost your retirement savings.

4. Create a Budget

Develop a realistic budget that accounts for income, expenses, savings, and discretionary spending. Regularly reviewing and adjusting your budget helps maintain financial discipline.

5. Invest in Yourself

Consider furthering your education or acquiring new skills that can enhance your earning potential over time.

Your 30s: Expanding and Protecting

1. Increase Retirement Contributions

Aim to contribute at least 15% of your income to retirement accounts. As your income grows, so should your savings rate.

2. Diversify Investments

Explore a mix of investment options, including stocks, bonds, and mutual funds, to balance risk and return.

3. Secure Adequate Insurance

Ensure you have appropriate health, life, and disability insurance to protect against unforeseen circumstances.

4. Plan for Major Expenses

Start saving for significant future expenses, such as buying a home or funding children's education.

5. Update Estate Plans

Create or update your will and designate beneficiaries for your accounts to ensure your assets are distributed according to your wishes.

Your 40s: Maximizing and Preparing

1. Maximize Retirement Savings

Take full advantage of retirement account contributions. If you're behind, consider catch-up contributions to bridge the gap.

2. Reevaluate Investment Strategy

As retirement approaches, reassess your investment portfolio to ensure it aligns with your risk tolerance and time horizon.

3. Focus on Debt Reduction

Work towards eliminating remaining debts, including mortgages and loans, to reduce financial burdens in retirement.

4. Plan for Healthcare Costs

Investigate long-term care insurance and other options to cover potential healthcare expenses in later years.

5. Engage in Financial Planning

Consult with a financial advisor to develop a comprehensive plan that addresses retirement, taxes, and estate considerations.

Your 50s: Refining and Securing

1. Catch-Up Contributions

Individuals aged 50 and over can make additional contributions to retirement accounts, providing an opportunity to boost savings.

2. Estimate Retirement Needs

Calculate the income you'll need in retirement and assess whether your current savings trajectory will meet those needs.

3. Consider Downsizing

Evaluate whether downsizing your home or lifestyle could free up resources for retirement savings.

4. Update Estate and Healthcare Plans

Review and update your estate plan, including wills, trusts, and healthcare directives, to reflect current wishes and circumstances.

5. Plan for Social Security

Understand how different claiming strategies can impact your Social Security benefits and incorporate this into your retirement planning.

Your 60s and Beyond: Transitioning and Enjoying

1. Finalize Retirement Plans

Determine your retirement date and develop a detailed plan for income, expenses, and lifestyle in retirement.

2. Manage Withdrawals

Create a strategy for withdrawing funds from retirement accounts in a tax-efficient manner to sustain your lifestyle.

3. Monitor Investments

Continue to review and adjust your investment portfolio to ensure it supports your income needs and risk tolerance.

4. Stay Active and Engaged

Consider part-time work, volunteering, or hobbies to stay mentally and socially active, which can also supplement income.

5. Review Legacy Plans

Ensure your estate plan is up-to-date and reflects your current intentions for asset distribution and charitable giving.

Retirement Milestones to Watch

Age 50: Catch-Up Contributions

At age 50, you're eligible to make additional "catch-up" contributions to retirement accounts, allowing you to save more as retirement nears.

Age 59½: Penalty-Free Withdrawals

You can begin withdrawing from retirement accounts without incurring the 10% early withdrawal penalty, though regular income taxes still apply.

Age 62: Early Social Security Eligibility

You can start receiving Social Security benefits, but doing so before your full retirement age will result in reduced monthly payments.

Age 65: Medicare Eligibility

At 65, you're eligible for Medicare. It's important to enroll during the initial enrollment period to avoid penalties.

Age 66-67: Full Retirement Age

Depending on your birth year, this is when you can receive full Social Security benefits without reductions.

Age 70: Maximum Social Security Benefit

Delaying Social Security benefits until age 70 increases your monthly benefit amount.

Age 73: Required Minimum Distributions (RMDs)

Starting at age 73, you're required to begin taking minimum distributions from certain retirement accounts, which are subject to income tax.

Managing Financial Windfalls

Receiving a raise, inheritance, or other financial windfall can be both exciting and overwhelming. Here's how to manage such events wisely:

1. Pause and Plan

Before making any decisions, take time to assess your financial situation and goals. Avoid impulsive spending.

2. Consult Professionals

Engage with financial advisors, tax professionals, and estate planners to understand the implications and opportunities associated with your windfall.

3. Pay Off High-Interest Debt

Use a portion of the funds to eliminate high-interest debts, freeing up future income for savings and investments.

4. Build or Enhance Emergency Fund

Ensure you have a robust emergency fund to cover unexpected expenses.

5. Invest for the Future

Allocate funds towards retirement accounts, education savings, or other long-term investment vehicles.

6. Treat Yourself Responsibly

It's okay to enjoy a portion of your windfall, but set a reasonable limit to maintain financial stability.

7. Communicate Carefully

Be mindful of how and with whom you share information about your windfall to avoid unwanted solicitations or expectations.

Conclusion

Financial planning is a lifelong journey that evolves with each stage of life. By understanding and implementing age-appropriate strategies, you can build a solid foundation, grow your wealth, and enjoy a secure and fulfilling retirement. Remember, it's never too early or too late to take control of your financial future.

You're not behind. You're just getting started.

Most people don't know this stuff—until they do. Now you do.

Clarity is confidence. And confidence is sexy.

Make one money move before you go to bed tonight. Just one. And then do another next week.

Made in the USA
Monee, IL
04 November 2026

67387578R00216